How to Get a Literary Agent

Michael Larsen, AAR

SOURCEBOOKS, INC.®
NAPERVILLE, ILLINOIS

Published by Sourcebooks, Inc.
P.O. Box 4410, Naperville, Illinois 60567–4410
(630) 961–3900
Fax: (630) 961–2168
www.sourcebooks.com

Larsen, Michael
How to get a literary agent / by Michael Larsen [Literary agents]
p. cm.
Originally published: Literary agents. Rev. and updated. New York : J. Wiley, c1996.
Includes bibliographical references and index.
ISBN-13: 978-1-4022-0560-6 (pbk.)
ISBN-10: 1-4022-0560-0 (pbk.)
1. Literary agents. I. Title.
PN163.L37 2006
070.5'2—dc22

                                            2005033519

Printed and bound in the United States of America
DR 10 9 8 7 6 5 4 3 2 1

Dedication

This book is dedicated to the writers it inspires to do their best work and show an affirming flame and to Elizabeth, my divine commission.

Contents

Prologue
Making Bigger Better for You:
An Instant Portrait of Publishing

**"Publishing today is show biz.
It's the same as the world of entertainment."**

—Agent Irving "Swifty" Lazar in *Swifty: My Life & Good Times*

Now is the best time ever to be a writer! There are more:
- subjects for you to write about
- ways to write your books, get help with them, or have them written for you
- options for getting your books published
- ways to use technology to make it easier and faster than ever to research, write, get feedback, build your networks, find an agent or publisher, and promote your books

But to help you understand how an agent can help you take advantage of the opportunities waiting for you, you need a short album of snapshots of an industry in transition that will give you a quick overview of the business. Placing writers and agents in the context of America's literary landscape will help you understand what they want to see, how to present it, and how they can help you.

We live in the age of what author and editor Ted Solotarff called "the literary-industrial complex." Here's a miniature portrait of the state of the industry as it lurches into an uncertain future:

- Six multinational conglomerates that I call the Six Sisters—News Corporation, Viacom, Hachette Livre USA, Holtzbrinck Publishers, Pearson, and Bertelsmann—dominate trade publishing (just as seven movie studios dominate Hollywood). Following them are about four hundred mid-sized publishers, not all of which publish books sold in bookstores, and more than seventy thousand independent presses and self-publishers.
- More than ten thousand new publishers opened their doors or portals in 2005.
- More than 175,000 books were published in 2005, more than half of them self-published.
- More than a billion copies of the near three million titles in print were sold.
- The industry generated sales of more than $25 billion by selling trade, mass-market, religious, professional, mail-order, and university-press books; textbooks; subscription reference series; books sold through book clubs; and new editions of previously published books.
- Trade books, together with the sales of mass-market books, account for less than half of the industry's sales.
- Big houses need big sales to sustain big overheads and placate their owners or stockholders, which creates a daunting challenge for first-time authors.
- Over the last decade, the number of independent bookstores was cut in half to seventeen hundred.
- Barnes & Noble sells more books than all independent bookstores combined. So powerful is Barnes & Noble that uncertain publishers will consult its buyers, each of whom has a specialty, about whether they should publish a book they're considering. The most important order for a book comes from Barnes & Noble, and how big the order is affects how publishers get behind it.

Barnes & Noble CEO Len Riggio complained about the high price of new books loudly but to no avail, so he took matters into his own hands: he started publishing books, and bought Sterling, which publishes one thousand how-to and reference books a year. It's a safe bet that none of them are overpriced.

Four customers—Amazon, Barnes & Noble, Borders, and the wholesaler Ingram—may account for 85 percent of a publisher's sales. Chains are responsible for as much as 80 percent of sales in some cities. This gives them the power to pressure publishers for promotional allowances for placing books up front and for greater discounts that in turn enable chains to sell books at greater discounts than independents can. And publishers' profits affect what they can offer writers—not bestselling authors, of course, for whom publishers will pay as much as they have to, but for books by unknown writers.

- Online book sales have grown to more than 15 percent of trade sales, which is where Amazon's Jeff Bezos predicted they would peak.
- Books face more competition from ways that consumers have to spend their free time and discretionary income.
- More than eight hundred thousand grassroots reading groups have become a force in building book sales.
- Over the last fifteen years, the amount of bookstore shelf space in the United States has quadrupled, while the number of readers has shrunk. So, the gap between the number of books published a year, the shelf space available for them, and the number of books sold is widening.
- Bill Gates predicted that we were coming to an "age of incredible disintermediation." It's here. At a big house, more than one hundred people will come between your manuscript and your published book. But thanks to technology, the only person who has to come between you and your readers is you, aided by the suppliers you use to help you self-publish your book.

- Publishing your own work gives you total control over the process, and it's easier and less expensive than ever. Done professionally, self-publishing is an effective way to test-market your book.

The right book at the right time—Dan Brown's *The Da Vinci Code* and Rick Warren's *The Purpose-Driven Life* leap to mind—can generate eight-figure, two-comma sales. In only ten years, the one hundred-plus books in the *Chicken Soup* series have sold more than one hundred million copies, an amazing achievement for editors Jack Canfield and Mark Victor Hansen. Then there's J. K. Rowling, whose attempt to write a story for her daughter to read transformed her from a single parent on the dole to a billionaire in less than a decade.

An Amazing Time to Be a Writer

Although some of these numbers are large, no book, author, house, nor even trade publishing as a whole is a major factor in the economy. And basically flat sales and the continually growing competition for readers' time don't bode well for the industry.

But the industry is evolving into something that will be better for writers and readers. More books on more subjects in more forms and formats are available to more people in more places, faster and with more discounts than ever.

Writers have more ways to communicate with their fans and to promote and profit from their books than ever. There are more ways to buy books than ever, and it's faster and easier to do it than ever—even months before they're published. This is an amazing time for you to be a writer!

Chapters 15-18 have more information you need about publishing, but where does this snapshot leave you? With challenges and opportunities you need to understand to find an agent and become a successful author. Onward!

Introduction
Read This Way

"I was so naive as a kid I used to sneak behind the barn and do nothing."

—Johnny Carson

Three Ways for You to Read the Book

There was once a sign on a church announcing the next Sunday's sermon. The sign read:

Everlasting Punishment
All are welcome.

I hope that you will find what follows more inspiring and pleasurable than punitive. You can choose between the following three ways to read it:

1. *Reader's choice.* Dip into it anywhere and just read what you want.
2. *A logical choice.* You are reading this book because you need a literary agent. Part 1, Hiring the Agent You Need, will describe how agents work and how to find one. Part 2, Understanding Your Agent, looks at what agents do and how to create and maintain a mutually fulfilling relationship with yours. Assume that I have structured the book in the most effective way, and read it in the order it was written.
3. *The author's choice.* What did the Zen master say to the hot dog vendor? "Make me one with everything." Part 3, The Prequel: What to Know

before You Go, can't make you one with everything, but it will provide you with a perspective on writing, publishing, and, most important of all, yourself.

Part 3 is really a prequel to the rest of the book. Before you start looking for an agent, before you even start writing, you need an overview of the world you hope to enter. Before you decide how you are going to read the book, ask yourself this question: "Am I ready for an agent?"

To find out if you are, ask yourself:

"Do I have a positive, yet realistic, perspective on the book business?" Chapters 14 to 17 will help get you started.

"Is my ability to write strong enough for my work to excite an agent?" Chapter 19 will help you understand how to develop your craft.

"Do I have literary and financial goals, and am I committed to achieving them?" Chapters 19 and 20 will help you provide some of the information about yourself that agents will hope you have when you contact them.

It may be more productive for you to read Part 3 first, then read Parts 1 and 2. If you can stand the suspense, save the last chapter, "Writing High: The End of the Beginning," for last.

Writers contact us feeling defensive because they don't know anything about agenting or publishing. Part of an agent's job is to help clients understand what they need to know to become successful writers.

I spend my life encouraging writers to make their nonfiction books as enjoyable to read as they are informative. Trying to meet that challenge myself, I use humor to help the medicine go down.

The playwright Tom Stoppard once said, "Every exit is an entry someplace else." I hope that in whatever order you decide to read the book, the end of it will mark your entry into the beginning of a successful career.

A Concluding Paradox

If you knew how lucky you are to be a writer at this exhilarating moment in history, you wouldn't read this book. You would consecrate every waking moment to writing and promoting your work. Yet the better writer you are, the more you need this book to help ensure that your books earn the rewards and recognition you deserve.

Part 1

Hiring the Agent You Need

Chapter 1
Making the Connection:
Using the Write Stuff to Attract an Agent

A *Writer's Digest* cartoon shows a room full of bullet holes and cowering on the floor in a corner is a hostage with his hands and feet tied and his mouth gagged. Next to him is a bearded young revolutionary standing in front of an open window, holding a rifle in one hand and shouting into a megaphone, ". . . five hundred thousand dollars in tens and twenties, a plane ride to Cuba, and a good literary agent!"

It's been said that an agent is like a bank loan—you can only get one if you can prove you don't need it. Writers, editors, and agents themselves help perpetuate the greatest myth in publishing: it's hard to get an agent. Nonsense! If you have a salable book, it's easy to get an agent, and it's easy to sell it. Writers find agents and sell their books themselves all the time. Writers sell more books than agents sell.

The more salable a book is, because of its literary or commercial value or both, the easier it is to find an agent and sell your book. Agents can only hope to make a living by selling books to the Six Sisters, and what's getting harder is writing a book that will appeal to them. And what's hardest of all is making a book sell once it's published.

You can find your agent the same way you can find a publisher: writing something salable and following submission guidelines in directories and on websites. Finding an agent is getting easier all the time. More than two thousand agencies in more than thirty-five states must find new writers to stay in business. If you have a marketable book, the challenge isn't finding an agent; it's finding a competent, reputable agent you feel comfortable working with.

Are You Ready for an Agent?

Random House Executive Editor Kate Medina warns writers to beware of "premature emission." When will you be ready to contact agents? When you have answered three questions.

1. Have you chosen the best option for getting your book published?

To answer this question, you have to set literary and financial goals for yourself. One of the reasons why now is the best time to be a writer is that you have more options for getting your books published than ever:

- You can collaborate with other writers in a co-op venture in which you share the production and marketing costs to create an anthology.
- You can pay for all of the costs to publish your book (but vanity publishing has no credibility in the industry).
- You can use subsidy publishing, which means that you pay part of the publishing costs (another option with no credibility).
- You can partner with a foundation that will support the writing and promotion of your book because it will further their cause.
- As mentioned earlier, you can self-publish your book using one or more of the following options:
  - photocopying your manuscript and binding it with tape or using a three-ring binder (a better alternative because material in a loose-leaf binder has greater perceived value);
  - publishing one copy at a time using print-on-demand (POD) technology;
  - using print-quantity-needed (PQN) for short runs;
  - using offset printing for longer runs;
  - publishing it online so it can be downloaded onto a computer, personal digital assistant (PDA), or another digital device, or with one of the more than four hundred e-book publishers, more than two hundred of whom will do it for free;

- publishing it in other media such as CDs, DVDs, combination CD-DVDs, software, or other forms such as calendars.
- You may be able to sell the rights to:
    - an online or offline trade or consumer periodical that will serialize it;
    - a publisher for a flat fee;
    - a small press, a niche or specialty publisher, or a regional publisher;
    - an academic or university press;
    - a professional publisher that publishes books for a specific field;
    - a mid-sized house;
    - one of the Six Sisters.
- You can work with a packager who provides publishers with a printer-ready manuscript or bound books.
- You can hire an agent to sell your books. In *The New York Agent Book*, former William Morris agent Joanna Ross observes that "agents are only avenues of opportunity"—and only one of the many avenues open to you.

Any option you choose will have trade-offs. When you're deciding about what to write and the best way to get it published, you have to take the long view as well as the short view. You're only deciding on the best choice for you now. If your first book sells well, you will have more options for your next book.

Why Publishers Buy Books
Among the reasons publishers buy books are:
- The book being sold may not be a big one, but the author has the potential to be a repeater who will turn out at least one bestseller a year.
- A successful but unhappy author at another house wants a new home.

13

- The author has a track record that assures the success of new books.
- The author will sell a lot of books and will obtain bulk orders for them.
- The writing is superb.
- Publishers love the book and think it will sell.
- They don't love it but think it will sell.
- They love it enough to publish it, regardless of its commercial potential.
- The author's platform—his or her continuing national visibility through talks, online and offline media, promotional partners, or businesses or nonprofits that will help him or her—assures success.
- The author's promotion plan guarantees the book's success.
- The author is a celebrity or media magnet who will guarantee enough publicity to make the book successful.
- The book deserves to be published because of its value to a cause or the country.
- An editor is passionate enough about it to overcome any doubts the house may have about the book.
- A new editor is building a list.
- Books on the subject or that kind of novel sell well.
- The house has published similar books with success.
- The book will be the first in a series with strong potential.
- The idea for the book is brilliant.
- The book is about a hot topic.
- The idea is about a trend.
- The title alone will sell books.
- The publisher thinks that the book will become an *evergreen*, a book that sells year after year.
- The book has subsidiary-rights potential.
- The book has school-adoption potential.
- The book is on a subject about which the house wants to build a list.
- Publishers want to keep the book and the author's future books out of competitors' hands.

- Editors discover the book on a trip to the London or Frankfurt Book Fair and think it will sell, are caught up in the excitement surrounding the book, or want to justify the trip.
- The house is sending the industry the message that because of new management or despite changes in the house, the house is a player.
- The author has a personal connection with someone in the house with the power to greenlight the book.
- The book is a potential prizewinner that will enhance the house's prestige.
- The house hopes to persuade big agencies to sell them more books.

This is not a definitive list, but if you were a publisher and wanted to stay in business, these are reasons that you would choose to do books.

Yes and No: Publishers who want to buy a book will always find reasons to justify the acquisition. As bestselling novelist John Saul observes, "If publishers don't want to buy a book in a heavily published field, they'll say, 'It's been done to death!' If they do want to buy it, they'll say, 'Always works!'"

The criteria that publishers consider in buying a book are the same as what you'll need to think about in choosing the best publishing option. Among these criteria are:
- how commercial your idea is
- how professional your writing is
- how promotable your book will be
- your ability to promote it
- how timely your book will be when it's published
- the size of the potential readership for your book
- the number of channels that can sell your book
- the book's subsidiary-rights and special-sales potential

- whether your book has the potential to be a series
- your ability to get a foreword and cover quotes
- the number of publishers who publish similar books
- whether chains and big-box stores will take it
- how much synergy you will create between your book and the other things you do that will enable you to sell and publicize it

What Agents Look For

Agents can only make a living selling to big publishers, all of whom are in New York, and mid-sized houses, most of which are in New York. That said, exceptions to that rule are:

- new agents who are building their client list
- agents who are earning enough income or who don't have to worry about making money, so they don't care how commercial a book is, only how good it is
- agents who specialize in a field, know all of the editors who will be right for a book, and will be able to sell a book quickly
- agents outside of the tri-state area who are more open to new writers than successful Big Apple agents are
- agents committed to a social, political, or environmental cause that a book will advance

Before you approach agents, you need to have a clear idea about the books you want to write and the author you want to be. The moment you have a complete novel or a nonfiction proposal that your networks assure you is 100 percent—as well conceived and crafted as you can make it—agents will be glad to hear from you.

Writers have asked us to read their first few chapters to see if they "should bother continuing." Getting feedback on your work is essential, but an agent's job is to sell books, not to read partial manuscripts and offer free advice about whether writers are on the right track.

2. Is your proposal or manuscript as salable as you and your networks agree it can be?

For fiction, you usually need a complete first novel and a synopsis; or a collection of short stories, most of which have been published, ideally in magazines that will impress editors.

You can't prove that you can sustain plot, character, and setting for the length of a novel until you do it, so first novels usually have to be finished. Publishers are offered too many completed novels for them to be interested in unfinished work by unpublished writers.

However, if you're planning a novel of six hundred pages or more, and you have two hundred smashing pages and an extensive, dynamite synopsis, your book might be an exception. But because of the trend toward shorter books, use the length of novels like yours that you love as models for how long to make your book.

For nonfiction, you need a proposal with an introduction with information about you and the book; an outline for each chapter—from a paragraph to a page in length, depending on the kind of book you're writing and how long your chapters will be; and, for most books, the best representative sample chapter and as much as possible of a finished manuscript for a narrative nonfiction book that you want to read like a novel.

For children's books, don't query for a picture book—send the text. For fiction, send three chapters and a synopsis. For nonfiction, send a proposal. Always include a SASE.

3. Is your promotion plan as long and strong as you can make it?

If you are writing a how-to book or any kind of nonfiction for a wide national audience, the promotion for which has to be author-driven, your promotion plan will be far more important than the content of your book in determining the editor, publisher, and deal you get.

The rising cost of doing business has made big houses less willing to build authors over several books before they write their breakout book. And because new writers don't usually have the promotional ammunition large publishers need, small, mid-sized, and university presses are seizing the opportunity to publish authors that big houses can't.

One reason that nonfiction writers, at least at the beginning of their careers, are luckier than novelists is that there are more ways to promote most nonfiction. But harder though it may be, promotion is just as important for fiction. The suggestions about promotion in Chapters 23 and 24 will help you think about how to promote your books.

Once you've answered yes to these questions, you're ready to find the lucky agent who's waiting to represent you.

Chapter 2
Can You Name That Tuna?
Eleven Ways to Find the Right Agent
for You and Your Book

Historical romance writer June Lund Shiplett stuck a pin into the list of agents in the trade dictionary *Literary Market Place* three times and hit my partner Elizabeth Pomada's name twice. That's how Elizabeth came to represent her.

Instead of calling first, one New York writer turned up on an agent's doorstep because he was researching agents in the main library on 42nd Street, and the agent was the closest one to the library.

Another new writer was looking for an agent in *Literary Market Place*. Her sister was on a diet, and she was making her a tuna fish casserole for her birthday. She looked at agents' names until she came to Frieda Fishbein. That's how Frieda Fishbein got to sell Colleen McCullough's bestseller *The Thorn Birds*.

If you're not psychic or cooking for your sister's birthday, here are eleven ways to find the agent who's out there waiting to sell your book. I've listed them, including the directories, in order of their effectiveness:

1. Referrals

The best way to get an agent's attention is if the first two words she or he hears or sees in a query letter are the name of a client, agent, journalist, author, bookseller, writing teacher, staff or freelance editor, or expert in the field who suggested you contact him or her.

The more important the person, the more eager the agent will be to hear from you and the faster you'll hear back from the agent. If a professional takes the time to read your work, and believes in it enough to let you use his or her name, agents will assume they're right and give it immediate attention.

Agents appreciate referrals. Even when they can't help the writers, they're grateful that professionals respect them enough to send writers to them. Agents don't ask references to judge whether something is salable because they may feel differently about it.

An agent's biggest challenge is finding salable books. Referrals are far faster than listening to phone calls and sifting through email, letters, proposals, and manuscripts, hoping to unearth the one writer in a hundred they can help. If the person writes a letter about your book to include behind your query letter, the first two words will still be the person's name.

Scouts are a more formal way of getting referrals. Agents may have scouts whose job it is to find and refer writers. Agents pay scouts part of the commissions earned by authors they refer.

Google as Bugle

Because a website is essential for authors, most published writers have them. So the fastest way to reach authors and establish a relationship with them is to Google them. You can Google any person or organization. Publishers' sites may have links to their authors' sites and blogs. Even if you don't find a site for authors, you will find other ways to reach them, if only by writing to their publisher, which you can also do by snail mail.

2. Your Networks

Your overlapping networks, online and off, will help you find your agent: speakers, writers, mentors, booksellers, publishing people, professionals in your field, a promotion network, and a mastermind group. Ask writing teachers about students who have gotten agents. (Chapter 20 has more about networks.)

3. The Association of Authors' Representatives (AAR)

If your networks can't help you, try the Association of Author's Representatives. The AAR is the best source of experienced, reputable agents. At the time of publication of this book, AAR has more than three hundred fifty literary and dramatic agents, and it continues to grow. The organization's website, www.aar-online.org, lists members and how to reach them. AAR's email address is aarinc@mindspring.com.

A Brief History of AAR

The Society of Authors' Representatives (SAR) was founded in 1928 and was made up of larger, older New York-based agencies. Founded in 1977, the Independent Literary Agents Association (ILAA) included agents in and out of New York. In 1992, SAR and ILAA merged to form the Association of Authors' Representatives.

The AAR meets regularly to discuss issues and opportunities in publishing and related media and has an excellent newsletter that is especially helpful for members around the country who can't attend meetings. AAR also lobbies publishers on issues of importance to writers.

To join, agents must have sold eighteen books in ten months, and members are obligated to follow the ethical guidelines in Appendix 3. Many competent, responsible, successful agents are not members of AAR, but AAR's code has helpful criteria for choosing an agent. One sign of agents' professionalism is that they adhere to AAR's code, even if they're not members.

Perhaps an agent who isn't a member of AAR may be willing to use it or incorporate the code into his or her agreement, modifying it as needed.

4. Writer's Organizations

Members of the Author's Guild, the National Writer's Union, the American Society of Journalists and Authors, the Women's National Book Association (which is open to men), and the other organizations listed in *Literary Market Place* are potential sources of leads and referrals. Their meetings, newsletters, events, and websites will also help you learn about agents.

5. Literary Events

Another reason why now is the best time ever to be a writer is the amazing array of sources that writers have for learning about agents, their craft, promotion, and the industry. In addition to the Web, there are writing classes, seminars, workshops, and conferences; books and magazines; publishing courses; and readings, lectures, book signings, and book festivals. These all present opportunities to meet or learn about agents from editors, authors, and agents themselves. They also give you the chance to ask if authors will let you use their names with their agents.

Agents go to events to find writers, and they expect writers to approach them and ask about representation. Agents are more approachable at conferences even if you don't have a one-on-one consultation with them. They're there to meet you. They will be more open to meeting you and hearing about your book than they are in their office, where they are responding to letters, proposals, manuscripts, phone calls, and emails; meeting with clients, new writers, and editors; and trying to read submissions.

You can mention your meeting whenever you are ready to query the agent. One writer queried us because she had seen us speak thirty years earlier. If only we could make all of our talks that memorable! (Must have been the striptease that did it.)

Visit www.shawguides.com for a list of conferences and workshops.

6. The Web

The exploding universe of cyberspace is already an inexhaustible source of information. It has classes, chat rooms, websites, e-zines, and blogs, all of which can help you find an agent.

If all you do is Google literary agents, you'll find more than 13,000,000 hits! Among the other sites to visit are www.authorlink.com, www.publisherslunch.com, www.publishersmarketplace.com, www.forwriters.com, www.sfwa.org, www.writersmarket.com, www.writers.net, and www.youcanwrite.com. Following the links on these sites will lead you to still more information.

Two cautions and a certainty:
- Websites disappear.
- The information you find on the Web is not guaranteed to be correct; unless you feel confident about the source of what you learn, verify it with other sources.

• New sites will appear before this book reaches your hands.

7. Directories

As the number of agents grows, so does the number of books for finding them. These directories have different strengths. They vary in the number of agents included, the kind and amount of information provided, and the guidance they provide about writing and publishing. The best ways to get the information you need: consult the latest edition and check the information in several directories about the same agent for a clearer picture of that agent.

Jeff Herman invites about two hundred AAR members and other agents he knows to be listed in *Jeff Herman's Guide to Book Publishers, Editors, & Literary Agents 200X*. Jeff's book offers agents the chance to give writers a sense of their personality by providing more than just the usual information about themselves. The *Guide* also has a book within the book: two hundred pages of advice about writing, agenting, getting published, and writing a proposal as well as a handy reference guide.

Writer's Digest Books publishes the *200X Guide to Literary Agents*, which lists more than six hundred literary and script agents. As the leading source of guidance about writing, Writer's Digest also provides a hefty helping of helpful information. You will find three features valuable:

• Entries include the most comprehensive list of subjects and kinds of fiction agents handle in any directory.
• The book also has an index list of subjects and kinds of fiction, and all of the agents who handle them. This is a fast way for you to zero in on agents who handle books like yours. Most agents handle adult fiction and nonfiction. But if you're writing in a specialized field, this list will enable you to find agents who represent books on your subject.

• Another index tells how open agents are to new writers.

The Writer's Digest guide also has a wealth of articles about what writers need to know about agents. It also lists contests, conferences, and production companies and has a resource section.

The Writer's Handbook 200X is edited and published annually by the Writer Books. The handbook provides information about one hundred fifty agents and also contains the most articles about all kinds of writing and includes markets for different kinds of writing.

The Agents Directory: Everything You Need to Know to Sell Your Book or Script by former *Writer's Digest* editor–turned agent Rachel Vater is a new addition to the genre. It has sixty pages of information about writing and agents, directories of literary and script agents, and lists of conferences and resources. Even with its sans serif typeface, it has the most readable layout.

Literary Agents: A Writer's Guide by Adam Begley is published in association with the New York-based group Poets and Writers. After explaining how agents work and how to find one, this guide contains a listing of about two hundred agents who do not charge to read manuscripts.

Literary Market Place 200X (LMP): *The Directory of the American Book Publishing Industry with Industry Yellow Pages* wins the doorstop award. It's so big—more than two thousand pages—that it's divided into two volumes. *LMP* is the comprehensive publishing directory. It includes basic information on more than six hundred agents.

These directories also have websites.

8. Magazines

The Writer, Writer's Digest, Coda, and other writing magazines have articles by and about agents. The trade magazine *Publishers Weekly* has a

"Hot Deals" column about agents' sales, a clue to how effective they are. *Publishers Weekly* also has a free daily e-zine. To subscribe, visit www.publishersweekly.com.

9. Publishers' Catalogs and Websites

The seasonal catalogs publishers use to sell new books may contain the names of the agents who control the rights on their clients' books. These catalogs are in libraries as are the directories listed earlier. You can also request catalogs from publishers. Publishers' websites will have more information about their books and authors, and perhaps, as I mentioned earlier, hyperlinks to authors' websites.

10. Books

Check the dedication and acknowledgment pages of your favorite books, competing books, and books on your subject. Grateful writers thank their agents and editors, and agents will think you're more professional if you mention one of their books. It's an indirect kind of referral.

Agents also write books and are as easily seduced by praise as you will be, especially if you can say that you're contacting them because of their book(s). Ken Atchity, Richard Balkin, Andrea Brown, Sheree Bykofsky, Sandra Choron, Richard Curtis, Arielle Eckstut, Jeff Herman, Jim Hornfischer, Susan Lerner, Noah Lukeman, Donald Maass, Evan Marshall, Peter Miller, Susan Rabiner, Amy Rennert, Peter Rubie, Harriet Wasserman, and Al Zuckerman are among the agents who have written books.

11. Media Exposure

Get published or get publicity about your work and yourself online or off. Agents and editors read media searching for writers and ideas. The right blog, article, or short story at the right time in the right place can sell a book. AAR member Sandy Dijkstra found Amy Tan because of a short story in *ZZYZZVA*, a San Francisco literary review.

Unhindered by space limitations, the Web offers new writers new opportunities to be published. The larger and the more prestigious or successful a periodical is, the better impression it will make on agents and editors. But getting published anywhere is better than not getting published.

Including a published article about you or your subject with your query letter adds credibility to you and your idea. If your article is long enough and strong enough, it can serve as a sample chapter for your proposal.

You can adapt these ideas to find a publisher.

Do They Really Need This Job?

There are more than two thousand agents, and the number keeps growing. How can you choose which agents to submit your work to? Use these criteria for starters:

- The size of the agency (discussed in the next chapter)
- The agent's previous publishing experience
- How long the agent has been in business (trade-offs discussed in the next chapter)
- The kinds of books the agent sells
- How many books like yours the agent has sold
- The number of books the agent has sold in the last year or so (too few may mean they're not active enough in the business; too many

may mean that you and your book won't get enough attention from them)

- The publishers the agent sells to
- How many books the agent is trying to sell at the moment
- How long the agent thinks it will take to sell your book
- Whether the agent is an AAR member
- If the agency has a website and if so, how effective it is
- The agency's promotional literature
- How active the agency is in your field

A Left-Coast Point of View

Elizabeth and I have a California approach to agenting. We like to handle books we like by writers we like and sell them to editors we like. When there's not a fortune involved, quality-of-life issues are important to agents and to editors as well. Writing and publishing a book may take two years, and since each book creates its own unique set of challenges, we want to be able to enjoy the process because of the people involved.

Simultaneous Submissions

Unless their guidelines say otherwise, you may submit query letters, proposals, or partial novels to as many agents or publishers as you wish simultaneously, letting them know that other agents have it.

Consider creating two or three groups of agents in order of their desirability, and approach the agents you'd most like to represent you first. Even if you strike out, you may learn something that will help you with the other groups.

If an agent responds to a query letter and requests an exclusive submission on a proposal or manuscript that other agents want to see, choose one of these responses:

- If it's an agent you really want to represent you, ask how long the agent wants. If he or she says a week, fine. If not, give the agent an exclusive for two weeks for a proposal or three to four weeks for a manuscript. If you don't hear back, notify the agent that you're sending it elsewhere, and go on to the next most desirable agent who is willing to read the manuscript if another agent has it. Assure both agents that you won't make a decision without consulting them.
- If more than one agent wants to represent you, and you can't decide which one to choose, tell the agents you are considering, and ask them if there's anything that they can tell you to help you make up your mind. This gives them the chance to express their feelings about your book, their hopes for it, and how they plan to sell it. If their answers still leave you undecided, consult your networks and perhaps their clients.

    Established agents may not want to be part of a multiple sub-mission of a whole manuscript. They don't want to spend the time to read a manuscript only to learn that they can't handle it. One way around this is just to submit to agents who don't mind being part of a multiple submission.
- Say, "I'm sorry, but as much as I'd like you to handle it, other agents have requested it." If the agent wants to represent you enough, competitors will still spur an enterprising agent to give it a quick read and get back to you faster than agents who are less excited about it.

When you decide on an agent, you owe it to any agents you haven't heard back from to let them know and to thank them for their time. The last impression you have of each other may in time become important if you ever have to switch agents.

Who Works for Whom?

Throughout the process of finding and working with an agent, always remember that your agent works for you. You are entitled to be satisfied with what your agent is doing on your behalf and how prompt and responsive the agent is when you communicate.

10 Ways to an Agent's Heart (They Do *So* Have Hearts!)

Like editors, agents love to get excited about their books and authors. This list of hot buttons for you to push captures what agents would like to find every time they start reading letters and submissions:

- Writers who have a great new idea for a series of books.
- Writers whose work everyone in the agency falls in love with because it's irresistibly beautiful, moving, funny, universal, timeless, and inspirational; has social value; and is commercial.
- Writers whose letters or proposals make it clear that nothing is more important than becoming successful authors.
- Writers who understand what's expected of them and what they can expect from an agent and publisher.
- Writers whose platform, media experience, and promotion plan guarantee that their books will be as successful as they want them to be.
- Writers who are always impeccably professional.
- Writers with whom the agent looks forward to working with for a lifetime.
- Writers who make the agent laugh.
- Writers who have an engaging voice.

- Writers who are approaching only that agent because:
  - they love the books the agent has sold, and they're hoping that one of the agent's authors will give them a quote for their book;
  - the agent's books are very successful;
  - they want to be published by one of the houses the agent sells to;
  - the agent's website or listing in a directory convinced them that the agent is the best one for them;
  - they met the agent at a conference, and the agent is excited about their book;
  - they have spoken to the agent's clients;
  - the agent is in AAR.

Writers understand the importance of an effective query letter, but its importance intimidates them because they're worried about doing it wrong. The next chapter will take the timid out of intimidation, because writing a query letter is as easy as HBC (the Hook, the Book, and the Cook).

Chapter 3
Getting Your Agent before You Know Who It Is:
Why Writing a Must-Read Query Letter Is Simple

"Dear Agent" and Other Letter Bombs

Once you have a list of agents to approach, it's time to make contact. Regardless of how they operate, most agents prefer to be queried by mail or email.

It's been suggested that for peace of mind, what we really need in our cell-phone-crazed world is a phoneless cord. We know an exasperated agent who once bellowed, "I want to be the only agent in the country with an unlisted phone number!"

If an agency is new, small, or outside of New York, try calling, but be brief and keep time zones in mind. And don't expect agents to return long-distance calls from strangers. Mention that agents may return your call collect if they wish, and that if you don't hear back, you'll try them again.

The First Law of Getting What You Want from People Who Don't Know You: make gatekeepers your allies.

As you create your career, you will want to contact people without having a referral. They may have gatekeepers, part of whose job it is to protect them from taking calls they don't want to take. You will encounter gatekeepers in every network you build. Befriend them, and they'll help you. One day, they may even become bosses, and they'll remember you.

The Second Law of Getting What You Want from People Who Don't Know You: Express your gratitude in a way that they will be glad to hear from you again.

When you reach agents' assistants, ask them to tell you if the agent will want to see your book and how to submit it. This should confirm what you've already found out. Get assistants' names and thank them by name for their help.

Agents' (and editors') assistants may determine the fate of your book. Novices work their way up to becoming agents by being assistants while they learn how to edit submissions and sell books. They find their first books by screening those that are submitted to the agents they work for.

Assistants at large and mid-sized agencies will screen your letter and your work for the agent they work for. The assistant may make the decision about it by writing a convincing reader's report about your book. The agent may only read far enough to confirm the assistant's judgment or may just take the assistant's word for it. On the other hand, if the assistant falls in love with your work, he or she may become your agent.

The Hook, the Book, and the Cook: Writing a Must-Read Query Letter

At the beginning of World War II, the English Prime Minister Winston Churchill asked the head of the British Navy for a statement about

England's preparedness for war—and he asked for it to be on one page. If England's preparedness for war can be summarized on one page, so can your book.

To be effective, your query letter must:
- generate as much excitement about you and your book as possible
- prove that you can write
- show that you're professional enough to know what agents need to know about you and your book
- provide agents the information they need in as few words as you can

Every word in your query letter is either helping to sell you or your book or it isn't. Every word counts. The first line of a query letter is more revealing than writers understand. For example, starting your letter with "My name is," "I'm seeking representation for," or "I have written a fiction novel" won't help you find an agent or editor. What's wrong with them?
- Agents don't need to know your name, which will be at the top and/or bottom of your letter.
- If agents are reading a letter from a writer they don't know, they assume it's a query letter.
- Avoid starting your letter with "I" or "My." Write about your book first, then about yourself.
- Writers who don't know that "fiction novel" is redundant probably don't know how to write one that's salable.

Obvious mistakes in a letter, proposal, or manuscript prove two things about writers, the first understandable, the second fatal:
1. They can't write at a professional level. This is usually the case at the beginning of a career. If they stick with it, they may be able to, which is one reason why our rejection letter in the next chapter is as gentle as we can make it.
2. They don't have the right readers to help them, and that's fatal. Getting feedback on your work and your query letter, which is a

sample of your work, is as essential to your career as writing and promoting it. You won't get your work right by yourself, but you don't have to. Get all the feedback you need, but do it before you submit your work.

Once agents and editors find something wrong with a query letter, the optimism with which they started reading it is replaced by a wariness that sooner or later will be justified by finding enough other mistakes to convince them to move on to the next letter.

Agents and editors reject close to 100 percent of the submissions they see, and they only read far enough to make a decision. If a query letter isn't well written, they won't read past it. They live by the prevailing wisdom succinctly put by agent Marcia Amsterdam that "if they can't write a letter, they couldn't write a book."

Cracking the HBC Code: Query Letters That Get Results

Writing a query is as simple as HBC: the Hook, the Book, and the Cook. It's a one-page letter with three or four single-spaced paragraphs and a space between paragraphs.

The Hook
The hook should contain at least one of the following:
- The name of someone who refers the agent to you
- A quote from someone who's read your proposal or manuscript and whose name or position will impress agents
- Media attention or another trend that proves the growing interest in the subject, but only if you're sure that the media will stay interested after your book comes out two years from now

- The most important reason your book will sell
- The opening sentence or a riveting paragraph from the manuscript
- Why the subject justifies a book

Give your hook the impact of the first paragraph of an article that must compel readers to keep reading. If it doesn't, they won't.

The Book

Include the following information, adapting it for your book:
- The title and essence of your book
- A brief synopsis of it
- Where it fits in the literary landscape in relation to other books and authors
- The size of the biggest markets for it
- How many pages the manuscript will be
- What you have ready to send that meets agents' guidelines, and anything more of the manuscript that you have ready to submit
- If your book will be the first in a series, mention it, and what, if anything, you have ready to submit for the next book
- The name of an authority in your field, an MD, an academic, a celebrity, or a bestselling author who has agreed to write a foreword
- The names of people who will give quotes

If color illustrations are an important element in your book, send a few representative samples with a hard copy of your query letter, and if you can, include a link to more of them.

Barking at the Wrong Moon

Of the thousands of submissions we get each year, many are from writers who haven't researched what we handle and how to approach us. This means that we get work that we don't represent such as poetry, children's books, and screenplays.

It also means that even if writers submit the kind of books we do handle, they haven't sent what we need to see and so are unlikely to have written something salable.

Writers prove that they're not ready for an agent by sending letters addressed to the agency, not either of us; both of us, instead of finding out which of us is the right person to contact; or both of us in separate envelopes—a waste of time for them and us.

How writers approach us is always a clue to their professionalism, which can indicate how well they write. When writers follow the guidelines in directories and on our site, they're more likely to have written something salable. We know instantly that the writers are professionals. They haven't wasted our time with words or information that we don't need, and they've sent us what we need to make a decision as quickly as possible.

The Cook

Include the following information if you can:
- Your credentials: degrees, research, and experience in the field
- If you're a published author, provide the info about your most recent or bestselling book
  - the title
  - the publisher
  - the year of publication
  - sales figures
  - the format: hardcover, trade paperback, mass-market paperback, or any combination
  - brief quotes or just adjectives from reviews
  - sub-rights sales such as movie, book-club, or translation rights if they'll impress recipients
- Your memberships in organizations in your field (which are more impressive if you've been an officer)

- The number of articles you've written and for whom (if you've had an impressive article about the subject of your book published, add it to your letter with the cover of the magazine)
- Your media experience
- Your speaking experience and the number of talks you give or the number of people you speak to a year
- The three or four most impressive things you will do to promote the book (vital info for promotion-driven nonfiction you want to sell to a New York publisher)
- A black-and-white head shot if your looks will be an asset in promoting your book
- Prizes, contests, and awards you've won (which are even more meaningful if you won them for the book you're submitting)
- The reason you're contacting the agent—what reasons will please agents besides a referral?
    - You heard the agent speak.
    - You read that the agent is going to speak at an event that you're going to so you can meet if the agent likes your work, and perhaps get feedback if the agent doesn't.
    - You love a book that the agent represented, and you're writing the same kind of book.

Email Submissions

Agents' listings will indicate if they're open to emailed submissions. A growing number of agents are. If you're not in the United States or Canada, submit the opening pages of your novel or nonfiction proposal at the bottom of an email query letter. Agents and editors only read far enough to make a decision, and they may not respond unless they're interested, so assume that no answer is an answer.

One agent we know only reads email that comes from a person or address she recognizes. And if your subject line doesn't tempt agents, they may not open the letter, so you won't know whether they've read it or how much of it they've read. This is why hard copy with a SASE remains the most reliable—if not the fastest—way to get a response.

Write nothing that is self-serving about you or your book, but quote the praise of an author or reviewer about you or your writing.

If you can, inject humor or a distinctive voice into your letter. But make sure that publishing professionals or writers whose opinions you respect agree that your letter works.

Because of viruses, agents and editors don't want attachments from strangers. But give them the choice of receiving your work in hard copy or as an attachment. Don't send a manuscript until an agent requests it.

Two query letters I only had to read first line of:

"Not that I compare myself with Shakespeare's Hamlet, but . . ."

"I have completed two novels. One is fiction. One is nonfiction."

Synopsis

After your letter, include a synopsis. Agents vary in how long a synopsis they prefer. Elizabeth, who does the fiction in our agency, just wants two double-spaced pages that tell what happens, including the ending of the book. If a client's novel has movie potential, she immediately approaches our coagents in Hollywood where, except for agents, people prefer reading treatments—synopses of scripts—to manuscripts.

When Pat Conroy's hefty bestseller *The Prince of Tides* was being sold to the movies, one of the producer's assistants said to Conroy, "I read it last night and it brought tears to my eyes."

Pleased but surprised, Conroy asked, "You read my book last night?"

"No," said the assistant, "I read the two-page treatment."

Relating your book to a successful book, movie, or author will clarify what your book is and the market for it. If, for example, your novel is a Spanish *Joy Luck Club* or a Ludlumesque thriller, agents will know immediately what to expect. Better yet is if you can combine two successful books or movies: "It's *Stars Wars* meets *Gone with the Wind*."

A Naked Bribe

When you send your manuscript, consider bribing agents with copies of your favorite book or the best example of a book like yours that made you want to write. Why?

- Your favorite book will give them an immediate sense of who you are as writer and your literary goals.
- They may not have read it.
- A book is a gift that will make you look both generous and professional.
- If they've read it, they may pass it on to someone else in the agency or return it in your SASE, and you can use it in your next submission. And your mutual admiration for the book may help start your relationship.

Make Your Letter Error-Free

Freelancers who sell articles with query letters know the importance of making them impeccable. Your letter is a sample of your writing. Spelling or grammatical errors or awkward, flat prose will guarantee your letter a quick click to the next email or an immediate nonstop flight to the circular file.

Regard a query letter as a piece of professional writing, since that's the business the agent is in and the one you are aspiring to join. If you've written a proposal, look at your query letter as the proposal for your proposal.

Agents are used to receiving multiple query letters, although we do begin to wonder when we get a query addressed to "Occupant." (Just kidding.) I'm used to my last name being spelled with an "o." Thanks to computers, we also receive queries that start: "Michael Larsen/Elizabeth Pomada" followed by a salutation that reads "Dear Ruth." However, AAR member Sheree Bykofsky reports, "I did get a great client this way and sold the book!"

The cliché about never getting a second chance to make a first impression is also true with agents and editors. An individually typed query creates a better impression than a photocopy, especially in the computer age. Many agents will not read past "Dear Agent," "Dear Sir/Madam," or "To Whom It May Concern."

Returning a manuscript with a letter addressed to "Gentlemen," Elizabeth wrote on it, "I am no gentleman!"

Most agents will look at query letters online but vary whether they accept downloads of proposals or manuscripts they want to see. Elizabeth doesn't want just a query letter. She wants a letter and the first ten pages of a novel followed by a two-page synopsis. And although she prefers hard copy, she will accept this material online if the writer is not in North America.

Agents may prefer to receive a hard copy of a proposal or manuscript instead of a hyperlink to your work, a reluctance that will disappear before the end of the decade. Downloading is a small challenge; tying up a printer and paying for what will probably be wasted time and paper makes agents reluctant to accept online submissions except from clients.

Nor can you assume that because agents or editors download a submission that they will read it right away. If you're a new writer, your work will be in a queue behind the work from clients, referrals, more promising submissions from new writers, and submissions that arrived before yours.

The more income agents are earning with their clients, the less eager they are to take on new writers and the harder it will be for you to break in. However, most agents or their assistants will read unsolicited queries, as opposed to unsolicited manuscripts. And all agents will take on a book that's so literary or commercial, it's impossible to reject. And if they have to, they'll recommend other agents to try. But unless an agent is interested in your book, don't expect an answer unless you include a #10 SASE.

Whether you call or write, don't ask to meet. Agents don't want to meet with writers until they've read something they want to handle. If an agent does want to represent you, do meet the agent if you can, even if it means a (tax-deductible) trip.

How to Avoid Spending Time and Money on a SASE

If you don't want to include a SASE, then include this line at the end of your letter: "I haven't included a SASE, so I only expect to hear from you if you're interested." The email equivalent of the SASE is to start your letter like this: "No response necessary unless you're interested."

R. K. Munkittrick wrote on a rejection slip to a poet who had submitted several poems to a magazine:

Please curb your doggerel.

—Robert Henrickson, *The Literary Life and Other Curiosities*

Unleashing the Doggerel:
How Not to Get an Agent

If a book is not well enough conceived or written, the writer won't get an agent no matter how hard he or she tries. But your book is, so all you have to do is avoid these mistakes writers make in approaching agents. They range in severity from pet peeves to grounds for summary dismissal.

- Don't ask what agents do; find out before contacting them.
- Don't send material the agent doesn't handle.
- Don't send anything handwritten.
- Don't visit an agent without an appointment or expect your work to be read while you wait.
- Don't use fancy typefaces.
- Don't offer a laundry list of different kinds of work.
- Don't send manuscripts or illustrations on odd-sized or colored paper.
- Don't submit a whole manuscript without permission.
- Don't turn a page upside down in the middle of a manuscript to make sure that the agent reads it.
- Don't neglect to include your address, phone number(s), or email address on the cover letter and title page.
- Don't call or write before you have a proposal or manuscript ready to sell.
- Don't call to see if a manuscript arrived, instead of enclosing a postcard or arranging for a return receipt.
- Don't call an agent at home, at night, or on weekends or holidays without permission.
- Don't call an agent while you're under the influence.
- Don't be dishonest about your work or yourself.
- Don't send a submission marked "Personal" or "Confidential."
- Don't put cute stickers, sayings, or drawings on the envelope.

- Don't take rejection personally and be rude. Agents aren't rejecting you; they don't even know you. They're only rejecting your work.
- Don't expect special treatment because your manuscript is a "guaranteed bestseller."
- Don't use shipping "popcorn."
- Don't call to inform an agent that the submission you discussed on the phone has been delayed. Agents don't sit around wondering about the status of submissions they haven't received from writers they don't represent.
- Don't expect to use your advance for next month's rent.

From the Need-to-No File

Among our unforgettable moments in querydom are being asked, "Do you take credit cards for your services?" and "I have a thousand-page manuscript—could you type it up for me?"; getting a call in which the writer said, "My idea is so good I can't tell it to you"; and receiving a messy manuscript filled with typos, errors in spelling, punctuation, or grammar with a cover letter asking us to "please excuse the lousy typing."

Ducking the Boomerang:
How to Submit Your Manuscript

Writer Karen Elizabeth Rigley once lamented, "Sometimes, it feels like I'm submitting boomerangs instead of manuscripts." To help avoid having agents bounce your work back at you or not return it at all, submit your manuscript properly.

- Whether you submit it online or off, make it look like it's worth the advance you want for it. How professional a submission looks is a good indication of how well it reads.

• Find out how agents you want to approach like to be contacted. Then submit what they need in the form they want to receive it to as many of them who accept multiple submissions of letters, proposals, or partial manuscripts as you wish. Although most agents accept email queries, check to see if they prefer mailed query letters. Many prefer a hard copy of a proposal or manuscript. This seems simple and clear enough to agents, but writers are endlessly ingenious in finding new ways to make mistakes when they contact agents.

Thanks to this book, that's one problem you won't have.

The appearance of your material reflects the professionalism with which you are approaching the agent, the subject, and your career. The way you submit your work is the tangible evidence of the care you have taken with the proposal or manuscript. The impression it makes of you will affect readers' reactions to your work.

One of our favorite William Hamilton cartoons shows an ambitious-looking young writer confiding to a lady friend over a glass of wine, "I haven't actually been published or produced yet, but I have had some things professionally typed."

Whether you do it yourself or have someone else do it, make sure your manuscript is impeccably typed (have proofreaders prove you're right).

To make your submission as easy as possible to read for people who read reams of paper a week:
• Type or print your manuscript immaculately on one side of 8½" by 11" twenty-pound bond paper.
• Type everything, including quotes and anecdotes, double-spaced.
• Avoid "widows" (a subhead at the bottom of a page or the last line of a chapter at the top of one).

- Use a standard, serif, pica—ten characters to an inch—12-point typeface like Courier. Serif faces, like the one you're reading now, are more readable.
- Don't justify the right margin.
- Type twenty-five sixty-character lines, or about two hundred fifty words on a page. Set 1¼" margins on the top and sides of the page.
- Insert a header in your manuscript. At the left margin of each page, half an inch from the top, type your last name. On the same line, at the right margin, type the number of the page.

"I've got all the pages numbered," bragged the writer ready to conquer the world. "Now all I have to do is fill in the rest." After you fill in the rest, be sure that your pages are numbered consecutively from 1 to the end of the manuscript, not by chapter or the parts of a proposal, so if the manuscript is dropped, it will be easy to reassemble the pages.

Getting the Write Words Right

Proofread your manuscript carefully and get eagle-eyed friends to review it. One person will not spot everything. If you're using a computer, proofread a printout to catch what you may have missed on the screen, like the extra spaces that sneak in between words. You will find different things on the computer than you do in type or that you will hear when your work is read aloud.

Check words like *their* and *there* that spellchecker software can't. When the *its* and *it's* are wrong, someone is usually using a spellchecker.

Three tips for proofreading your manuscript:

1. Try proofreading your manuscript backwards so you will proof the manuscript, not read it.
2. Run a finger under the words and read them aloud softly.

3. Read the manuscript aloud or have someone read it to you. If it's a novel or narrative nonfiction book, you'll get ideas for passages to read at book signings and help make the job of whoever narrates the audio version of your book easier.

Packing Your Submission

Once you've got your submission ready, you should take the time to package it correctly.

- Submit your manuscript unbound, without staples, paper clips, or any other form of binding. Send high-quality photocopies of your text and illustrations or duplicates of slides. Never submit original artwork. Always keep a copy of anything you submit handy in case an agent or editor wants to discuss it.
- If you're sending a proposal, a children's book, or a short sample of the manuscript, you may use a rubber band or paper clip. But for a more professional look and greater protection in case you want to resubmit the material, insert it in the right side of a colored, double-pocket construction-paper portfolio.

Type the title and your name on a self-adhesive label and stick it on the cover. Use the left pocket for writing samples or illustrations and for the SASE. Include your name, address, day and evening phone numbers, and email address on the title page and on all correspondence.

- Don't send a diskette or email your manuscript until an agent requests it.
- Package your material neatly and carefully. Agents and publishers do not assume responsibility for lost or damaged manuscripts. For a short work, use a manila envelope, or, for greater protection, a #5 mailing bag. Enclose another stamped, self-addressed mailer if you

want the material returned. If you don't need the manuscript back, just enclose a #10 SASE to ensure a response.

You can arrange for a return envelope and postage through FedEx, United Parcel Service, or the post office. Without a SASE, an agent or editor will probably not respond or return your submission.

- Never send loose stamps; they can get separated from the manuscript.
- Don't use metered postage for the SASE.
- Use self-sealing envelopes and mailing bags. They make an agent's job easier and faster.
- Package your submission as simply as you can. It shouldn't take an agent longer to open the package than it does to read the manuscript. We once received a manuscript that was wrapped in plastic, put in a box, wrapped in foil, covered in a sheet of plastic bubbles, put in *another* box with shredded paper, wrapped again in brown paper and again with wire, and then the edges were taped! A sure-fire candidate for instant incineration.

Five staples will seal a mailing bag effectively. Avoid string or tape, and don't tape letters to the outside of the package. As one agent puts it, "The easier your package is to open, the easier it is for an agent to like you."

Send your cover letter and SASE inside the package with your proposal or manuscript so agents won't have to put them together.

- Don't send revisions, additions, things you left out, or address changes after you submit your work. Assume that agents don't keep a log of the thousands of submissions they receive a year. Playing match-up will not endear you to them.
- If you don't need the material back, say so. Agents recycle paper, and since mailing in both directions costs more and can damage a manuscript, it may make more sense to reprint what you submit than to ask for its return. But include a #10 SASE if you want a response.

You may prefer to include a self-addressed postcard with your address and the agent's name on it. We prefer a #10 business SASE in which we send our printed rejection letter, occasionally with a handwritten note:

- explaining why we're rejecting the book;
- suggesting changes to make the book more salable and perhaps asking to see the proposal or manuscript again if the writer makes them;
- requesting to see the writer's next book;
- suggesting publishers or agents to try.
- If you're sending a complete manuscript, insert it in a box, and use a #6 or #7 mailing bag, depending on the length of the manuscript.

Don't call to see if your submission arrived. It interrupts agents and wastes their time. To be certain your material arrived, use a delivery service that requires a signature; spring for a return receipt from the United Parcel Service or the post office; or use a paper clip to attach a SASP, a postcard you've filled out to your cover letter. Fill in your address and write the agent's name and this message on the back:

We received your submission on_____

We will get back to you by_____

Name_____

- Allow two to four weeks for a response to a query letter, two days for an email. If an agent requests a proposal or a partial or complete manuscript, find out how long the reading will take by visiting their website. Call or write if you haven't heard by that time. Allow for mailing time.

Don't try to guess when you sent your material. Either keep a copy of the letter handy or make a note of the date it was mailed and the date by which you expect a reply on your calendar as a reminder to follow up.

A six- to eight-week turnaround is typical, but agents vary in how quickly they process submissions. If you haven't heard in eight to ten weeks and are not satisfied with the reason why—a vacation or business trip can slow agents down—ask for the manuscript back or notify the agent you're submitting it elsewhere.

Calling will annoy agents, and it won't get you a faster reading. Agents receive a steady stream of mail and email. Priority is given to those from clients and those who come with recommendations. Then they plow through the rest in the order received, unless a cover letter excites them.

The industry obeys Murphy's Laws:

"Everything takes longer than it's supposed to."

"Anything done to speed up the process makes it worse."

The next chapter describes what happens when the response finally arrives.

Chapter 4
Joining the "2 Percent" Club:
A Crash Course on Rising from Rejection
to Acceptance

One day I received a package, similar to those I use to mail manuscripts, containing my book. Instead of fighting with the tape and staples, I decided to cut it open. My seventeen-year-old son watched as shredded grey stuffing fell from the cut packaging to the floor.

"Now that's I what call a rejection," he said. "They burn the manuscript and send you the ashes."

—Marion Eckholm, *Writer's Digest*

A Celebration of Rejection

Over the years, we've developed a macabre fascination with rejection. The next time you're feeling bad about your work being rejected, remember the trials of these bestsellers:

- *The Good Earth* by Pearl Buck was returned fourteen times and went on to win the Pulitzer Prize.
- Patrick Dennis said of his autobiographical novel *Auntie Mame*, "It circulated for five years through the halls of fifteen publishers and finally

ended up with Vanguard Press, which, as you can see, is rather deep into the alphabet." This illustrates why using the alphabet may be a logical but ineffective way to find the best agent or editor.

- Twenty publishers felt that Richard Bach's bestseller, *Jonathan Livingston Seagull*, was for the birds.

- The first title of *Catch-22* was *Catch-18*, but Simon & Schuster planned to publish it during the same season that Doubleday was bringing out *Mila 18* by Leon Uris. When Doubleday complained, Heller changed the title. Why 22? Because S & S was the twenty-second publisher to read it. *Catch-22* has become part of the language and sold more than ten million copies.

- Mary Higgins Clark was rejected forty times before selling her first story. One editor wrote, "Your story is light, slight, and trite." More than fifty million copies of her books are now in print.

- Before he wrote *Roots*, Alex Haley had received two hundred rejections.

- Robert Pirsig's classic *Zen and the Art of Motorcycle Maintenance* couldn't get started at one hundred twenty-three houses.

- John Grisham's first novel, *A Time to Kill*, was declined by fifteen publishers and about thirty agents. His six novels have more than sixty million copies in print.

- A total of one hundred forty-four publishers couldn't digest *Chicken Soup for the Soul*, compiled by Jack Canfield and Mark Victor Hansen, before it became a huge bestseller and spawned a series that in 2005 had expanded to one hundred books that have sold more than one hundred million copies.

- The *Baltimore Sun* hailed *Naked in Deccan* as "a classic" after it had been rejected for seven years by three hundred seventy-five publishers.

- Zelda Sayre wouldn't marry F. Scott Fitzgerald until he sold a story, and he papered his bedroom walls with rejection slips before he won her hand.

- Dr. Seuss's first book was rejected twenty-four times. The sales of his children's books have soared to two hundred million copies.
- Louis L'Amour received two hundred rejections before he sold his first novel. During the last forty years, Bantam has shipped nearly three hundred million of his one hundred twelve books, making him their biggest-selling author.
- If you visit the House of Happy Walls, Jack London's beautiful estate in Sonoma County, north of San Francisco, you will see some of the six hundred rejection slips London received before selling his first story. If you want to know how much easier it is to make it as a writer now than it was in London's time, read his wonderful autobiographical novel, *Martin Eden*. Your sufferings will pale compared to what poor Martin endured.
- British writer John Creasy received seven hundred seventy-four rejections before selling his first story. He went on to use thirteen pseudonyms to write five hundred sixty-four books.
- Eight years after his novel *Steps* won the National Book Award, Jerzy Kosinski permitted a writer to change his name and the title and send a manuscript of the novel to thirteen agents and fourteen publishers to test the plight of new writers. They all rejected it, including Random House, which had published it!
- And my all-time favorite: the *New Yorker* rejected a short story by Saul Bellow *after* he won the Nobel Prize for Literature.

Throughout this book, you will see humorous rejections from our collection. If you're going to be in any of the creative arts, you have to take to heart the poet Robert Service's belief that "rebuffs are merely rungs on the ladder of success." Look at rejection as *selection*, as a way of helping you pick the right agent and editor for you.

The Right to Be Wrong: Why Manuscripts are Rejecteb

"Rejection is one hundred percent guaranteed
in the writing profession."

—Gregg Levoy, *This Business of Writing*

Agents reject submissions for many reasons that have nothing to do with the quality of the work. Since most reasons don't reflect the proposal or manuscript's quality, if an agent rejects your work, go on to the next agent. Believe the agent is wrong if you wish, but don't expect an explanation about why your submission was rejected.

"I know it's not perfect," you may be tempted to reply, "but how am I going to make it better if agents won't tell me what's wrong with it?"

To which an agent might respond, "Telling you what's wrong with your work is not my job until we're working together. If you're not paying for my time, how can I justify adding to the time I've wasted reading your work by telling you why and risk giving you the impression I want to start a dialogue? What I *have* to do to make a living is find the next book I can sell ASAP."

If you didn't notice the typo in the subhead of this section, write the word *rejected* five times on the blackboard.

Going in Style: A California Rejection

A writer at the Santa Barbara Writers Conference once quipped that people become agents for the same reason that they become dentists: they like to inflict pain. Yet when it comes to enduring rejection, nobody tops literary agents. Editors come closest because editorial boards turn them down all the time.

Being writers as well as agents, Elizabeth and I are especially sensitive to rejection. Here is the rejection letter we send out:

Dear Writer:

Many thanks for sharing your idea or your work with us. Alas, we must reject what you have been kind enough to submit. We only handle adult book-length fiction and nonfiction. We are declining either because you submitted something else, or we can't help you achieve the success you want for your book.

Like the rest of the arts, publishing is a very subjective business. Even though we have written or coauthored fourteen books, most of which have been successful, we still get rejected. And although we have sold books to more than one hundred publishers since 1972, our clients' work is still rejected. Nor do all of the books that we do sell succeed.

We must find new books and writers to stay in business, and we love to get excited about them. But the only way we can make a living is by selling books to the large and mid-sized New York publishers, and selling small books by new writers to big publishers is becoming more difficult. So finding new writers is the hardest part of the job, and it's getting harder.

Like editors, we receive thousands of submissions a year and reject more than 90 percent of them. This forces us to use a form letter. But rejecting manuscripts that become successful books is a publishing tradition. And a rejection may have nothing to do with the quality or salability of your work.

So assume we are wrong. Persevere until your books reach the goals you set for them. We usually can't suggest a publisher or agent who might be interested in a writer's work, but directories, your publishing network, and the Association of Authors' Representatives will lead you to the agent you need. Persistence rewards talent. We can't make a living saying no, but as author Joe Girard says, "Every no gets you closer to yes."

Many thanks for giving us the opportunity to represent you. We wish you the best of luck with your writing career. Our website, www.larsen-pomada.com, has information you may find helpful.

Yours for Good Books that Sell (Especially When They're Yours!),

Elizabeth Pomada and Michael Larsen

Sailboats and Recipes: Making Your Submission Stand Out

How can you make your submission stand out and rise to the top of the agents' piles faster? Consider these suggestions that supplement the recommendations for what to include in a query letter in Chapter 3:

- Start your query letter with the name of one of the agent's clients—the more valuable the better.
- Offer a fresh, unique, original, highly commercial idea.
- Make your writing as irresistible as your networks assure you it can be.
- Include the number of major markets that you will get yourself to on publication to promote your book. (You can Google a list of them or check in the back of *Guerrilla Marketing for Writers*.)
- Mention the number of books that you will sell a year at your talks.
- If you're aiming at big houses and you're one of the few writers who can offer a matching promotion budget, ballpark the cost of your promotion plan, and if it's $20,000 or more, include the number.
- Come up with a brilliant title.
- Imbue your writing with your voice so you shine through.
- Indicate that it's a single submission because you know about and are eager to work with the agent.
- Include an eye-catching cover design.

- Be passionate about writing and promoting your book and about any books that the agent represents that are like yours.
- Include an attention-getting device. Someone once sent us a flower pot with five-foot-high dried branches sticking out of it and fake $100 bills hanging from the branches to suggest his book was going to be an evergreen money tree.

Imagination is more important than money: aim for something small and relevant that can be included easily with your submission. The goal is relevance and imagination, not making a financial sacrifice to impress an agent. (If you're writing about food, don't send homemade food. Anything edible must have the manufacturer's wrapping on it.)

These ideas will only help you if you have a salable book. None of them is necessary. If you do none of them but have a salable book, you'll still find an agent.

Another way to receive a faster reading: if the agent is in a city that you will be traveling to, the agent may be willing to read your work before you arrive so you can meet if the agent is interested.

A Hitchhiker's Guide to Asking the Right Questions

One summer while I was in college, I hitchhiked from New York to San Francisco. It enabled me to experience for the first time how vast, gorgeous, and for the most part empty the United States is.

A writer in search of an agent is also like a hitchhiker on the publishing highway, holding up a manuscript in hopes of being picked up by an agent and a publisher. Many cars may pass you by before one stops, and you never know how long or enjoyable the ride will be. But sooner or later, if you keep writing, you'll find the rides you need to reach your destination.

When an agent likes your work and wants to represent you, meet the agent if you can. It will be easier for you to size up an agent and establish a rapport in person than over the phone.

Meeting an agent is a chemistry test that both of you have to pass. Visiting will also give you a chance to see the office and the books the agent has sold and to meet the staff. If the agency has more than one agent, be sure to meet the agent who will be working on your book.

There's no certainty that your courtship will lead to a happy working marriage, but prospects for a successful relationship will be enhanced if you are familiar with your agent's experience, personality, and operating procedures. You should know what you need from the agent and what the agent will do for you.

The AAR has a list of questions to ask agents interested in representing you. The list is in Appendix 2, and it's followed by additional questions you may find helpful. Used together, the answers to the questions should help you determine whether you are talking to an experienced, reputable agent. You don't have to ask these particular questions or limit yourself to them. Directories may also answer some of them.

But when an agent expresses an interest in taking you on, satisfy yourself before you agree—as you would before hiring a doctor, lawyer, or accountant—that the two of you can work well together.

The bigger and more established agents are, or the more modest the books they are asked to represent, the less amenable they may be about having to prove themselves to new writers. No agent likes to be grilled, but you're entitled to an agent who isn't half-baked.

When it comes to getting to know your agent, style is as important as content. Find out as much as you can about agents before you approach them. During your first conversation, only ask about what you need to know but haven't learned from other sources. Talking to one or more clients will also help answer your questions.

If an agent promises you the moon, head for the nearest egress. If an agent decides not to represent you, tactfully ask why. You may not change the agent's mind, but the feedback may help with your next interview.

If Once Is Not Enough: Interviewing More Than One Agent

A store in San Francisco once sold T-shirts that read, "Life is one audition after another." Should you interview more than one agent before making a choice? No and maybe.

You can send multiple query letters and multiple samples of a novel, informing the agents that it's a multiple submission. But agents may only take the time to read a whole manuscript if they have it on an exclusive basis.

So if more than one agent requests the whole manuscript, research the agents enough to pick the one you would most like to represent you. If the relationship doesn't work out, go on to the next agent who asked to see it.

If you're writing nonfiction, you can send queries, or start with just your proposal, to as many agents as you wish simultaneously, if they're willing to consider a multiple submission. If more than one agent wants to represent you, researching the agents in directories and through your professional network will help you clarify which agent to choose.

Whatever an agent says or does should make as much sense to you as it does to the agent. Trust your instincts and use your common sense.

Chapter 5
A Study in Read and Green:
Six Criteria for Choosing the Right Agent for You

DREAM JOB OPPORTUNITY

Literary Agents Needed Now

Start a new high-income, low-risk career today! Enter the glamorous, high-stakes world of big-time publishing. No waiting! No experience, training, testing, or degree necessary. Salary potential unlimited. If you have stationery, a computer, email, a phone, and a table, you can be a literary agent now!

Be in constant demand by America's millions of writers! Get paid to read potential bestsellers! Meet new writers eager to become clients! Be wined and dined at glamorous restaurants by New York editors eager to work with you! Get invited to chic publishing parties! Feast on juicy gossip!

Become indispensable to eternally grateful authors! Have books dedicated to you! Make a fortune with your stable of bestselling authors! Become a power broker in the industry! Be quoted in columns! Have stories written about you! Sell your books to the movies and meet the stars! Write your bestselling memoirs!

Set your own hours! Sleep late! Wear whatever you like! Take long vacations! So don't delay—start the moment your business cards arrive!

(Realists need not apply.)

How Agents Become Agents

Many agents succumbed to their own version of this fantasy. If you like books, have an entrepreneurial spirit, and, ideally, a working spouse who will be delighted to support you for five years until you start to make a living at it, being a literary agent is tempting. Discovering wonderful new writers and helping them get their books published is a noble ambition and the best part of the business.

Of course, there are some days when, if agents were asked how they became agents, they would answer, "Just unlucky, I guess." But most agents, like most editors, do the job for love, not money. They do it because they love books and they like helping writers.

Agents are as diverse, independent, and individualistic as the writers they represent. Part of the reason for this is that just as anybody is free to write books, anybody may agent them. This explains why many agents, who may think big, start small and work out of their homes.

AAR member Sandra Dijkstra, who represents Susan Faludi and Amy Tan, believes that becoming an agent is only a matter of Cartesian logic. The French philosopher Descartes believed: *Cogito, ergo sum*—"I think, therefore I am." Aspiring entrepreneurs around the country are saying to themselves, "I think I'm an agent, therefore I *am* an agent." Only time and their bank accounts will tell if they are right.

The low start-up costs, lack of licensing requirements (except for movie agents), deceptive simplicity of the business, and the glamorous aura of publishing continue to attract new agents. So agents vary enormously in their qualifications, how they work, their ability, and their sense of responsibility.

Former Editors

There are as many ways to become an agent as there are agents. The traditional and still best path to agenting goes around an editor's desk. As you will see in Chapter 18, your editor is the in-house agent for your book. So an agent who has been an editor, especially one at a large trade publisher, has a big head start in gaining the experience needed for the job. Being an editor provides on-the-job training in working with writers, negotiating contracts, and nurturing authors through the publication process.

Working for an Agent

Next to being an editor, the best way to learn how to be an agent is to work for one. At the bi-coastal William Morris agency, aspiring agents start out in the mailroom or as assistants. Sheree Bykofsky became an agent while working for a packager. After selling four books in one month, she incorporated.

Other Publishing Positions

Working for major publishers in other positions also enables agents to learn how publishing works and build a network of editors and other publishing people. Successful agents have learned about the business as sales reps, subsidiary-rights salespeople, publicists, promotion directors, and house counsels. Appendix 3 is an outline of the publishing process, a fascinating, complex undertaking filled with opportunities for mistakes as well as creativity.

Bookstore Insiders

Booksellers learn on the front lines what flies and what dies. This is excellent experience for developing a sense of the kinds of books sales reps can convince booksellers to stock and what motivates people to lay down hard-earned money on books.

Legal Know-How

Lawyers who become agents may not have a publishing background, but they bring knowledge of contracts and negotiation that makes them effective at the bargaining table.

These are only the most obvious ways to learn about agenting. There are others such as being an author or a writing teacher or working in the movie business or in other media, such as a magazine editor or a journalist.

Those who join the ranks lacking both publishing experience and ability account for much of the turnover in the agency business. Like writers, the survivors all toil at the same job, but no two of them do it exactly alike.

Comedian and author Steve Allen once returned a manuscript sent by a hopeful writer with the following note:

"I thought you'd like to see what some fool is sending out under your name."

Mix and Stir: The Ingredients for a Working Marriage

What are the qualifications for being an agent? Since the relationship between a writer and an agent, like that between a writer and an editor, is a working marriage, the qualities needed include the same virtues that help to sustain any marriage: honesty, intelligence, compassion, friendliness, trust, patience, confidence, initiative, responsiveness, reliability, promptness, courtesy, respect, enthusiasm, chemistry, a sense of humor, loyalty, faith in you and your work, and optimism tinged with fatalism.

An agent needs to have:
- a knowledge and love of writing and books and the desire and ability to represent different kinds of books and authors to different kinds of editors and publishers
- the ability to keep track of a changing mélange of meetings, phone calls, clients, correspondence, submissions from writers and to editors,

deals, projects in different forms and stages, editors and other in-house people, sub-rights contracts, and contacts in the trade and consumer media

- the ability to judge books and advise writers how to make their work more salable
- a knowledge of the publishing business
- a knowledge of and credibility with editors and coagents
- a knowledge of contracts and how to negotiate them
- the ability and willingness to be tough on a writer's behalf
- curiosity about anything that could wind up between covers
- persistence and creativity in trying to sell a property and in following up on royalty statements and sub-rights sales
- the recognition that helping to shape a writer's career is a serious responsibility that agents must live up to if they expect to keep clients

> "The single most abominable rejection I have ever heard of a writer receiving was this: *Dear Mr. Andrews: We cannot use the paper you sent us. You wrote on it.*"
>
> —Gregg Levoy, *This Business of Writing*

Their Way or the Highway: Why Agents Are Like Books

"If the phone doesn't ring, you'll know it's me."

—Anonymous

Every book is a book, yet every book is different. So it is with agents. They vary in their personalities, backgrounds, and in the size and location of their agencies. This leads to a wide spectrum of approaches to running a business. Agents vary in:

- the services they offer
- their competence
- the books they handle
- their tastes, interests, and literary judgments
- the number of writers they handle
- how they want to be queried
- what they request in an initial submission
- how involved they get with the publishing process
- how they submit books
- the number of editors and publishers they deal with
- how many publishers they try before giving up
- whether they charge fees, what they charge them for, and how much they are
- their commissions
- whether their agency agreement is oral or written
- the terms of their agreements, which are discussed in Chapter 6
- when, how, and how much they like to communicate with clients
- how long they take to respond to submissions
- whether they accept multiple submissions

A woman submitted a novel to an agent, and two months later, she called to see what had happened to it. The agent drew a blank.

"Was it a romance?" he asked.

"No," she said.

"Was it a mystery?"

"No."

"Was it historical?"

"Well," said the writer, "it wasn't when I sent it."

Agents vary in how strongly they have to feel about a project to handle it. Some agents will only represent books they love. Others live by the Hollywood adage: "Sell it, don't smell it."

Agents may specialize in children's and young adult books, in nonfiction, or in literary, commercial, or genre fiction such as romance or mysteries. But most can't afford to or don't want to specialize and will consider adult fiction and nonfiction for the general public. Many agents for adult books also handle children's books. Some handle textbooks, articles, short stories, and even poetry. The *Guide to Literary Agents* lists the kinds of books agents handle.

Six Questions to Ask Yourself about the Agent You Want

Answering the following six questions will enable you to assess the kind of agent you want to represent you. When you find an agent willing to work with you, your answers will help you evaluate the likelihood of a happy marriage.

1. What qualities do you need in an agent?

When you are looking for your first agent, what you need from the relationship may be hard to decide. But to avoid being disappointed, try to figure out the kind of relationship you want with your agent, and then find one who you think will satisfy your needs.

One AAR member spoke for her colleagues when she said, "I'm somewhere between a lawyer and a shrink." A writer once confessed to HarperCollins VP Carolyn Marino, "John Doe's my agent, but I'm afraid to call him." If you need a lot of personal attention or handholding, don't choose an agent who prefers to keep the relationship strictly business.

It's been said that 93 percent of what is remembered when you speak is not what you say but everything else about you: your appearance, your gestures, the tone of your voice, and your friendliness. When you meet people, you tend to make either a head connection or a heart connection with them. When you connect both ways, you have the chemistry for an enduring relationship.

Friendliness is a quality essential for some, unimportant for others. One of the top agents in the business once told me that he had no interest in being friends with his clients. His job was to make money for them, and that was his sole concern. A writer once gushed to me about her well-known agent, "I love him. He's the only person I know who's meaner than I am."

In *Beyond the Bestseller*, Richard Curtis's excellent inside portrait of publishing, he refers to a successful agent "with a tongue like a trash can."

Sandra Dijkstra tells the story about a client of hers who was discussing her with a friend, and the friend said, "Everyone says she's a bitch." "Yes," the client replied, "but she's *my* bitch." If you want a shark in your corner, find one.

2. Do you want to work with a large, medium, or small agency?

Most agencies are one- or two-person shops. There are more than one hundred medium-sized agencies that have three to six people on staff. The twenty large agencies with eight or more people have subsidiary-rights specialists for first-serial sales and movie, foreign, and other rights. They also represent their clients as lecture agents.

Two large agencies, William Morris and International Creative Management, have offices in New York and Los Angeles and abroad. They are talent agents as well as book agents and represent actors, screenwriters, producers, and directors whom they can call on to "package" a movie deal—that is, bring all the bankable elements together to get financing and distribution for a movie.

Large agencies have lawyers on staff that review and negotiate contracts, which may save writers legal fees. While agents in small agencies have to monitor their clients' financial affairs, large agencies have accounting departments that enable the agents to concentrate on servicing their clients and selling their work.

These high-powered agencies have overheads to match their clout and are more eager to find commercial properties that they can recycle in other media than they are to find small projects by new writers with little sub-rights potential.

A writer once came to us after leaving the top man at a large agency feeling he was neglected because he was "a small fish in a big pond." Or as another writer delicately put it, "I believe my potatoes were too small for their baronial tables."

But the prestige of being represented by a large agency such as Curtis Brown, International Creative Management, Janklow & Nesbit, Sterling Lord Literistic, William Morris, or Writers House opens doors for clients because they represent so many bestselling authors that publishers are always eager to see whatever they have to sell.

The same consolidation that has affected publishers, booksellers, wholesalers, and mass-market distributors has also affected agenting. In his first-rate book *Writing the Blockbuster Novel*, AAR member Al Zuckerman, president of Writers House, estimates that about twenty agents account for 90 percent of the bestselling novels.

Editors may offer agents at large agencies larger advances than they would offer small agencies for the same book. But publishers are buying books, not agents, and they will pay any agent whatever it takes to acquire a book they want. What agents bring to the table is the ability to judge what a book is worth and to extract that sum from a publisher. Al Zuckerman believes that, caught between authors wanting bigger advances and editors wanting smaller ones, agents have to have the best judgment about what a book is worth.

The risk of poor communication arises between the writer and the agent in large agencies, because different agents who may be on oppo-site coasts handle various sub rights. You can minimize this problem by establishing effective lines of communication with your primary agent, the one who takes you on.

Your goal is to find an agent you will enjoy working with and who will do an effective job for you. If your book is salable enough, you will find an eager agent at any size agency. Whether you choose to look for a big, medium, or small agency will depend on your assessment of your needs and your book.

If you are a new writer, you may find small agencies:

- more open to new writers and less profitable books
- more reachable by phone
- less harried and more accessible, especially if they're out of the pres-sure-cooker atmosphere of the Big Apple
- able to respond to your submission more quickly because they have fewer submissions
- more likely to be concerned about the quality of your relationship as well as your work

3. Are you willing to pay a reading fee?

Back in the days before paperback auctions, agents' megabuck demands, and conglomerate mergers, publishing was a nice, quiet "gen-tleman's business." But even today, discretion and gentility are still expected of agents in acquiring clients. Literary agents expect clients to find them through listings in directories, referrals, their websites, and their presence at literary events. They may contact writers whose arti-cles, short stories, or books they've read, or people about whom articles have been written.

One of the most successful agents in the country outside of New York charges an annual $250 client fee to cover postage, photocopying, and long-distance phone calls. Most successful agents keep track of expens-es incurred on their authors' behalf and either deduct them as their income is received or bill their clients if there is no income from which to deduct the expenses.

Like editors, established agents receive thousands of submissions a year. Whether or not they earn a living from agenting, agents may feel entitled to a fee for the time spent reading and critiquing what they regard as unsalable work. Some agents just charge unpublished writers; some refund the fee if they decide to handle the book or if it is sold.

When Elizabeth and I started our agency in 1972, we wanted to see everything. After a year or so, we realized that we had read over one hundred fifty manuscripts and found only two worth handling.

To staunch the flow and, we naïvely hoped, improve the quality of submissions, we decided to charge a $25 fee for reading complete manuscripts, which is what Elizabeth was being paid to review books for the *San Francisco Chronicle*, and to refund the fee if we handled the project. Alas, the jewels and refunded fees were few, and after a year or so, we could no longer afford the time.

We don't charge reading fees now, but Elizabeth looks at only the first ten pages and a two-page synopsis of a completed novel or a proposal for nonfiction. One respected Big-Apple agent only asks for the first two pages and a synopsis.

To avoid the possibility of impropriety, AAR members are forbidden to charge reading fees. If you're dead set against paying a reading fee, don't. Hundreds of agents don't charge one. In fact, Writer's Digest's *Guide to Literary Agents* is divided into two groups of agents: those who charge reading fees and those who don't. But doing so doesn't automatically brand an agent as dishonest.

There are able, responsible agents who charge reading fees and may edit your manuscript or publicize your book for a fee or a larger commission. You can't expect an agent who doesn't charge a fee to edit your work. If they take on a writer, most agents will at least provide feedback that their clients can use to make their work more salable. They may also suggest you work with a freelance editor.

Before sending your work to an agency that charges a reading fee, find out if additional fees are required for editing or reading a revision, whether you will receive a critique of your manuscript, and if and when the agent refunds the fee. Be a wary consumer, as you are with any new product or service you try, until you're convinced that you are dealing with an experienced, reputable agency.

At one point, however, one agent was asking writers for a 15 percent commission, for $100 a month, for a minimum contribution of $100 for a trip to New York, and to pay for dinners the agent had with editors. The author was also expected to do the initial mailing of the manuscript at the agent's direction!

There is nothing illegal about this, because agents are free to work any way they want. It's been said that you have to risk your life to feel alive. Agenting books is rarely life-threatening, but there is usually an element of risk.

Writers risk their time writing their books; agents risk theirs by trying to sell them. Traditionally, agents' basic overhead, apart from expenses arising directly from representing their authors, has come out of their income, not their writers'.

If the book doesn't sell, both are out the time, effort, and overhead they gambled on the project. This has always been the premise of the writing and agenting professions.

Risk is one of the most exciting aspects of writing, agenting, and publishing. Books by bestselling authors sometimes fail, while new writers come out of nowhere and build a nest on the bestseller list. I hope your book will be one of the surprises.

4. What commission are you willing to pay?

A cartoon once portrayed a group of agents sitting around a table, with one of them saying, "We've got to figure out a way to keep these damn writers from getting ninety percent of our income!"

The profession of agenting started in England in the 1880s because of mistreatment of authors by publishers, the growing value and complexity of subsidiary rights in England and America, and the protection of authors' rights provided by the first American copyright law.

In the 1880s, a lawyer in London named A. P. Watt used to bill authors for his services. When they didn't pay, he had his authors' earnings sent to him, deducted a 10 percent commission, and then forwarded the balance to the authors.

Paul Reynolds, the first American agent, began his fifty-two year career in 1891. Mark Twain was one of the first American authors to have an agent.

In the United States, the number of agents started growing after World War I. With few exceptions, the 10 percent commission held firm until the 1970s.

The rise in commissions accelerated during the recession in the early 1980s. Hit by rising costs, shrinking advances and royalties, lower bookstore sales, a proliferation of agents, and the greater difficulty of selling books to penny-pinching publishers, agents were pushed into raising their commissions. So just as publishers (and everybody else, it seemed) raised their prices, agents started to raise their commissions.

Agents have increased their commissions out of need, not greed, and some (including us) absorb costs such as postage, long-distance telephone calls, and perhaps photocopying, previously charged to authors.

Agents are still free to charge whatever writers are willing to pay. (Movie and talent agents are limited by law to 10 percent.) As mentioned earlier, agents who provide editorial or legal assistance may charge a commission as high as 25 percent. The commission you pay should seem fair to you.

5. How important is an agent's experience?

"Judgment is what you get from experience. Good judgment is what you get from bad experience."

—Anonymous

Should you sign up with a new agent or approach those who have been around a while? An agent's stock in trade is his or her contacts; knowledge of writing, books, publishing, contracts, and selling subsidiary rights; and ability to work with writers and publishers. An agent can acquire much of this knowledge only through experience.

But publishing experience doesn't guarantee you an effective agent, and the lack of it doesn't preclude someone becoming an accomplished agent, if the person is capable of learning the trade. The trade-off between established agents and new ones is that although the former bring knowledge and experience to the table, new agents:

- are more open to new writers
- can respond more quickly
- have the drive to establish themselves
- are more open to new ideas because they may not know what they can sell
- have more time to devote to editing and selling their books
- bring the passion of a neophyte to their new calling

These virtues can make up for the difference in experience.

However, unless you have confidence in your agent's ability to negotiate a contract and he or she has negotiated deals the same size as yours with publishers like the one who wants to buy your book, ask him or her to consult with a more experienced agent or an intellectual property attorney to ensure that the contract will be as finely tuned as possible when it reaches you.

6. Does your agent have to be in the Big Apple?

New York harbors the greatest concentration of literary agents in the world, and more keep joining their ranks. But Andrea Brown in Salinas, California; Sandra Dijkstra in Del Mar, California; Frederick Hill and Bonnie Nadell, who have offices in San Francisco and Los Angeles; Jillian Manus in Palo Alto, California; Jan Miller in Dallas; Amy Rennert in Tiburon, California; and Raphael Sagalyn in Bethesda, Maryland, are proving that agents don't have to be in the Big Apple to flourish.

Ultimately, agents don't sell books and writers don't sell books. Books sell books. Editors are just like you. Either they respond to a book or they don't, and no one can make that happen. The power of agents and publishers comes from the words of their writers. As AAR member Molly Friedrich once said, "Agents gain leverage by being right."

An editor reads a proposal or manuscript and decides either from a literary or commercial point of view, ideally both, that the book is worth publishing. It makes no difference whether the manuscript arrives from across the street or across the country or even whether it comes from an agent. Writers sell thousands of books a year.

The reason that New York is the capital of publishing is its unique concentration of:
- writers
- agents
- publishers
- bright, creative people who come from around the country to work for them

- review and publicity media
- publicists
- radio and television networks
- trade and consumer print media
- subsidiary-rights buyers
- suppliers who service publishers
- the world's leading financial center, which provides the capital that lubricates this high-powered engine of commerce
- writers' organizations
- literary events

This exciting mix propels publishing forward in search of the next hot book. Publishing people generate ideas, deals, and an insatiable craving for marketable goods, services, and personalities. Some agents fill their lunch calendars months ahead, others lunch with editors once or twice a week, and still others avoid the ritual altogether, preferring two quiet hours to work.

AAR member Susan Ann Protter was lunching with Michaela Hamilton, now editor-in-chief of Kensington Books. Mike, a cat fancier, mentioned that she was looking for a mystery series featuring cats. This was catnip for Lydia Adamson, one of Susan's authors who went on to write three series.

So lunches and parties help keep agents up-to-date on editors' needs and the latest gossip, and ideas are hatched and deals consummated over the Dover sole, but few agents, if any, make their living over lunch. They make it by phone, email, snail mail, UPS, Federal Express, fax machine, and burning the midnight oil.

During one of our regular trips to New York in the early eighties, a paperback editor was wining and dining us in a chic midtown bistro. We were delighted when she informed us that she wanted to buy a historical romance series and then speechless when she didn't want to negotiate the deal. She refused to talk terms over the Beaujolais and insisted that we wait until she returned to her office and then call her from a phone booth!

Through publishing events and proximity, New York agents have more access to:

- book editors for selling books, hatching ideas that lead to deals
- magazine editors for trying to get assignments, reviews, and first-serial sales
- other media people
- scouts for foreign publishers
- editors visiting from elsewhere
- movie and television buyers based in New York

However, don't assume that because agents are in the Big Apple, they see everyone they need to and know what's going on. As one editor-in-chief noted, "There are New York agents who are out of it."

Over the years, writers around the country have approached us because they were put off by the impression of the New York publishing world as an impenetrable monolith. They didn't understand the perpetual scramble agents and editors endure in search of salable books.

We were once talking with a well-established New York agent who said that she had nothing to sell. All of her writers were working on books, so she was sitting around waiting for a book to turn up that she could sell.

Writers contact us saying that New York agents don't return phone calls. One AAR member who responds to every letter admits, "I don't return calls from people I don't know unless they are with a publisher, producer, or studio." But New York is the most competitive place in the world to be an agent. This means that most New York agents are at least as anxious as agents elsewhere to find new writers. If you want an agent in New York, stifle your fears and plunge into the fray.

Remember, agents don't work for publishers; they work for their writers. And although many writers prefer an agent closer to home, ability and compatibility matter more than geography.

The Worm in the Apple

Life is a series of trade-offs, and while being in New York makes agenting easier, it also makes living harder. New York doesn't start things; it commercializes them. In manufacturing terms, the rest of America is the Research & Development Department; New York is Marketing & Finance—it's the executive suite.

Publishing people go to the same parties, see the same people, read the same media, and live the same urban or suburban lifestyle. This breeds provincialism that makes them all the more receptive to new writers and ideas.

Finding the Right Fit

Wherever your search for an agent takes you, keep in mind these enduring truths about the breed:

- Like editors, agents don't go into the business to get rich. They are agents because they like books and they like people. Publishing is a people business sustained by profit, passion, psychic rewards, and personal relationships.
- Like writers, editors, publishers, and books, agents aren't perfect. Each is a unique blend of strengths and weaknesses. Don't look for perfection. Look for a good fit with your work and your personality.

Happy hunting!

Chapter 6
Taking the Vows for Your Working Marriage:
The Author-Agency Contract

"A verbal agreement ain't worth the paper it's printed on."

—Samuel Goldwyn

In the past, agents preferred handshake agreements. Many still do. But most agents have written contracts. Large agencies have always had them, and movie agents in California are required by law to have them.

Agents who prefer not to have a written contract believe that trust is the foundation of a happy working marriage. If agent and author trust each other, no written agreement is necessary. If they don't, it's time to get a divorce. New agents often start out feeling this way, and then decide to have a written contract to protect themselves, usually after an author has left them without justification.

For Butter or Verse: Covering the Basics

Some agents supplement their oral understandings with a letter of agreement. Even if your agent doesn't use a written contract, he or she should be willing to draw one up and sign it if it's important to you.

Traditional marriage vows commit the bride and groom to stick it out "for richer or poorer, for better or worse." To include everything that can befall a relationship in wedding vows is impossible. For an agency contract to provide for every contingency that can affect the working marriage between you and your agent is equally impossible.

But a contract can cover the basics and help to avoid misunderstandings that lead to problems. Your contract should spell out the obligations of both you and your agent while the contract lasts and after it ends. It should also describe how you can terminate the contract.

Questions about the agent-author relationship don't arise when all is well. But when a real or imagined problem crops up, writers wonder what their obligations are to their agents. One of life's lessons learned through bitter experience is that you avoid problems by minimizing risks. When your future or large amounts of money may be at stake, do you want to rely solely on your assumptions, your memory, and the goodwill of your agent to protect your interests? A working marriage consummated with a mutually satisfactory contract helps avoid problems and provides the means to solve those that do arise.

Just as no two agents are alike, no two agency agreements are the same. They vary in length, thoroughness, tone, what they cover, and clarity. Some are written in legalese, others as a letter between author and agent.

Your ability to change your agent's contract will depend on your value to the agent and how much the agent wants to represent you. But even if you are a new writer approaching your first agent, you are entitled to a contract that you think is fair, and you should settle for nothing less.

Whatever form your contract takes, you and your agent should reach an understanding on the following twenty-one points:

1. The Confirmation of Your Agent

Unless you and your agent agree otherwise, your agent will expect to have the exclusive right to sell all of your work and your literary services throughout the world. This means that even you can't sell your own work, only your agent can. If a publisher asks you to write a book or offers you a contract, you are obligated to refer the publisher to your agent.

2. Your Agent's Right to Use Coagents
One clause will mention the agent's right to hire coagents, who are specialists that help with subsidiary rights such as film or foreign rights.

3. Your Agent's Fiduciary Responsibilities
Agents have two big incentives: they want to keep clients and they want to make money, which they do by placing their clients' work. But the contract between you and your agent creates a fiduciary responsibility on your agent's part.

Your agent is obligated to act with the highest level of loyalty, fidelity, and good faith in representing you and your work. You have the right to expect honesty, confidentiality, and professionalism.

4. What Your Agent Will Represent
An agreement can be limited to specific projects or kinds of writing or to a specific territory, such as North America. But an agent will have the first opportunity to represent or the right of first refusal on all of a client's literary work in all forms: books, plays, screenplays, essays, articles, short stories, and poetry in all print, broadcast, electronic, and merchandising media throughout the world. This includes material you write or coauthor and that you are commissioned to write.

The exceptions to this include work that is already committed to another agent or buyer, writing you produce as part of your job, and other projects or kinds of writing you and the agent agree to exclude.

If you are selling first-time North American serial rights to short pieces for a one-time payment, the negotiations are much simpler than for a book. You have less need of an agent, especially if you're a freelancer who already knows the editors.

Even if your short stories or articles sell for four-figure sums, agents may still be unwilling to handle them, because their commissions won't justify the time spent placing them. But if your agent is earning enough commissions from your books, he or she may be willing to take care of less profitable work as a courtesy.

Some of AAR member Susan Ann Protter's clients regularly make four-figure sales to national magazines. They submit their articles but ask Susan to handle the negotiating and make sure that they get paid. If you write short stories or articles and your agent doesn't handle them, you may want to ask if your agent will help you on this basis. Large agencies have specialists who sell book excerpts to magazines and may also represent their authors' articles.

If you are a screenwriter and you already have an agent for your screenplays, the agent you find to sell your novel may agree to exclude screenwriting (and perhaps motion-picture rights to your novels) from the agreement. Or if your agent wants to represent your novels, but you also write poetry or short stories, which the agent doesn't handle, you should be free to sell them on your own or through another agent.

Since the agent is trying to establish your reputation and may not be making any money in the attempt, or since the agent's efforts have made your other work more salable, the agent may want commissions on work that you sell for yourself or through another agent. You will have to decide whether your agent's efforts on your behalf justify the agent receiving commissions for work sold without the agent's help.

5. How Long the Agreement Will Last

Oral or written agreements last only as long as both parties want them to. Your right to leave your agent is part of the fiduciary relationship. Written contracts may last indefinitely, with the writer given the right to end the agreement with thirty or sixty days' notice. This is, in effect, a one-book contract because, in addition to being able to leave your agent at any time, it leaves you free to go to another agent with your next book.

A contract may state that it lasts for a fixed period of time—one or more years—at the end of which the writer can cancel the agreement or do nothing and let it be extended automatically for the same period of time. Because the relationship is a fiduciary one, you may leave your agent at any time.

6. Your Agent's Right to Represent Competing Books

An agency agreement may include a clause allowing your agent to handle books competitive with yours. Agents vary in their willingness to represent competing books.

Timing may be the determining factor. If your agent is trying to sell two competitive books at the same time, he or she is faced with the problems of which editors to show which project to and in what order. The same problems may arise in selling first-serial and subsidiary rights. Also, part of your agent's fiduciary responsibility is to inform clients about potential conflicts of interest.

If one of the books has already been sold or published, handling a second book on the subject may not impair an agent's effectiveness in representing the first book. But if a second project is clearly competitive with one an agent is already handling, the agent must notify the writers. If both clients are agreeable, the agent is free to handle the second manuscript.

The second author will benefit from the agent's experience with similar books. Publishers who were outbid for the first book may be interested in the second. On the other hand, if your agent has tried unsuccessfully to sell a book like the one you're proposing, your agent may be able to save you time by telling you to change the book or go on to the next project.

Snoopy receives a rejection letter:

Dear Contributor:

Thank you for submitting your story to our magazine. To save time, we are enclosing two rejection slips: one for this story and one for the next one you send us.

7. Your Agent's Commission

This clause specifies your agent's commission, 15 percent for domestic sales. Some agents charge as much as 25 percent if they provide other services such as publicity.

If your agent uses a network of foreign agents to handle foreign sales, it will specify the foreign agents' commission on such sales, usually 10 percent. Your agent may reduce his or her commission to 10 percent, which will bring the commission to 20 percent. Some agents work through American coagents who charge 20 percent, bringing the total commission to 30 percent. Agents usually split their normal commission with their movie agents, but may add 5 percent for their coagents, bringing the total commission to no higher than 20 percent.

The commission clause may also indicate that commissions earned by an agent do not have to be returned for any reason. For example, if an agent sells a book, receives the commission on the first part of the advance, and either the author doesn't deliver the manuscript or the publisher decides it's not satisfactory and the author must return the advance, what should the agent do?

Nothing. The agent has done his or her job by selling the book. If the writer doesn't produce or the manuscript is unsatisfactory, it's not the agent's fault, so why should the agent be penalized by having to return the commission? This is a black-and-white situation.

Other circumstances may not be so simple, and, regardless of this provision, an agent may be willing to return a commission if the author repays an advance and the circumstances warrant it. Some agents take the position that if the writer has acted responsibly, the agent will repay the commission when the writer returns the advance.

8. The Agent as Conduit

Publishing contracts will contain an agent's clause, stating that your agent represents you and enabling your agent to act on your behalf and receive income earned through the contract. Your agent deducts the commission, and forwards the balance to you.

Agents who don't have written contracts know that when they sell a book, the publisher's contract will include an agent's clause. Appendix 2 contains two sample agents' clauses.

Publishers prefer this system because agents protect them from writers claiming they never received money due them and because agents serve as knowledgeable mediators if questions arise. And as conduits for an author's income, agents are certain to receive their commissions.

Agents maintain a separate agency account so their clients' income won't be mingled with their own. The money in this account belongs to the agent's clients, not the agency, so that if the agency goes bankrupt, client income is safe.

This is a standard practice not usually mentioned in an agency agreement, but you should feel free to confirm it. New agents may not have a separate account because they may not receive enough income to justify opening one. State laws about bank accounts also vary.

9. Remittance Time

Dorothy Parker once said that the two most beautiful words in the English language are *check enclosed*. The contract should specify how soon your agent will forward your income and royalty statements to you after receiving them. Ten working days is usually enough time for checks to clear in an agent's bank. However, a check in a foreign currency may take months to clear.

10. How Expenses Will Be Paid

An agent will pay for local phone calls and ordinary mailing expenses. Your agent may expect you to pay for part or all of the other expenses, such as messengers, long-distance phone calls, faxes, cables, overseas or overnight mailings, photocopying proposals or manuscripts, mailing costs for multiple submissions, buying books and bound galleys of your manuscript set in type, and legal advice.

Your agency contract should indicate what expenses you will pay and when. Whether or not it's stated, it's understood that your agent will not commit you to a large expense without your approval.

11. Checking the Books

You are legally entitled to examine the entries in your agent's books relating to the income from and expenses for your work. If your agent is absorbing expenses, there will be no need to check them, and there may be no books to check. You should receive an itemized list of the expenses deducted from your income. If an agent resists your right to see the financial records being maintained on your behalf, head for the nearest exit.

12. Your Freedom to Sign the Agreement

The agency contract should indicate that you are free to sell your work and sign the contract. This protects your agent from conflicts caused by a previous buyer or agent.

13. The Right to Assign Income from the Agreement

Your agent does not have the right to transfer you as a client to another agency without your approval if he or she sells out, moves on to something new, becomes ill, or passes away. However, like you, your agent has the right to assign income to others. Agatha Christie assigned the income on her plays and mysteries to her nephew to lessen the burden of inheritance taxes.

14. Your Freedom to Assign the Agreement

Although the relationship between you and your agent ends if either of you dies or is incapacitated, the agreement may state, as a publishing agreement does, that its terms are binding on your heirs or anyone to whom you give the proceeds of the book. Continuing income from authors' estates can be a major source of regular income for an agent. Knowing that one's literary affairs will be well taken care of can be a source of comfort for writers.

15. Which State Law Governs the Agreement

This indicates which state's laws will be used to interpret your contract if a dispute arises. Usually, it's the state in which your agency has its head-quarters.

16. Changing the Agreement

Neither you nor your agent can unilaterally change the contract. You must both sign all changes and additions to the agreement. Each of you will have a signed, dated copy of the contract.

But as your career develops, what you need from an agent may change. For example, you write nonfiction books and your agreement states that your agent will handle all of your work, but you want to write children's books or fiction, an area in which your agent has no experience. You should be free to find another agent for your other work.

17. When a Problem Threatens Your Working Marriage

"The only sure sign that a man is dead is that he is no longer capable of litigation."

—the *Encyclopædia Britannica*'s entry on death

If a marital spat comes between you and your agent, the agreement should provide a method for resolving it. The simplest way is for you and your agent to agree to discuss the problem in person, by phone, by mail, or by email. If you both conscientiously try to solve the problem in a way that is fair to both of you, you may find an equitable solution to the problem.

A compromise will be less emotionally and financially costly than a fight.

For a problem the two of you can't handle, consider these alternatives:

- Use a mutually satisfactory mediator. This person can be a judicious, knowledgeable publishing professional or an experienced mediator, whom you can find through the publishing, arts, or legal community. A mediator will help you find a solution. This enables both of you to control the outcome.

- Use an arbitrator from an organization that supplies them. The best known of these groups is the American Arbitration Association. This approach can be less time-consuming, costly, and technical than litigating, but as with a mediator, the results hinge on how competent and knowledgeable the person is.

- The longest, most painful, and potentially the most expensive possibility is litigation. Since anyone can hire a lawyer at any time, this possibility doesn't have to be mentioned in the agreement.

18. Getting a Friendly Divorce

As mentioned earlier, you can end your agency relationship at any time. If the time to leave your agent arrives, you won't want to prolong the relationship or slow down the progress of your career. Make the transition to another agent as quickly and painlessly as possible so you can get on with selling your work.

The only question is how soon you can leave the agency with a minimum of problems. An agreement with no fixed duration will provide for ending the relationship with a certified letter in a certain period of time, usually thirty or sixty days. This allows time for submissions to be sold or returned and for the agent to notify coagents to wind up their activities. It will also give you time to look for another agent.

But if you are between books, and your agent or your agent's coagents aren't trying to sell your work, a thirty- or sixty-day waiting period isn't necessary. Write a letter saying you're leaving and the date the termination becomes effective.

If you terminate a contract without cause before it expires, you may be liable for commissions your agent would have earned had the agreement run its course.

19. After You Separate

This clause explains your agent's rights and responsibilities after the agreement ends. Agents usually continue to receive their authors' income from sales already concluded. However, if you prefer, your agent can arrange with your publisher to have separate checks and statements sent to both of you.

In any event, your agent has the right to receive the commission on all projects already sold and those on which negotiations began while the agent represented you.

Just as it is part of your agent's fiduciary responsibility to inform you about all offers, your agent must also, upon request, return manuscripts you have submitted and furnish you with copies of rejection letters. The letters will be helpful if you decide to pursue the sale of your book, since you or your next agent will not want to submit your manuscript to an editor who has already rejected it. Chapter 11 also discusses ending the agreement.

Another rejection slip for Snoopy:

Dear Contributor:

Thank you for submitting your story. We regret that it does not suit our present needs. If it ever does, we're in trouble.

20. Subsidiary-Rights Sales after Your Agreement Ends

Another issue to resolve when you leave your agent is the sale of subsidiary rights. If the agent had let the publisher keep all of the book's subsidiary rights, then the agent would share in them, because the agent continues to receive commissions on contracts that you have signed. However, your agent tries to retain subsidiary rights for you. Agents try to sell those rights, and forward the proceeds from those sales to you as soon as possible.

Like publishers, agents need sub-rights income to help sustain their businesses. Since your agent made those rights sales possible by the initial sale of your book, and then kept those rights out of the publisher's hands for you, he or she may feel entitled to keep representing such rights or to receive commissions on them regardless of who makes the sales. You may save aggravation and money later by clarifying this when you sign up.

The film or foreign rights to a book may be more valuable than the American book sales. Agents make a living by encouraging writers who produce not just one book, but many books, with both backlist and sub-rights potential. This potential may grow over time, as the author's career develops and new possibilities like electronic rights emerge.

If, for example, you become a famous novelist, the foreign and film rights for your previous books may become valuable years later.

If you've written a nonfiction book that's gone out of print, and your agent has had the rights for the book reverted to you, renewed interest in the subject or a successful new book may make it possible to get the book republished.

If you are leaving your agent, your former agent may be willing to split commissions on future deals for rights with your new agent. The trade-off here is that although your first agent will make less money, the income will come in with no effort or expense on that agent's part.

Another alternative is to pay two full commissions, which will be worth it, if you're receiving a smaller percentage of something rather than a larger percentage of nothing.

On the other hand, even though you've left, your first agent may still want to sell the subsidiary rights for previously sold books. Your new agent may be working with some of the same movie and foreign coagents as your first agent, so if trust or ability was not what separated you, there may be no advantage in trying to withdraw subsidiary rights from the first agent. You and your new agent must decide how to proceed.

21. One Clause to Avoid
Some agents charge monthly retainer fees to help minimize their risk. If you can afford to subsidize your agent and are otherwise satisfied with the agent's honesty, reputation, experience, and ability, then it's up to you to decide whether you want to pay your agent a salary.

Signer Beware

One of the ways in which the AAR is serving the agenting community is by having a code of ethics (Appendix 3). The code establishes standards members must meet.

No other standard exists for what agency agreements should cover to help you judge another agreement an agent presents to you. Your agent should be willing to explain any clauses that are not clear to you and to alter the agreement to your mutual satisfaction. But you have to be a careful consumer, just as you would when signing any business document.

If you have concerns about the agreement and the agent isn't willing to discuss them or make what you feel are reasonable changes, consider these suggestions: research agreements in books, talk to other professionals in your networks, check online, ask writers' organizations for help, or hire an attorney who knows publishing to go over the agreement with you.

Appendix 4 has a Writer's Bill of Rights and an Agent's Bill of Rights that provide guidelines for what you and your agents can reasonably expect from each other, regardless of what the agent's contract says.

A Modest Proposal

This chapter cannot be the final word on agency agreements, but it will provide a basis for understanding your relationship with your agent, for discussing questions if they arise, and for going your separate ways as painlessly as possible. The agency agreements in Appendix 5, including ours, will give you an idea of what such agreements look like.

If you and your agent trust your instincts, use your common sense, and act in good faith, you will both be doing your part in establishing a lasting working marriage.

Chapter 7
Life after Yes:
Eleven Steps to Matrimonial Bliss

"Marriages are made in heaven and consummated on Earth."

—John Lyly, British writer

The Eleven Virtues of a Dream Client

Congratulations! You have found an agent who has taken you on and is trying to sell your book. You are both reveling in the honeymoon: the confidence, enthusiasm, good will, and anticipation that follow the consummation of your working marriage.

As with any marriage, the challenge now is to make your working marriage with your agent as fruitful and rewarding as possible. The best way to accomplish this is to be a dream client. What's a dream client? For agents, they are writers who:

- know who we are and approach us in a professional way with fresh ideas, impeccable writing, and enthusiasm
- write irresistible books that everyone who reads them loves
- are patient, faithful, grateful, creative in coming up with fresh ideas, conscientious about writing and rewriting, and are tireless promoters
- understand that our working marriage is a collaboration and provide whatever support and ideas they can to help us
- are totally committed to developing their craft and career
- deliver a book a year, on time—each book better than the last

- understand that we want them to be satisfied with our efforts
- call us when they need us
- mention us in their dedication or acknowledgment pages
- become lifelong friends
- write so well and are such wonderful people that they inspire us to be dream agents

One of the things that makes our list eccentric is what's *not* on it: money.

How can you become a dream client?

1. Write Well and Often

Write your books as well as you can, and write at least one book a year. Make your agent, as well as your editor and your readers, eager to see your next book. Also remember that an agent's credibility is on the line with every submission he or she makes.

A writer sent the manuscript for his novel to a publisher and on the envelope, he wrote: *FISH INSIDE. DELIVER IN FIVE DAYS OR NEVER MIND.*

He got a message back: *PACKAGE DELIVERED IN FIVE DAYS BUT HAD TO OPEN THE WINDOW ANYWAY.*

2. Deliver Your Books on Time

There are enough challenges in publishing a book. Unless you have no alternative, don't add to them and risk a rejection by being late with your manuscript.

3. Communicate Only When Necessary

Kendra Marcus, a children's book agent in Orinda, California, once faxed a children's book to an editor on a Friday morning and sold it that afternoon. Your book will probably take longer. So one point to settle when your agent starts to submit your work is when you can expect to hear from him or her. Unless it's for personal or social reasons, call or write your agent and expect contact only when it's necessary.

Regardless of how big an author becomes, agents can't devote all of their time to one client. Your agent may be your only agent, but you are not your agent's only client. However, agents are not mind readers. If a problem arises with your book, your editor, or your publisher that you can't handle, contact your agent. Never assume your agent knows about the problem. Don't delay, hoping it might go away by itself. Don't beat your head against a wall trying to find the solution by yourself.

Part of your agent's value to you is his or her experience. Maybe your agent has dealt with the problem before and knows how to solve it. He or she may be able to show you why it really isn't a problem, or why it's an opportunity in work clothes.

Calling your agent about every small frustration will damage your relationship. However, if you have a serious concern, tell your agent about it immediately. Don't be defensive in your relationship. You don't work for your agent—your agent works for you. But also keep in mind that until your agent sells your book, he or she is working for free. When you do contact your agent, be cheerful and optimistic. Ask if there's any way you can help.

4. Live and Help Live

"Live and help live."

—Miriam Viola Larsen, a good poet, a great mother,
and an inspiration for what I do

When you start working with your agent, agree on how your agent will submit your work, whether one or more copies will be submitted at a time, and when you will hear from your agent. Agents vary in how they like to get back to writers, and writers vary in how anxious they are to hear what's happening with their work. Once you establish a satisfactory way of working with your agent, be patient. If it stops working, change it.

5. Try to Forget about Your Manuscript

Once your agent begins submitting your manuscript, try to put it out of your mind. Publishing is a slow business, and the movement of paper through the labyrinths of the publishing behemoths is slowing down even more.

You and your agent both want to sell your book as quickly and as well as possible. Your agent will be delighted to call you with good news the moment there is any. While you're waiting:

- If you have a brainstorm on how to make your proposal or manuscript more salable and your agent agrees with you, revise it and get it back to your agent.
- If your book isn't finished and you have faith that it will sell, continue to work on it.
- Keep reading about publishing and promotion, and refine your promotion plan.
- Start your next book.
- Go on vacation.

6. Celebrate When Your Book Is Sold

When your agent sells your book, show your appreciation. A bottle of champagne, celebratory meal, or flowers will do nicely. Oxford University Press Editorial Director Peter Ginna feels that personal letters are more meaningful. The goal isn't to make a grand gesture, just to express your gratitude. The best gifts may be a simple handwritten thank-you note, and recommendations to other writers.

7. Acknowledge Your Agent

Like most people, agents like to see their names in print. Thanking your agent in your dedication or acknowledgments will bring added pride and pleasure to your agent every time he or she thinks about your book. When people ask Elizabeth and me if we have children, we say no, we have books instead. Your book is your baby, but, like you, it's also part of your agent's extended literary family.

8. Promote Your Books

This essential activity is discussed in Chapters 21 and 22.

9. Use Your Agent Reflex

Your agent reflex: if an editor approaches you and wants to buy your book or wants you to write one, talk about the book but not about the money. Memorize this line, and use it: "Gee, that sounds great, but if you want to talk about money, you'd better call my agent." Here's hoping you need your agent reflex often.

Even after your book is sold, don't talk to your editor about money without asking your agent. You may do yourself more harm than good.

10. Trust Your Agent

Trust your agent to work well on your behalf. You will have the final say about selling your book. Esther Newberg, a senior vice president at International Creative Management, believes that "it's passion that makes a book work." So you might, for example, fare better at a smaller house or with a smaller advance but with a more passionate editor. Have faith in your agent's instincts as well as your own.

11. Be Faithful to Your Agent

Agents take on new writers in the hope that they will become better at their craft and more profitable as clients as time goes by. If your agent gives you a reason to leave, you should do so without hesitation. But to leave an agent who is doing an effective job is to deprive the agent of commissions earned partly because of the agent's commitment to you and your career.

A publishing paradox: every book is a book, but every book is also a unique combination of author, subject, timing, agent, editor, and publisher. Harmonizing these elements so a book is as successful as it can be is always a creative challenge for everyone involved. Agents who help their authors do it well earn the right to a lasting relationship.

Mae West once quipped, "Marriage is a great institution, but I'm not ready for an institution." If you're ready, then be prepared to enter into this secular state with the belief that marriage is not a 50-50 proposition. Make it a 100-100 proposition by doing all you can to help it survive and thrive. You and your agent have to be equally committed to do whatever it takes to create and sustain an enduring relationship.

Part 2

Understanding Your Agent

Chapter 8
Transforming a Writer into an Author:
What Your Agent Does before the Sale

"Everyone lives by selling something."

—Robert Louis Stevenson

The Recipe for Publishing Success

"Do you need an agent? No. You don't need an agent. You don't need a dentist either. You can fill your own teeth."

—Mystery writer James Frey

An Englishman once observed that "a baby is a big noise at one end and no sense of responsibility at the other." But your book *is* your baby. You give birth to it twice: first as you're writing it and again as your publisher midwifes its coming into the world. And you want it to be as successful as possible.

You may think that it doesn't matter who publishes your first book or how much you get for it as long as it's published. If so, you don't need an agent. Bestsellers and books that become classics do get rejected. But I believe that if your book is good enough, anybody can sell it, because any likely publisher will buy it.

But the recipe for success in publishing is complex and involves many people. It calls for thirty-one ingredients, the best possible:

1. author
2. idea
3. manuscript
4. agent
5. editor
6. publisher
7. deal
8. design
9. production
10. subsidiary-rights sales
11. marketing plan with trade and consumer advertising, publicity, and online and off-line promotion
12. space and copy in the catalog
13. marketing materials
14. reception at sales conferences
15. lay-down or sell-in by the sales reps to stores
16. sell-through by bookstores with minimal returns
17. reprinting to keep the pipeline supplied with books
18. warehousing and order fulfillment
19. staff and/or freelance publicist
20. author platform
21. press/speaker kit
22. trade and consumer promotion by the author and the publisher
23. reviews
24. location in bookstores' displays
25. use of handselling, shelf-talkers, and author events by booksellers
26. sales to libraries
27. use by schools and book clubs if the book is suitable
28. accounting
29. timing

30. luck
31. word of mouth and mouse

Then add the contagious enthusiasm of everyone involved in editing, selling, reviewing, and promoting the book, and your readers. All of these elements have to be mixed well and served at just the right time. The publishing process adds incalculable spices that complicate this recipe and affect sales:

- Editors have their own tastes and publishing houses their own character and employees.
- Editors and publishers do certain kinds of books better than others.
- Although there may be more idealism in publishing than in any other business, editors and publishers vary in their ability and sense of responsibility as much as agents and writers.
- You cannot determine if a publisher will be right for you from its size, its location, or its books. As I mentioned earlier, it may be better for you to have a big book at a little house than a little book at a big one where it will get lost.

The Roles of an Agent

How can you acquire the best possible editor, publisher, and deal for your book? Here's how your agent can help you:

An Agent Is a Mediator

"What publishers do you work for?" This is a question that probably every agent has heard, so as I mentioned, you need to know that agents don't work for publishers, they work for the writers they represent. They are mediators between two realities: you and the marketplace.

An Agent Is a Scout

Agents are the eyes and ears of the publishing business, perpetually on the lookout for salable books. Your agent is a scout who knows what publishers are looking for, which editors can best judge the salability of your work, and which houses can do the best job publishing it.

An Agent Is a Filter

Agents are filters for editors. Editors know that submissions from agents are far more likely to be salable than those from writers. So editors— those who even read submissions from writers—read agented submissions first because they'll be more likely to buy them and because if other editors have them, they may try to take them off the table with preemptive offers (a subject discussed in Chapter 9).

An Agent Is a Guide

Your agent guides you through what may seem to be alien territory. Your agent can explain what you need to know about agenting, publishing, and the craft of writing to help ensure your success.

Editors don't have the time to answer all of an author's questions throughout the publication process. Although they are also busy, agents work for their writers, so they make time.

There's a cartoon in which a writer exults to a friend, "I just got paid for my manuscript. My agent paid me five dollars to take it someplace else."

An Agent Is a Midwife

In *Beyond the Bestseller*, Richard Curtis notes that during the paperback boom of the sixties, the role of agents expanded beyond encouraging writers and protecting their interests. Publishers came to depend on agents to help them fill their growing lists.

By reducing the burden on editors to bring in books and develop writers, agents became more powerful by becoming more involved with generating ideas, their clients' writing, and shepherding their clients' books through publication. Before then, books had to be finished before being sold, but agents started selling books on the basis of partial manuscripts, outlines, or even one-page presentations.

Today, your agent is a midwife whose editorial guidance can help you give birth to your idea by turning a loser into a winner. Your agent can save you time and frustration by reading your work and judging its salability. Your agent nurtures both you and your books as they make their way through the world of publishing.

It's tougher than ever to sell the work of new writers to major houses. An agent's advice can make the difference between a manuscript with potential and a successful book. Submissions reach our doorstep in one of these conditions:

- Hopeless: either we don't think it's salable or it's not right for us
- Hopeless but: the book isn't salable but the writer may be, and we ask to see the writer's next book
- Salvageable: the material has possibilities, and we discuss with the author how to make it publishable
- Ready to submit: the proposal or manuscript is good to go

If writers need help editing their work, we recommend freelance editors. The least expensive way to get editorial help is to build a network of other writers who can help you, and to join or start a writer's group that meets weekly to critique each other's work.

An agent who knows books and publishing can make a world of difference in helping a writer tailor a book to suit publishers' needs. Whether it's a catchier title, a more marketable angle, the addition of a missing element, or smoother prose, by the time an agent sends out a proposal or manuscript, it's stronger and more salable than when it arrived.

Writers sell their books to small and mid-sized houses all the time, but one thing they can't do is understand how editors and their colleagues will judge a submission. Agents who have submitted books that were accepted and rejected will have a far more refined sense than writers of how editors will respond to a book and what it needs to be worth as much as writers want for it.

A final rejection for Snoopy:

Dear Contributor:

Thank you for not sending us anything lately. It suits our present needs.

An Agent Is a Focal Point for Subsidiary Rights

Chapter 6 notes that your agent will expect to handle all of your work in all media throughout the world unless you agree otherwise. As soon as your agent starts representing your book, the agent will develop a plan for selling subsidiary rights.

One successful agent has a three-pronged approach to selling rights. First he sells the American rights, then the foreign rights, and then he approaches Hollywood. He uses the momentum of one sale to help make the next.

If your book has strong enough subsidiary-rights potential, your agent will start selling the rights before your book is sold to a publisher. If a property or an author is salable enough, an agent can start stirring up interest even before having a manuscript to sell.

Foreign and movie sales may not become possible until an author's books sell well or even hit the bestseller list. Before and ever after publication, your agent follows up on new opportunities for subsidiary-rights sales, sending new information about your books to coagents as it becomes available.

An Agent Is a Matchmaker

Your agent knows which editors and publishers to submit your project to and, just as important, which to avoid. The relationships between a writer and an agent, editor, and publisher are a series of simultaneous working marriages that have both personal and professional aspects. When your project is ready to be submitted, your agent discusses with you how best to proceed. Your agent continues to send out your manuscript until it is sold or as long as your agent feels that he or she can sell it.

Like agents, editors reject more than 90 percent of what they see. A manuscript may be first-rate but unsalable because publishers feel, perhaps wrongly, that it doesn't fit the needs of the marketplace, competes with one of the publisher's books, or will be published too early or too late for the book to succeed.

Agents vary in the number of publishers to whom they will submit a manuscript, depending on a book's commercial potential, how many publishers they deal with, the feedback they receive, how many publishers exist for a book, and how much they like it and the author.

Some agents will sell a book to any publisher, good or bad; others will sell only to publishers they know will do a book well. We know an agent who submitted books to just four major houses. If none of them took it, he returned the project. Other agents will keep trying for years.

A Home at Last

On March 3rd, 1987, Elizabeth was discussing an offer for a literary first novel, and I was listening to her half of the conversation. I picked up the thick file of correspondence about the book and started turning the pages. I finally got to the last page, which was the cover letter with which the author had submitted the book. Lo and behold, the author had submitted the book on March 3rd—March 3rd, 1977! It took a decade for Elizabeth to find a small literary house to make a low four-figure offer for the book, but what a joy it was for both the author and us. And the book got a nice review in the *New York Times*.

An agent may send out one, two, or three copies of a proposal or manuscript, or as many as thirty copies in a multiple submission.

For a book with bestseller potential, an agent may conduct an auction, giving publishers a date and ground rules ranging from simple to complex for bidding against one another on a project. With the writer's approval, the agent may simply opt for the house that makes the highest bid or may let editors know that the author will evaluate various aspects of the deal, including the editor and the house, in determining the best offer for the book.

An editor's skill and passion may be more important than the size of the advance. That's one reason why, if possible, you should visit editors who want to buy your book before accepting an offer. If you're writing a cookbook, there's usually only one editor at a house who does them. Your agent can only submit your proposal to the cookbook editor. The best deal and the best house may not also include the editor you'd most enjoy working with.

Talking to editors about their vision of your book and its potential, seeing their offices and their books, meeting other people on the staff is a valuable opportunity to decide if the chemistry is right for your working marriage with an editor and publisher. It's also a great opportunity to learn about how publishers work.

An Agent Is a Shock Absorber

Many books are never sold, despite an agent's best efforts. Rejections can crush a writer, but for agents, absorbing turndowns is just a disagreeable part of the job.

After a series of rejection slips from publishers, Nobel Prize–winning novelist John Steinbeck wrote to a friend:

It is nice to know that so many people are reading my books. That is one way of getting an audience.

An Agent Is a Negotiator

When a publisher does make an offer for your book, your agent is a negotiator who hammers out the most favorable possible nuptial agreement for your working marriage with your publisher. When your agent receives the contract, it is reviewed clause by clause. No contract arrives ready to sign. If your agent is dealing with a publisher for the first time, the contract review usually leads to one or more long letters, faxes, or phone calls about changes.

The time it takes to negotiate a contract depends on a combination of factors unique to every sale: the book, the size of the deal, the timing, the people involved, and the house. The contract for your book is between you and your publisher, so your agent cannot sign it for you. The meaning of a contract's clauses may be obscured by legalese (cynics say intentionally), but with your agent's help, you must understand, approve, and sign it. You will be responsible for the literary, financial, and legal obligations it contains.

Calculating Unseen Value in an Offer

There's much more to consider in deciding what will be the best combination of editor, publisher, and deal. Here are issues to consider besides the advance when choosing your publisher:

- Royalties for the hardcover, trade, and mass-market paperback editions
- How much lower your royalties will be when your book is sold at high discounts
- How your advance will be paid
- Which subsidiary rights you keep
- The splits on sub-rights income between you and your publisher
- Bonuses for one-time, revenue-generating events like a movie sale or an appearance on *Oprah*
- Escalators for hitting a bestseller list

- The number of promotional copies you'll receive
- The publisher's track record in your field
- Your chemistry with the editor and other people in the house
- How much time your editor will devote to editing your manuscript
- How committed the house is to your book
- What the house will do to promote your book (which may change)
- When your book will be published
- Whether the house wants other books in a series and how many
- Where the publisher is located

There may be other issues that relate to you or your book. If your agent has already sold books to the editor or house, you will benefit from that experience. Your agent will help you weigh the tradeoffs in an offer—and there are always tradeoffs.

Interlude 1
Paper Cuts:
A Terrible Day in the Life of an Agent

William Targ, the editor who bought Mario Puzo's *The Godfather* for $5,000 after two editors had turned it down, once remarked, "The trouble with the publishing business is that too many people who have half a mind to write a book do so."

If the Moccasin Fits

"Help me never to judge another until I have walked two weeks in his moccasins."

—Sioux prayer

These words of wisdom may keep you from making a mistake in working with your agent. You hired your agent, the agent works for you, and you have the right to be satisfied with what your agent is doing for you.

But you may destroy a salvageable marriage by harboring unrealistic expectations or not understanding your agent's job. Looking at your relationship from your agent's point of view will help you appreciate an agent's problems and concerns. In this interlude and Interlude 2, on a terrific day in an agent's life, you can try my eight-and-a-halfs on for size.

A terrible day in the life of an agent may include any of the following hassles, a composite day-in-the-strife. They are disguised to protect the guilty.

If, as most agents do, you work for yourself, agenting can be isolating. An agent who is very happy living on a mountain in the Southwest works alone and never meets his clients or the editors he sells to. He prefers doing everything by mail and email.

But wherever agents are, they represent writers around the country (and sometimes beyond), so most of your work is done by phone, mail, and email. There are the writers represented on one side, the buyers on the other, and the agent in the middle.

The people, the phone calls, the paperwork, and the details are endless. And if agents don't sweat the small stuff, sooner or later it will come back to haunt them and cost them time, money, clients, or embarrassment.

After plodding my way through far more fruitless emails than I would like, I start playing my daily game of email and telephone tag with people I need to reach. The only editor who isn't on another call, not in yet, or at a meeting on this cold, rainy Monday in January blithely announces that the deal we negotiated last week is still not definite because it needs the approval of a management committee. (An editor usually gets house approval before making an offer.) Now I have to tell the author that the deal she and I thought was firm still has to be approved.

I spill my coffee on a manuscript as I grab the first call of the day. It's immediately clear that picking up the receiver is my second blunder. In fact, I'm convinced my real mistake was getting out of bed.

"What do you mean, you don't feel the vibrations are right for me to represent you?" I ask incredulously after a client says hello to say goodbye.

"Well," she continues with a West Marin airiness, "my moon is rising, and since I was born on the cusp, my astral guide assures me that it would not be good for you to represent me."

What's a star-crossed Capricorn to do? I've been fielding this laid-back Libra's questions for two years while she labored on a how-to so far out I thought it just might be in. Finally, I get to read it, and shock of shocks, it looks salable. Now, thanks to a rising moon, my hours on the phone and my reading time have come to naught—another portent for a bad day.

One of our coagents in Hollywood calls with a news flash: three days before the camera was set to roll, a movie based on one of our books has been killed because one of the studio's blockbusters bit the dust on opening day. The project, which took more than a year to nudge this far, is as good as dead.

The next call is from a seething client who's had it up to here with the subject of an autobiography on which she's collaborating and with me for bringing the two of them together. A minute after I finally put the receiver down, the subject of the autobiography also calls in a royal snit, and complains that the writer smokes too much and is dictatorial about how the book should be written and unwilling to make changes since she is "the writer."

"Whose story is it, anyway?" she demands to know. It's going to take some heavy three-way palavering to keep this project on track, and they haven't even finished the proposal. I promise both of them I'll get back to them soon, wishing it could be in a decade.

Another marriage made in helvetica: as if by black magic, the next call is a conference call with two other angry collaborators whose unholy alliance is disintegrating at warp speed. I'd put together a guy with a story to tell and one of our writers. The guy is unhappy with what the writer is producing. The writer hasn't been able to pull out of the guy what she needs and has used up more time than the pittance the guy is fronting for what a sample chapter justifies. Both of them feel like they've been taken advantage of, and nothing I can do can make it right for either of them. Fade to black.

Daily, two-foot stacks of mail arrive in at least three installments: UPS, package mail, and everything under two pounds in the mailman's big blue bag. Overnight mail and other mail services also give our doorbell a workout.

With a dull thud, the mailman deposits today's hefty stack of morning mail, containing fifteen queries with sample chapters, nine queries without sample chapters, seven rejects for books we've spent too long submitting in vain, four manuscripts, two proposals, and the usual clump of media, bills, and letters.

Eagerly awaiting the arrival of the first bound copies of a promising first novel, I tear open a mailing bag and sure enough, it's the book. But when I open it up, pages fall out of it! The bindery screwed up, and I have to hope that the author doesn't become unglued and that this disaster didn't ruin every book in the first printing.

The mail also includes this missive:

Dear Mike:

Just wanted to let you know that a writer friend put me in touch with Crapshoot Books, who bought my book. What do you think of that? Another friend who's studying accounting took care of the contract. Many thanks for your help.

"Many thanks," he had the chutzpah to write! For the past four months, I read this turkey's manuscript, made extensive suggestions for revisions, read a revised version, made further suggestions, read a third version, and sent him our agency agreement, which he never signed. He doesn't even understand that he's taken advantage of my time, for which I won't be compensated. All I can do is count my blessings and hope that Lady Luck knows she owes me one.

The next call comes from a weeping, frustrated author on the road who, because her publisher stopped promoting her book, set herself up with a full schedule of media appearances, only to find out that no stores have books—not even the store where she's having a signing. After a heavy dose of verbal TLC, she is ready to continue to shoulder the boulder up the mountain.

The mail isn't finished with me yet. A note from an editor brings news of this disaster: a beautiful art book I was looking forward to seeing has been doomed by a typhoon. You may wonder how a typhoon can ruin a book. It's easy when it's a gift book being printed in Hong Kong. A delay in printing and shipping the book means that it won't reach stores in time for the holidays, a disaster for gift books.

I receive a call from an editor being driven berserk by a client. The client had found some inconsequential matter that she regarded as sufficient reason to badger us at least once or twice a week. Not satisfied with how we were negotiating her contract, she badgered the editor about it. I dispatch a letter giving her sixty days' notice.

My job is to be a marriage broker, to arrange happy, productive working marriages between writers and editors. This time, we got the right editor—it's the author who blew it. I feel sorry for the editor. I'll have to figure out how to make it up to her so she'll remain receptive to our other writers.

Still more gloom from the mail pouch: our agency agreement allows clients to end the agreement with sixty days' notice by registered mail. Signing for a registered letter from a client always causes an uneasiness fulfilled by a writer's saying goodbye. Today is no exception. We tried for three years to sell a science-fiction novel for a guy in Montana and finally succeeded, beyond our expectations, because the editor who bought it wanted a series. The series didn't make the author rich, and he decided that his career wasn't moving far enough, fast enough, and it was our fault.

Our agreement makes it as easy as possible for clients to fire us because we don't want unhappy clients. But we always hope to have the opportunity to respond to a client's problems to see if we can solve them or if there is a solution to the problem other than time and perseverance.

I open the next letter while eating lunch at my desk—a soggy tuna fish sandwich on cold toast. An editor is rejecting the finished manuscript of a specialized how-to book that took twenty-three submissions and more than a year to sell and is unlikely to be sold elsewhere. The excuse the editor is forced to use is that the illustrations are late. The real reason: her publishing house has been gobbled up by a larger one with no interest in the subject. And although there's a chance that we could cajole the house into doing the book, they would kill it with indifference. I am left with the joyless task of informing the author, haggling about repaying the advance, and finding a new home for the book.

I stab myself with a staple as I open a jiffy bag sealed with twenty staples instead of the five it requires.

The mail does bring a check. That's the good news. The bad news is that the check came about because the numbers on an author's royalty statement made us holler, "Tilt!" and we're still wondering if the author got all the royalties due to him. There's another check, this one postdated! The needy author will be thrilled. Maybe she can postdate a check for her landlord.

I place a call to the last of ten editors considering a proposal and learn that it's on its way back. It's a book I'm very excited about, and editors are returning the project with rejections so good you could frame them, but they just can't convince the marketing department that the book will sell.

Near the end of the day, I have the depressing task of calling one of our Hollywood agents to let her know that our client has made his choice between the two movie offers for his book. One was for a small but fair sum from an earnest young producer with no credits, the other for twice as much money from an Oscar-winning director. Our client chose earnestness, which in this case cost him and us money and cost the project the clout of a proven director. Melancholy proof that sometimes, agents can be only as effective as clients let them be.

My day ends, as most days do, by reading a succession of queries and proposals, all of which have only one virtue: they fail to keep me awake.

To top off this terrible day, the phone wakes me up five minutes before midnight. Judging from the background noise, it's someone in a bar who sounds totally sloshed. He wants to know if I would be interested in seeing a bestselling novel he is thinking (!) of writing. I force myself to tell him politely to call back between nine and five.

Since I'm now awake, I decide to take a stab at one last manuscript to try to salvage something from what has been a thoroughly dismal day. Numbed by the inadequacy of what I have endured so far, I start reading…

(To be continued in Interlude 2)

Chapter 9
The Publishing Contract:
Tiptoeing through a Diamond-Studded Minefield

"The writer, owing to his temperament, his lack of business training, and his frequent isolation from other members of his profession, is especially unfitted to drive a good bargain with those who buy his manuscripts."

—From a pamphlet issued by the Author's League of America, 1912

"Every profession is a conspiracy against the laity."

—George Bernard Shaw

When an Editor Says Yes

"You know that book we spoke about last week? Well, I brought it up at the editorial-board meeting this morning and got a go-ahead. I'd like to make you an offer for it." The longer an agent waits to hear those words, the sweeter they sound. Usually, when an offer is made, the editor has already spoken to the agent to:
 • verify that the book is still available
 • see if any other offers have been made on the book

- let the agent know that the editor is in the hunt, so that if the book is being considered by other houses, the agent won't accept another offer (unless it's a preemptive offer) without first talking to the editor
- find out what kind of advance the agent is looking for, to make sure that it's in the same ballpark as what the editor is thinking about offering—just as it's essential for you and your agent to share the same literary and financial goals for your book, both of you must also accept your editor's perspective on your book's potential
- tell the agent when to expect a phone call about the house's decision

Striking a Deal

"Trust in Allah but tie your camel."

—Arab proverb

When the editor calls back, buoyed by the victory of getting the book through the editorial board and eager to make an offer, the discussion will cover the following deal points:
- Your advance
- The payout: how many installments your advance will be paid in
- Your royalties
- Subsidiary rights
- In a hardcover contract, how paperback income will be split if the house sells mass-market or trade-paperback rights
- Issues particular to you and your book such as the discounts on books you buy or out-of-pocket costs you need

The conversation may also cover issues such as:
- advance escalators for appearances on the bestseller list

- an advance escalator on a movie sale
- a promotion budget
- a first-printing guarantee
- a bonus for appearing on a talk show

After the agent and editor discuss the essential points of the deal, the agent gets back to the author, and then continues to call the other publishers who bid on the project until all houses have made their final offers. It may take more than one call to agree on the deal points with the winning publisher.

You Snooze, You Lose

One way publishers avoid bidding against competitors is to preempt a book: bid on the book first with an offer that the author can't refuse. The offer has to be big enough to convince authors and agents that they may not do as well as the preemptive offer if other publishers don't bid or don't make as high a bid.

The agent may suggest holding out for a bigger advance and will tell the author to consider how desirable the house and editor are. It's a judgment call, and agents help clients weigh the pros and cons of the situation, taking into consideration:

- the editor
- the publisher
- the house's track record with similar books
- how committed the house is to the book, which may be more important than the advance
- the royalties and sub-rights splits
- the markets for the book
- if the house is bidding for more than one book
- the agent's knowledge about and experience with the house

If you and your agent don't think a preemptive offer is high enough, you can make a counteroffer, and if necessary, negotiate the difference. Or you may reject the offer but give the editor a topping privilege, meaning that no matter how high the bidding goes, the editor can top it by ten percent.

This can be frustrating for other editors interested in the book. One editor complained about receiving a book at 9:00, and by the time he called the agent at 11:00 to express interest in the book, another house had already preempted it. The hotter the book is, the faster publishers pounce on it.

The resourceful house Grove/Atlantic wanted to buy *Cold Mountain*, which they rightly believed would be a bestseller. But they knew that they couldn't outbid their bigger rivals for it. This situation arose during the week between Christmas and New Year's, the slowest week in the year—so slow that some big houses close their doors. What enterprising Grove/Atlantic President Morgan Entrekin did was make a preemptive offer of $125,000—a great price for a first novel but a pittance for a bestseller, especially compared to the $8 million that Random House gave Charles Frazier for his second book. The catch was that Frazier had to accept Entrekin's offer that week, and it worked.

If the agent already has sold books to the publisher, the agent may know how much flexibility the editor has to improve the offer. When you, your agent, and your editor agree on terms, the editor emails them to the contracts department, and they integrate them into a computer-generated contract. If your agent has sold books to the house, the agent will have established the agency's boilerplate that your publisher may use to prepare the contract for you to sign. At a large house, it may take two months or more for the contract to reach your hands.

If more than one house makes an offer, your agent will continue to call from house to house until editors have made their final offers for the book.

You may feel that it will be better to accept a lower offer from an editor you will enjoy working with more and a house that will do a better job with your book, making you more money in the long run. It's your call to make. Choosing the best editor and publisher is easy for an agent.

A contract is a diamond-studded minefield that divides a finite sum of money between two parties. Since contracts are written by publishers, they are loaded with potentially explosive clauses that contain opportunities for your publisher to profit at your expense. Publishers exist to make a profit, so they try to retain as much of the money a contract generates as they can.

They do this by trying to:
• hold down advances and royalties
• retain as many subsidiary rights as they can
• maximize their share of the income from these rights
• tie up the author's next book
• include clauses that benefit them by lowering the author's income

They can't readily get concessions from their printers or their customers, but unsuspecting authors are fair game. Simon & Schuster asks for theme-park rights. More than one publisher has a contract giving themselves world rights for the universe. Now that's thinking ahead!

One author admitted that she signed a contract offering a $1,000 advance with a 2 percent royalty because, she says, "I thought that's what everyone got. I didn't know you could negotiate."

Publishers' contracts run from five to thirty-six computer-generated pages. Their function, once they're filled in with terms, is to establish a mutually satisfactory basis for your working marriage with your editor.

Contracts protect both parties. But for new writers, a long document written in legalese can be intimidating. Publishers may have more than one standard contract. We have heard of an editor who used to keep three sets of boilerplates on hand, and whether he was buying a book from a new writer, an experienced writer, or an agent determined which one he pulled out of his desk drawer.

The Hired Lung: The Agent as Haggler

Negotiating with writers puts editors in a schizophrenic position. Editors and writers share an interest in working together as closely as possible to create the best possible book and then make it succeed. Editors want to establish lasting relationships with writers, and they know that haggling about money or taking advantage of an author's naïveté will hurt their chances to do so.

Yet editors are paid by publishers, not by writers, and part of what they get paid to do is buy books as cheaply as possible. Responsible editors know that they will be trying to increase their houses' profits at the expense of writers, so they resolve this dilemma by recommending that writers find an agent. Editors may suggest agents to contact.

Business, like politics, is the art of the possible. The sale of your book will take place or fall through depending on the ability and willingness of your publisher, your agent, and you to agree on a deal. Agents have an obvious interest in wangling as much money as possible out of publishers: the more money their clients make, the bigger their commissions. Here are the points covered in any negotiation:

Your Advance

"Will you be needing an advance?"—Alfred Knopf's advice to editors on what to ask prospective authors after lunch. Why? "You'd be surprised how often they say no."

This dialogue goes back decades, but it captures the mercantile mindset: buy as much as possible for as little as possible.

Bill Gates is the richest man in the world. But when he sold his first book, *The Road Ahead* (on the basis of what one editor in the running called a "thin" fifteen-page proposal), he insisted on a $2.5 million advance. Then he gave it away to charity! Why would anyone want $2.5 million and then give it away?

The answer: "The more they pay, the more they push." If a large house spends even $100,000 on a book and it doesn't work out, they write it off as part of the cost of doing business. If it's a hard-soft deal, they'll hope to make some of it back on the paperback edition. If not, maybe they'll make it back on the author's next book. But if a publisher shells out a million or more on a book, they can't ignore it. They have to do what they can to recoup the advance and make a profit.

The Art of the Possible

The practice of publishers paying authors an advance against anticipated royalties from a book started in the 1870s. Ever since, books have earned income to recoup the advance in two ways: royalties from sales of copies of the book, and sharing the income from the licensing of rights and any other commercial uses of the book.

After you receive your advance, you will not receive any more money from your publisher until your book earns back your advance from royalties or subsidiary-rights sales. The bigger your advance, the more copies your book will have to sell or the larger the sub-rights sales will have to be for your book to earn out.

Agents can assess the present and future value of a book and an author, but they can't pull rabbits out of hats. New writers often say to us, "Well, since it's my first book, I guess I won't get much money for it." Probably not. But a publisher will gamble whatever an agent or competing bidders convince them that your book is worth, regardless of whether it's your first book or your fourth.

In fact, it can be *harder* to sell a second novel than the first. When a sales rep sells booksellers a second book, they call up on their computers what the first one sold and order accordingly. If a first novel fails, publishers may ask authors to change their names so they can have a second chance to be promising first novelists.

The traditional yardstick for determining advances is the amount of royalties authors will earn the first year from the first break-even printing. In the early forties, the average advance was $500. Now most first-time advances from major houses are in the $10,000 to $25,000 range, but the advance for a genre or literary novel may be less than that. Advances for children's books range from $2,500 to $5,000 but can go up to six figures.

A Horse That Finished First before Leaving the Starting Gate

The Horse Whisperer, an unfinished novel by British screenwriter Nicholas Evans, was sold to Disney for $3 million. The momentum of this sale led to an auction and a $3,150,000 sale to Delacorte. With foreign rights, *The Horse Whisperer* garnered more than $10 million in sales before it was published. Between the book being a bestseller in hardcover and paperback, $3 million was a bet that paid off.

How Your Advance Will Be Paid

Advances are usually divided into two or more parts, depending on the size of the advance. One common payout is half on signing and half on acceptance of the manuscript.

But the larger the deal, the more installments it will be divided into. When Carl Sagan made the $2 million deal for his bestselling first novel *Contact*, he chose to have the advance paid evenly over ten years.

The tougher the book business is and the larger advances are, the more parts publishers will want to divide them into.

Your Royalties

Your royalties will vary according to the format of your book, the discount at which it is being sold, and how and where it is sold.

Trade royalties are usually based on the list or cover price of your book, so if your book cost $20, and you were earning a royalty of 10 percent a copy, your royalty is $2.

Specialized publishers and some trade publishers base royalties on the net price of the book, the discounted price they receive for the book. If booksellers buy your $20 book at a discount of 40 percent, they pay $12, and if the royalty rate is 10 percent of net receipts, the royalty is $1.20—a difference of 40 percent. To make a net royalty comparable to a list-price royalty, an agent will ask that it be doubled. Lower royalties kick in for books sold at a discount of 50 percent or higher.

Hardcover Royalties

Although around the turn of the twentieth century, hardcover royalties ran as high as 25 percent, they are now usually:
- 10 percent of the list price on the first five thousand copies sold
- 12½ percent on the next five thousand copies
- 15 percent thereafter

Successful authors command a straight 15 percent royalty or higher. Royalties for cookbooks or illustrated books that cost more to design and produce than a book with just type may be less than normal.

Trade-Paperback Royalties

Royalties vary from publisher to publisher, but range from 6 to 10 percent of the list price. A typical royalty scale may start at 6 percent and rise 1 or 1½ percent after ten thousand to twenty thousand copies. It may escalate again after another sales plateau is reached. A straight 7½ percent royalty is generally what New York houses prefer.

Mass-Market Royalties

Royalties on rack-size books also vary, running from 4 percent to as high as 22 percent of the cover price for a blockbuster. A royalty of 8 percent on the first one hundred thousand to one hundred fifty thousand copies, and 10 percent thereafter, is typical. The bigger your book, the higher the royalty your agent can demand.

The defining differences between trade and mass-market paperbacks are size, price, publication, and distribution. Mass-market books fit into the racks in fifty thousand outlets including airports, drugstores, and supermarkets. They have a relatively narrow price range. Trade paperbacks can be any size or price. Like magazines, pocket books are published on a monthly basis and distributed to outlets by IDs, independent distributors. Only four distributors control 91 percent of the business.

Publishers in Chains

Three customers—Amazon and the "Killer B's," Borders and Barnes & Noble—generate more than half of many publishers' sales. Powerful customers can put pressure on publishers for higher discounts and more promotional money, and publishers have to do whatever they can to placate them. Where does the money that publishers yield to their biggest customers come from? It can come from higher cover prices and publishing more books, writers who receive lower advances and royalties, and keeping subsidiary rights. Publishers, in turn, put pressure on writers and agents to accept lower advances and royalties, give up subsidiary rights, and tie up authors' future books. This is why you need an agent who can withstand that pressure, who knows where the give is in a contract, and who will stand up for your interests.

Subsidiary Rights

The Association of American Publishers reports that most trade publishers don't sell enough copies of their books to make money, so for their books to be profitable, they must sell subsidiary rights.

The growing importance of subsidiary-rights income has increased the determination of publishers to hold onto whatever rights they can, even if they don't know their value or how or when they will exercise them. Agents try to prevent publishers from encroaching on rights traditionally withheld for writers.

As Martin Levin notes in *Be Your Own Agent*, publishers don't buy books. They acquire the rights to publish books and to serve as the authors' agents in selling subsidiary rights. Your book will have primary and secondary subsidiary rights. Your publisher will expect to control the right to sell primary subsidiary rights for:

- book clubs
- condensed versions of the book
- anthologies
- reprints if your book is a hardcover, or hardcover publishers if you're selling to a paperback house
- excerpts after publication, called second-serial rights
- reproduction of part or all of the book without changing it, in all media, including records, films, microfilms, and other means of information storage and retrieval.

Secondary Rights

Your agent will to try to retain the secondary subsidiary rights for your book, including:

- first-serial rights: excerpts before publication
- foreign rights
- dramatic rights in all media: film, television, CD, DVD, radio, and theater

- merchandising rights, also called commercial exploitation, including products such as T-shirts, coffee mugs, calendars, and towels

Your agent will withhold for you all rights not granted to the publisher. The subsidiary rights your agent retains for you may be worth more than the rights you grant to your publisher. However, they may not become valuable until your work becomes popular or the interest in the subject of your book revives for some unexpected reason, perhaps decades from now. Your agent will stay alert to possibilities for exploiting all rights to your book. Chapters 6 and 8 discuss subsidiary rights.

The New Wild, Wild West: Electronic Rights

Publishers have won the right to extend their right to sell display rights—reproducing a book as-is by a book club, for example—to cyberspace. They have now extended that right to include e-books and whatever other devices emerge in the digital revolution.

Publishers will also ask for multimedia rights—the right to combine your text with material from other content providers such as video, audio, graphics, animation, and photography. Your agent will try to withhold these rights for you. They are closer to dramatic rights than simply reproducing the text. Movie people will also want these rights, so giving them up may affect your ability to sell the movie rights to your book.

The Paperback Split

When a hardcover house sells the paperback reprint rights, the traditional split with the author is 50-50. With sufficient leverage, this can be pushed up in steps to a 70-30 split in your favor.

Agent Peter Matson obtained the ultimate paperback split. He sold William Morrow just the hardcover rights to a John Irving novel for $1.3

million, leaving him free to sell the paperback rights separately to Bantam for another $1.3 million.

If circumstances warrant, your agent will request approval or at least consultation on the paperback sale.

Issues Particular to Your Book

If you are signing with a publisher because of an outstanding editor, your agent may try to insert a clause in the contract giving you the right to go with the editor if the editor switches houses before your book goes into production.

The special issues that contracts can cover are as varied as the writers who sign them.

Reaching for the Stars

If your book generates enough interest, your agent may be able to obtain the following clauses for you:

• Expense Money

Your agent may be able to get you additional money to cover part or all of your out-of-pocket expenses such as travel, illustrations, and permissions costs.

• Bestseller Escalators

This escalator and the next one usually only come into play with potential bestsellers: when your book appears on the *New York Times* or *Publishers Weekly* bestseller list, the publisher increases your advance to a fixed ceiling—$50,000, for example—depending on your book's position and longevity on the list.

- Movie Escalators

    A movie escalator is a fixed sum—perhaps $25,000—paid when a movie based on your book goes into production.

- Promotion Budget

    A rarity in contracts, this commits the publisher to spending a minimum sum to promote your book.

- First Printing

    Again, only big books need apply for a contractual commitment to the size of the first printing, and if a book is big enough, the commitment isn't necessary. But large publishers do base their advances partly on the royalties generated in the first year or by the first printing.

    Editors often estimate the printing and the other deal points in a computer-generated P&L (Profit and Loss statement) or proposal-to-publish form they have to fill out to persuade the editorial board to buy a book. Your agent will ask about the estimated first printing and cover price to see if your advance is in line with your anticipated royalties.

Printing estimates are as definite as April weather until shortly before the presses roll. Unless a publisher is committed to force-feeding books into the stores, the first printing of your book will equal the advance sale or *laydown*—the number of books the sales reps have gotten into the stores—plus additional copies to cover initial reorders.

Translating from Legalese into Legal Tender

After discussing the deal with your editor, your agent will go over it with you and discuss what changes might be possible. Usually editors don't have a great deal of latitude in upping an offer, but your agent will try to better the deal.

Even when the terms of the deal are settled, the negotiations are usually not finished. If your agent has dealt with your publisher before, it may be possible to use a previous contract as a boilerplate and just fill in the information pertaining to the new book. Your agent will check the last contract a client signed with the publisher and negotiate necessary changes.

When it's not possible to use a previous contract as a model, after the foregoing points have been agreed on, the editor sends your agent the filled-in contract so that your agent can review the rest of the clauses.

This leads to at least one long phone conversation or an email listing the changes your agent wants. Sometimes someone in the publisher's contracts department goes over the offending clauses with your agent, and they thrash out a contract you can live with.

Other Important Contract Clauses

Your contract may contain anywhere from ten to more than one hundred clauses. The most important clauses are:

- the grant of rights
- copyright
- delivery of the manuscript
- approval or consultation on the manuscript, title, and cover
- revised editions
- the warranty and indemnity clause that covers your legal responsibilities for your book
- the option clause covering one or more future books
- the right to examine the publisher's books
- author's copies for promotion
- the obligation to publish in a specified time
- the reversion of rights to you
- termination of the agreement
- the agent's clause, two samples of which are in Appendix 2

Your agent may also be able to negotiate for special riders favorable to you.

Hiring an Intellectual Property Attorney for the Contract

If you place your book yourself, you can hire an intellectual property attorney to help you negotiate the contract. However, lawyers don't read your work, so they can't evaluate an editor, publisher, or offer in relation to better alternatives. That's not their job.

What an attorney can do is go over the contract with you to help get you the most favorable terms, and perhaps negotiate on your behalf. But once the lawyer's hourly fee is paid, you won't have to share your income. Before and after contract negotiations, you're on your own. You won't have an advocate during the publishing process.

Volunteer Lawyers for the Arts has enlisted attorneys around the country who will accept reduced fees. For assistance, call (212) 319-2910, or Google them to find the office nearest you. Some agents are also lawyers and provide both services. But beware: literary law is a specialty. If you're going to use an attorney, make sure it's someone who knows publishing contracts.

Reading Between the Lines

Negotiating a contract can take minutes or months. But when your agent, your publisher, and, most important of all, you are happy with the results, congratulations are in order. You may have turned a minefield into a potential gold mine.

Chapter 10
Following the Money:
What an Agent Does after the Sale

"There was once a cartoon showing a hulking gorilla saying to a writer, "I realize it's unusual for an agent to charge seventy-five percent, but I assure you I'm worth it."

The Agent as Advocate

The moment your book is sold, you are no longer just another writer. You are an author! Friends in and out of the literary community accord you a larger measure of respect.

From idea to bookstore, publishing a book usually takes a year and half to two years if your book will be published by a big or mid-sized house.

Problems may arise about revisions; a late, rejected, or undelivered manuscript; your editor's leaving the company; the title; cover design; lack of promotion; or a delayed or faulty royalty statement. Your agent is your advocate and a creative problem solver.

Choosing When to Sell Subsidiary Rights

Chapter 8 described what an agent does about selling sub rights before your book is sold. After publication, your agent continues to pursue the sale of rights to your book that your agent has withheld on your behalf.

While agents can sometimes solicit interest in or sell sub rights to a project with a proposal or a finished manuscript, unless a book is very timely or commercial, the time to begin is when the manuscript has been accepted and is in its strongest, most salable form. Foreign agents may prefer to wait for bound books. The two areas an agent will want to explore as soon as possible are first-serial sales and a movie sale.

Promo Pieces: First-Serial Sales

First-serial sales can be a source of income and publicity. Such sales are more likely for a nonfiction book than a novel from which it may be difficult to cut a strong slice. Agents may contact magazines, starting with those boasting the highest circulations and first-serial rates, and offer them the right to excerpt your book in one or more article-length excerpts.

Local periodicals may buy your work because you're a local writer. National periodicals will only be interested if the subject will appeal to a large audience. But more than three thousand special-interest magazines—for skiers, car buffs, parents, Net surfers, photographers, and so forth—need material. Although they may not pay much, they will reach a receptive audience for a book on the subject.

Cyberspace is infinite. There are more places for excerpts to run, including your website, and excerpts can be as long as you and whoever hosts the site think people will keep reading. A few publishers have put all of all their books online for free, and book sales went up. People started reading them and decided they didn't want to read the whole book online or printed out, so they bought the book.

10/40 & Out: Making a Living on Surfer Time
America Online has a 10/40 law. They estimate that you have ten seconds to capture the attention of Net surfers and forty seconds to keep it before they move on, another incentive to make your book and your website as visually appealing and enjoyable to read as you can.

Books arrive in stores about a month before publication, later on the West Coast if books are shipped from warehouses in the east. The ideal time for an excerpt to run is on publication, when books are in stores, so that readers who enjoy the excerpt can run right out and buy your book.

Because it takes fewer online sales than bookstore sales for a book to become a bestseller, getting as many buyers to the same online bookseller at the same time is the easiest way to create an online bestseller. This will encourage your publisher to keep pushing your book and book buyers to keep buying it.

A magazine pays more for first-serial sales than for second or post-publication serialization because they have it exclusively. Different magazines may run different sections of a book concurrently, and the same material may run simultaneously in noncompetitive media such as newspapers in different cities.

However, first-serial sales are chancy. Magazines are flooded with material, and editors have been known to take an idea submitted to them by a freelance writer and assign it to a staff writer whom they're already paying or a freelance writer with whom they've already worked. They may also decide to save money by waiting until after publication or just interviewing the author. Since many first-serial sales are made for less than a thousand dollars, they generate more publicity than income.

It may make more sense for the author to let the publisher license first-serial rights:

- If the book is heavily illustrated, it may be more practical for the publisher to provide illustrations to magazines.
- If the book is being rushed to press, there may not be enough time to sell excerpts, because big magazines have six-month deadlines. So, given the shortened production time, a publisher may be better able to meet a magazine's deadlines.
- The publisher may have a crackerjack first-serial person.
- A book's first-serial potential may not be large enough to warrant an agent's involvement.
- On a big book, a publisher may insist on controlling first-serial rights so it can integrate those sales into its overall marketing plan.

There are some trade-offs. If your publisher keeps first-serial rights, your share of the income may be used to repay the advance. If your agent handles them, your income will be forwarded to you as it's received. Also, although the author usually gets at least 75 percent of a first-serial sale, the split between writer and publisher can range from 50-50 to 90-10. If you're a freelancer, you may be able to make your own first-serial sales, so discuss this possibility with your agent.

Life at Twenty-Four Frames a Second

You may not need an agent to sell your book, but you *must* have one for TV or movie sales. Studios and producers won't consider unagented material for fear of being sued if they make something similar to a book they rejected. Bestsellers are sold in auctions for seven-figure sums. Most books, however, are optioned for six months or a year for 10 percent of the sale price—for example, $50,000 against $500,000—if the movie goes into production. The sale price may also be 10 percent of the film's production budget. The producer can extend the option for the same amount of time and money.

The option gives the producer time to get a script written, interest actors and a director, and obtain financing from one of Hollywood's Seven Sisters, the major studios that dominate the movie industry: MGM, Paramount, Sony/Columbia, Twentieth Century Fox, Universal, Walt Disney, and Warner Bros. Interest may come from stars or other proven pros who have their own production companies on studio lots and give the studios first crack at the movies they make. Or interest may come from one of the many independent producers, the independent publishers of Hollywood. If it's going to be a TV movie, the producer will try to interest a network. The big payoff comes if and when the cameras start rolling, and the producer antes up the purchase price for the film rights.

You may also get a percentage, usually 2 to 5 percent of the net profits after the costs of making, distributing, and promoting the film. Since most movies are a triumph of technique over content, the accounting may be the most creative part of making them—your percentage will be meaningless unless the movie is a blockbuster, and maybe not even then. *Forrest Gump* cost less than $100 million to produce and made $622 million, but until Winston Groom's attorney stepped in, the producer claimed there were no net profits.

Nine out of ten options don't get picked up, but when they lapse, another producer can option the book. A novelist we know had enough novels published that he could live just on the option money for his books.

The industry's dealmakers are constantly making deals for movies that wind up not being made. This is why Oscar-winning director Billy Wilder said that in Hollywood, "they spend twenty percent of their time making movies and eighty percent of their time making deals."

Getting a script, a director, actors, financing, and distribution and then making a movie is a three-to-five year process that costs an average of more than $100 million. Then it takes another eighteen months more before it's completed and released, and then another two-comma sum goes into marketing and distribution.

The Big Scream: Dying for a Movie

If your book has movie possibilities, your agent will start talking it up to coagents. We once received a funny, imaginative novel called *Me Two* about a dying old millionairess who lives in a penthouse and hires a swami to transport her soul into the body of a beautiful young nurse who will inherit her fortune. But when the moment comes, the swami trips, and the millionairess's soul falls off her penthouse into the body of a drunken bum in the alley below. This leads to humorous complications and a love story with a happy ending.

At the same time we started submitting the manuscript, we also started approaching producers with the project. The first producer to see the manuscript optioned it. And although we never sold the book—comedies are hard to sell in hardcover or paperback—you may have seen what Kings Road Productions did with the manuscript in the Lily Tomlin–Steve Martin movie *All of Me*.

More than two decades after the movie came out, there was interest in remaking it, and because of the success of the Broadway musical based on the movie *Dirty Rotten Scoundrels*, the producer also wanted theatrical rights.

A *New Yorker* cartoon shows a Hollywood agent sitting across a table from a writer, saying, "There are two ways we can go here. You can have one percent of the gross or ninety percent of the net."

If you can't be a "grosser" like Julia Roberts or Toms, Hanks or Cruise, and get a piece of the gross receipts, the purchase price is all you can expect to receive. In Hollywood, net profits usually means no profits. Even if your agent can get you the job of writing the screenplay, it will be a futile effort predestined for the circular file, because the producer will hire a professional screenwriter to rewrite it or start from scratch. No producer will put the fate of a fortune's worth of celluloid into a novice's hands. It's not personal; it's strictly business.

Unless you are a superstar like Michael Crichton or John Grisham, you will have no control over the process. Time, money, power, ego, uncertainty, and the craziness they generate give rise to the cliché about how a writer should respond to a movie offer: take the money and run. John Irving's Oscar for *The Cider House Rules* was a first for a writer who wrote the screenplay of his own book.

Booray for Hollyword

United Artists was all set to start filming one of our books on a Monday. The Friday before, *Heaven's Gate*, one of the most expensive, all-time stinkaroos, had opened—a disaster for United Artists and for our author. They stopped production on all of their movies—proof once again that only the past is relatively certain.

Speaking at the San Francisco Writers Conference, producer Lloyd Silverman told how it took ten years to make *Snow Falling on Cedars*. It wasn't made because it sold four million copies, and it wasn't sold because it spent seventy-two weeks on the bestseller list. It was made because Scott Hicks, who won an Oscar for directing *Shine*, wanted to direct it and because Frank Marshall and Kathleen Kennedy, who had produced George Lucas epics, wanted to produce it. It was made because to them, the studios couldn't say no.

This process convinced Silverman that Hollywood's Seven Sisters only greenlight movies when they can't say no to the people who want to make them. Sometimes they say no even then. Even though Warner Bros. had been working with Clint Eastwood for decades, they still didn't want to do the Oscar-winning *Million Dollar Baby*.

Like writers, moviemakers start with blank screens they have to fill with something salable. And like moviegoers, readers vote with their eyes. And from their judgment, there is no appeal. If a book has strong enough movie potential, agents may take it to Hollywood first to build the book's value. If a book has movie potential, someone will buy it, but movie interest may not develop for decades.

Your book may have to wait until you're famous, public interest changes, or the right actor, director, or producer goes wild for it. It took seven decades for Edith Wharton's wonderful novel *The Age of Innocence* to be transformed from paper into celluloid—and look how long it took the Bible.

From the moment your agent starts trying to sell your book as a movie until audiences determine its fate, moviemaking, like the rest of the arts, is an unpredictable endeavor. Another reason writers should be aware of what happens in the Big Enchilada is that the movie business and the book business are much alike. Add a zero or two to what publishers pay and you have Hollyword, a book-movie combo with great potential for synergy. The uncertainty, rising costs, competition, and the star system that afflict the movie business also dominate publishing. Two of New York's Six Sisters—HarperCollins and Simon & Schuster—are part of conglomerates that also own movie studios: Twentieth Century Fox and Paramount.

And although Hyperion is only a mid-sized house, it's owned by Disney, and it may be doing the most to take advantage of the potential synergy between New York and Hollywood. One example of the potential synergy is Tim Allen simultaneously having the number one book from Hyperion, movie from Disney, and TV show on Disney's ABC. Jackpot!

Random House formed an alliance with Focus Features to develop movies from their books and books from the movies that Focus Features makes. The quest for synergy marches on. For a very enjoyable tour of La-La Land that has a lot of resonance for writers, read Oscar-winner William Goldman's *Adventures in the Screen Trade*. His opening salvo about the wisdom of moviemakers: "Nobody knows anything!"

Foreign Rights

When your book is ready to be sold abroad, agents will contact their counterparts around the world to see if there's any interest in the project. Unfortunately, most books are written in a particular literary and cultural context and don't travel well. Brand-name authors sell abroad, but most books on gardening, cooking, sports, and pop psychology don't interest foreign readers.

Solid nonfiction with enduring value, such as science, history, memoirs, biographies, mathematics, technology, business, film, art and illustrated books, and books about big ideas of universal interest are among the subjects that will sell abroad.

Also salable are books that suit a particular country's tastes and interests:
• The French and the Japanese love mysteries and jazz.
• Genre romances are popular in many countries.
• Scandinavians golf in the snow and are eager to learn American techniques.
• The Germans and Japanese love science fiction and have the income to buy illustrated books.

Books on American culture may do better in English because many book buyers interested in them read English.

Top New York agent John Brockman sells directly to foreign publishers, sometimes before approaching American publishers. This helps to establish the value for a book and build momentum for the American sale.

Industry buzz on a book or a pre-publication review in *Publishers Weekly* will spark foreign interest. A successful launch in America or an author's growing popularity over time may also do the trick.

In every country except the United States and England, where Charles Dickens had perhaps the first literary agent, agenting is a relatively new profession.

In Japan, France, Italy, and Germany, agents sprang up after World War II, when publishers began to acquire American books.

As noted earlier, American agents usually split a 20 percent commission, sometimes 15 percent in Britain, with their overseas colleagues. Some American agents who specialize in selling foreign rights charge 20 percent to which the author's agent adds 10 percent, bringing the total to 30 percent.

Because of the smaller book and subsidiary-rights markets overseas, advances and royalties for most foreign contracts are smaller than in the United States. Books are usually more expensive abroad, where people also have less discretionary income. Translating a book may make it 25 percent longer, and translation costs affect royalties. In Japan, translators are so important that their names may be more prominent on book covers than the authors'.

Views from Abroad

Our English agent, David Grossman, says, "In many ways, British publishing practice is far more conservative than in the United States, which is a reflection of a society in which the past usually counts for much more than the present or future." This is also true for France and Italy.

William Miller, an agent in Japan, feels that "the agent working in Japan is not merely acting as a business aid to an author but as a bridge between Japan and the rest of the world over which business can travel."

Bestsellers command hefty advances in major markets, and while they don't usually match American numbers, if your book is sold to half a dozen countries, *mucho dinero* may be heading for your mailbox. We've sold Cherie Carter-Scott's #1 *New York Times* bestseller *If Life is a Game, These are the Rules* in more than thirty-five countries. There are two French editions and two Chinese editions. Seven years after it was published, our coagent for translations, Chandler Crawford, continued to make sales.

Books, movies, rock, Levi's, television, and the Internet have helped make the international language English and the global culture American. Eastern Europe and China's acceptance of copyright has opened new markets for American books. It is easier than ever for the right book to change the world. Phillip Roth once said, "Once a book is published, the world edits it." All those solitary months in front of a computer screen will be worthwhile when you start receiving letters and emails from fans around the world.

An Agent Is a Sentinel

What will your agent do for you after the sale? Your agent will:
- keep on top of publishing news and trends that might create opportunities for you and your books
- be an early reader of your work and provide feedback on it
- be a sounding board for your ideas and perhaps give you ideas

- be a mentor who helps direct—or if necessary redirect—your career
- stay in touch with editors and perhaps obtain assignments for you
- investigate merchandising rights if your book sells well enough, and words or images from your books have the potential for products like calendars, coffee mugs, or T-shirts
- perhaps arrange collaborations between you and someone with an idea who needs a writer
- testify on your behalf if your book generates litigation

Your books may generate paperwork and opportunities decades after they're published. It may be possible to resell out-of-print books and sell movie and foreign rights. Foreign-rights sales will mean supplying coagents what they need, ferrying contracts and other paperwork from where they originate to clients, figuring out exchange rates for currencies, keeping track of printings, checking royalty statements, chasing overdue income, and shepherding American and foreign tax forms. These obligations require accuracy, devotion to detail, and time. It will simplify your life if your agent takes care of them for you.

Your agent will remain an oasis of sympathy and encouragement, a morale booster, and a confidant who will help you survive the slings and arrows of personal and literary misfortune. He or she will continue to act on behalf of you and your heirs.

Erasing the Line between Client and Friend

An agent isn't a tax expert, a savings-and-loan, or a personal assistant. But one of the joys of the profession is that enduring friendships develop between writers and agents that can blur the line between duty and affection. Mutual dependencies created by time or fortune may affect how you and your agent relate to each other.

How Agents Are Like Publishers

Literary agencies are businesses that must make a profit to survive. Agents also have to balance serving the needs of their clients with maintaining their relationships with the publishers they sell to.

Like publishers, agents:
- are motivated by love or money or both
- need big books to make big bucks
- love to get excited about their books and authors
- must do a good job if they expect to receive a writer's next book
- start working with a writer hoping to establish a permanent relationship that grows more profitable and creative as the writer's career develops

For most agents, the hardest part of the job is finding good books to sell. If you can write and promote books that meet the needs of the marketplace, the Age of Information will be a golden age for you. Your literary agent will help you get your share of the gold.

Interlude 2

Hooked on Books:

A Terrific Day in the Life of an Agent

(Continued from Interlude 1)

. . . a first novel called *The Kryptonite Kid* that is written in the form of letters from a seven-year-old boy to Superman. Is he kidding? How is he going to bring off a 210-page novel (I always check page length) out of a kid's letters?

But by page 20, I'm hooked. And by the end of the book, he has made me laugh and cry by using the simplicity of a child's letters to provide insight into sex, God, religion, innocence, love, family, school, growing up, and small-town life. It's a timeless, universal, enthralling novel that will appeal to kids as well as adults.

As I read it, it thrills me to know I am discovering a major new talent. Names of editors who will love the book spring to mind unbidden. It's the same phenomenon you experience when you love a book: people you want to share it with leap to mind. When I finish the manuscript, I can't wait to share it with Elizabeth and meet the author.

The discovery of the manuscript in the wee hours of the morning after a horrendous day is only the start of a perfect day-in-the-life.

It's a glorious spring morning. The sky is clear, the air is crisp, and the sun is turning new leaves brilliant green. After walking to the waterfront to admire the spectacular beauty of San Francisco Bay, I put on Mozart's Clarinet Concerto, pick up the *Chronicle*, and find a glowing review of one of our books, a sign of glad tidings to come.

The day's reading, mail, meetings, and phone calls yield:
• an irresistibly moving, inspiring, and commercial book
• a book that will change the world or at least improve it
• checks, large and small, for domestic and foreign sales—especially welcome are the checks you don't expect
• a letter from a new writer or editor who turns out to be a wonderful human being and a first-rate professional
• calls from new writers who say an author, agent, editor, bookseller, or reviewer we admire recommended the agency
• a contract negotiation in which we obtain at least a degree of satisfaction on all of the changes we request
• an offer for a book that exceeds our expectations
• news of a first-serial, foreign, movie, book-club, or a seven-figure paperback reprint sale
• a meeting with a writer who has rewritten a proposal exactly as I requested and that I know I'll be able to sell

Our English agent calls to announce that he has just sold the English rights to a novel before pub date. The author is so pleased that he brings over a bottle of Dom Perignon to celebrate.

An editor calls to wrap up an auction that leads to a six-figure deal. I call the author in Cincinnati, and he reports that he is going full steam ahead on the book so he will finish it earlier than the contract calls for. Agent and editors love writers who do more, better, and faster than they have to. It inspires me to do better.

"You know," he asks, "what the best thing you and Elizabeth have done for me is?"

"What?" I ask.

"Your success with my books has given me the freedom to write without having to worry about the rent, and that's the greatest gift you could have given me. I just want you to know that I really appreciate all that you've done for me."

"Your talent and your fans liberated you," I tell him. "We were just the key that unlocked the cell."

I'm delighted that we've helped free him to write, and the kindness of his words makes me misty-eyed. His ability to write and willingness to endure rejections and hang on for four years until his work gained in popularity are what won him his freedom. Getting his books to a receptive editor and publisher helped, but ultimately, it was book buyers responding to his gifts as a storyteller who freed him to write.

Agents thrive on a fascinating paradox: every day is the same and every day is different. You do the same things, but what you have to do varies every day, as does every book and every writer. The projects with which you're involved are in different stages of development. And there's a constant stream of new ideas and new writers whizzing by, hoping to interest you. If you are excited by new ideas, it's impossible to stagnate or become bored. The years fly by. I love ideas and helping writers develop them into salable proposals that will help them achieve their goals.

If, as most agents do, you work for yourself, you have the freedom to work in whatever way brings out the best in you and your clients, and as soon as your income allows, you can handle only books you are passionate about.

Katharine Kerr, another one of our favorite authors, calls. She fulfilled many a Midwest housewife's dream by plunking her typewriter down on her kitchen table and turning out her first fantasy novel. In England, her books are bestsellers, and she's been called "Tolkien's heir" and "the queen of Celtic fantasy." Her thirteen-book series exploded out of a short story she wrote in 1982—twenty-four years later, she was still writing it. She's feisty and brilliant, and it's always a pleasure to hear how she's coming along on her next opus.

The mail brings a two-book contract from a hot new publisher. The cover letter includes the following paragraph:

It is a pleasure to do business with you. The proposals you have provided for my consideration are polished and comprehensive. Your expertise in preparing authors for the publishing process has facilitated my decision-making and acquisitions activity. Additionally, a number of the proposals you represent have very strong market potential. I look forward to our continued communications.

Today's UPS delivery includes an advance copy of a book just off the press. The jacket looks super, and I open the book and see this:

Words would get in the way were I to try to articulate what I feel for Elizabeth Pomada and Michael Larsen who have become much, much more than my agents. This kind of recognition is one of the joys of an agent's life. Only a handful of us get rich from the job, so, like writers, the rest of us need all the psychic rewards we can get.

When a writer cares enough about the editorial help you've provided and the two-and-a-half years you've spent selling the book, sustained only by your friendship and conviction, to write that, you know that regardless of how well the book does, it was time well spent. Apart from the writers it persuades to contact you, it proves once again that you are doing what you were born to do.

The book became the first in a string of bestsellers, and there are few greater joys in life for an agent or author than seeing your first book on the *New York Times* bestseller list. It justifies your faith in the book, the author, and the publisher's ability to make it work.

Bob Stinnett, the author of *Day of Deceit: What Roosevelt Knew about Pearl Harbor*, has three of the top ten spots on Amazon's list of books about Pearl Harbor. The new trade paperback is in the top spot followed a ways back by the audio version and the hardcover.

Now it's time to meet one of the best editors in the business for a long literary lunch, which traditionally involved martinis and short, unproductive afternoons. But because we only work when we're awake, and we have an afternoon and night's worth of work ahead of us, mineral water and cappuccinos all around are the potables of choice.

The editor has an idea for a series of books, and is looking for a writer who can write and promote them. We have the perfect writer for the job.

By the end of lunch, I feel exhilarated. Once again, I know that despite the hard knocks, being in the book business is the only way to make my living.

On the basis of what she called "the best proposal I've ever seen," a hardcover editor made a substantial offer for a book. She rides home on the train with a mass-market editor. When I get back from lunch, she calls gleefully to let us know that, six weeks before the book is going to be published, the mass-market editor is so excited about the book that she has made an opening $100,000 offer for the paperback rights.

The mail brings *Publishers Weekly*, the cover of which has an effective ad for one of our books, the opening shot of a $100,000 promotion campaign.

Jay Conrad Levinson, the author of *Guerrilla Marketing*, gives a seminar at the Mark Hopkins Hotel and gives away a list of 555 ways to earn extra money. I take it home, and when I take another look at, I say to myself, "That's a book!" And sure enough, it becomes one.

On the acknowledgments page, Jay thanked "my high-determination, high-imagination literary agent . . . the person who suggested the book to me in the first place, then coaxed and coddled it to its place in your hands." At this writing, I've been working with Jay for almost thirty years, and there are more than twenty-five books in what seems to be an endless series. Jay was even kind enough to let me use the brand he built to coauthor one for writers.

A dream client forwards an email she received suggesting changes on her manuscript that includes these words: "What a wonderful, wonderful, wonderful book! I had so much fun reading it—the messages come through so beautifully and with such a message of hope. This is truly a book that is going to make the world a better place. What a joy it is to work on! You did a spectacular job on the manuscript and it will be a pleasure to publish."

The widow of an author calls after receiving a royalty check to thank us again for getting her husband's work republished. We were pleased that books of enduring value have a way of surviving neglect.

Finding an editor or reader who loves your book as much as you do is guaranteed to send chills up and down your spine. And the editor backs up her feelings with a solid advance, along with consumer promotion and first-printing commitments. That's my kind of phone call!

Our evening's festivities begin when one of our authors, who has written a book about her adventures as a commercial fisherwoman, arrives with a thirty-pound albacore tuna! She takes one look at our combination of delight and chagrin and—bless her heart—decides that she'd better clean it for us. We feast on the freshest sashimi we've ever tasted. Ah, the joys of living and working in the country's second-largest publishing center.

One of our writers is a literary artist who writes six days a week and settles for nothing less than the best work of which he is capable. During dinner, the most delectable course is the pleasure of his company. His desire to promote his books and his dedication to writing for posterity as well as to make a living illuminate our lives and make for an inspiring evening.

At the end of the day, we go to a sneak preview of *All of Me,* a comedy made from one of our books. It's wildly funny, and we are the only people in the place who cheer during the titles when the phrase "Based on the novel by . . ." flashes on the screen!

Like editors, agents have to make a living from their efforts, but they are motivated more by ideas, writing, passion, and the transforming power of books than they are by profit. They share the goal of producing books that inform, entertain, inspire, and endure. And discovering new writers is the best part of their job.

New ideas, books, writers, and editors are always enriching our lives, in both senses of the word. It's very fulfilling to be needed and to help talented writers gain the rewards and recognition they deserve.

If you can't write books, the next best thing is helping writers to create them by being an agent or editor. If their books stand the test of time, a little of their immortality rubs off on us.

Imagine making a living reading and buying books (and they're tax-deductible!). I have never met anybody whose job is a better blend of change, beauty, variety, new ideas, pleasure, excitement, the unexpected, challenges, creativity, meeting people, friendship, social value, and stimulation.

My faith in the value of life and books, writers, and publishers restored, it's home to hit the manuscript pile again, hoping to find another artist before sleep overtakes me.

Book lovers do it between the sheets, and they never go to bed alone.

Chapter 11
Terminal Transgressions:
What to Do if Your Working Marriage Fails

"Marriage is grounds for divorce."

—Sam Levenson

Seven Potential Problems with Your Agent

The beginning of your working marriage with your agent is the honeymoon, when everything is fine because you're both on your best behavior. The agent is submitting your book and you are both eager with anticipation. If the book sells, you're both delighted because it proves the two of you were right about the book and each other.

If it doesn't, the agent's interest may wane. You may realize that although you were right about your book, you were wrong about your agent. This could happen after a month or a year. It could happen with your first book or your twelfth.

As in any marriage, your relationship with your agent will go through a period of adjustment, and you may experience ups and downs that can befall any continuing relationship. However, even the most promising marriage can turn sour. The day may come when you decide that your agent is wrong for you, that, as someone once said, "Marriage isn't a word—it's a sentence." If that day comes, it's time to think about divorce.

Other than flagrant violations of professional ethics, what reasons justify leaving your agent? The following seven situations indicate that you have a problem.

1. Your Agent Never Contacts You

Don't expect an agent to be constantly checking in with you to make sure everything's okay. However, your agent should inform you promptly about significant developments regarding your work. He or she may only call with good or helpful news, which may be a long time coming.

At the same time, if you never hear about the progress of your agent's efforts, you may rightly wonder what, if anything, is going on. Avoid this problem by establishing at the outset when you should expect to hear from your agent. If your agent repeatedly fails to abide by the arrangement, find out why and change either the system or the agent. Your agent is not a mind reader. Call or write if you have a question about your work, but until your agent has sold something for you, don't expect too much in the way of handholding.

2. Your Agent Doesn't Answer Email, Letters, or Phone Calls

What would you do if your doctor, lawyer, accountant, or anyone else you hire to work for you doesn't return your phone calls? You'd fire them.

In addition to being a bestselling author, Michael Korda was the editor-in-chief of Simon & Schuster—and he returned calls the day he received them. If he can, anybody can. Agents make their living by mail, email, and phone. They are extremely sensitive about editors getting back to them. If your agent wants to represent you, your agent will answer your calls and email. If not, hire one who will.

However, trust your agent. Don't become upset if you don't receive an instant response. Find out why. Was the agent ill, very busy, out of town? A responsible agent will have a satisfactory explanation. If not, and poor communication becomes a habit, it's time to move on.

There is a divide between fiction and nonfiction. Unless they think a book has bestseller potential, agents only submit one or at most three copies of a novel. Agents use multiple submissions for most nonfiction. The more salable books are, the sooner agents hear from editors. But editors should respond within two months. So, for a nonfiction book, you should expect to hear from your agent either when the book sells or when your agent has heard from all of the houses that received the proposal.

3. Your Agent Is Not Actively Pursuing the Sale of Your Work

If your manuscript has become a doorstop in your agent's office, it's not doing either of you any good. Find out what the agent plans to do with the project. Has it been seen by all the likely editors? If you have an agent who is not in New York, is he or she waiting to discuss the project with editors in person?

Agree at the beginning of your relationship on the best strategy for selling your book, and if that doesn't work and you or your agent can't come up with a second line of attack, you should be free to seek another agent or pursue the sale of the property yourself.

If agents temporarily run out of editors to whom to send a project, they may tell writers to take a shot at selling the book themselves without obligation to the agency, and if they succeed, they can decide at that time if they want the agent to take over. Meanwhile, if agents find a new editor or imprint, an editor they know changes houses, or they hear about a house needing such a book, they will let the author know they are submitting it. Sometimes, a book only needs time and patience to sell.

Just because your book hasn't sold doesn't inevitably mean that you should switch agents. Writing your second book may be the best way to sell your first book. Time away from it may allow the market for your book to improve, for you or your agent to come up with a more salable approach to the subject, or for the success of your second book to make your first book salable.

Agents want to represent authors, not books. They're in it for the long haul. Even if a first book doesn't sell, the author will learn from it, so the second one will be more likely to. If it does, it makes the author's past and future books more marketable.

4. Your Agent Is Vague about His or Her Activities

If your agent doesn't seem to know what's going on with your book or you're not getting definite answers to questions about your work, find out why. If you're not satisfied, find yourself another agent.

One writer to another:

"What is your relationship to your agent?"

"Hand to throat."

5. Your Agent Does Not Want to Handle New Work

You've written a book or proposal that you're very excited about, but your agent either doesn't like it or doesn't think much of its chances. If your agent's arguments about the project's weaknesses don't convince you, what do you do? If it happens once, let your agent continue to handle projects under way and try to find another agent for it or sell it yourself. If your agent continues to reject your work, maybe you should be looking for one who's more in tune with the direction your work is taking.

6. Your Agent Is Unable to Sell Your Work

Matching your book with the right time for its publication, the right editor, and the right house may take a phone call or, through no fault of your book or your agent, years. As long as your agent believes in your book and is trying to sell it, he or she deserves the right to keep trying.

7. You Outgrow Your Agent

Suppose you are a new writer represented by a small new agency and, to everyone's surprise, your first book takes off and hits the bestseller list. If the book's success is just a fluke unlikely to repeat itself, consider yourself lucky and stick with your agent. However, if you expect to turn out a string of bestsellers, each with strong movie and foreign-rights potential, then you may have outgrown your agent. You may decide that you need a larger agency or just an attorney to negotiate contracts.

One of the unhappy realities of publishing is the R&D (research and development) factor: successful writers switching from the small agencies and publishers that develop them to big agencies and publishers. If you have a bestseller, agents will start contacting you. But regardless of your sales, if you feel that your career has developed beyond the point where your agent can represent you well, it's time to change agents.

The Path to Freedom

If a problem arises between you and your agent, here's how to solve it.

Meet with Your Agent

If that will be too painful, call or write. If your agent has acted conscientiously on your behalf, you owe your agent the opportunity to discuss the problem with you.

Make sure that your networks agree that your concern is justified. If they do, try to find a mutually satisfactory solution to the problem. If you can't, or if after a fair trial within a mutually agreeable time period, the solution doesn't work, it's time to end the relationship.

But in fairness to your agent, don't approach or commit yourself to a new agent until you've given your present agent a chance to remedy the situation. Ending a basically sound relationship in a moment of pique and turning to a second agent who may turn out to be less satisfactory may not be a wise decision.

Notify the Agent of Your Decision

Your agent's fiduciary relationship with you requires that the agent stop acting on your behalf immediately when you request it. Request it in person or by sending a certified letter explaining the problem and your decision to end your relationship. Allow up to sixty days for responses to work the agent has submitted and has the right to a commission on, even if someone else negotiates the contract.

If you meet with the agent, follow up your conversation with a certified letter confirming any new terms you agree on during your conversation. If you are determined to leave your agent, you can. You may have to consult a literary attorney if your agent offers resistance.

Your agent will continue to be entitled to receive earned commissions and, unless you agree otherwise, to receive checks and royalty statements, and to represent you on the subsidiary rights for the book.

Publishing is a small world whose denizens thrive on their insatiable appetites for that delectable delicacy: gossip. Avoid becoming known as a difficult author or an agent-hopper.

Code Makers: AAR's Code of Ethics

The code of ethics for Association of Authors' Representatives in Appendix 3 sets reasonable standards of conduct for agents whether or not they are members of the group. If your agent is a member of the organization and crosses the line, contact AAR. AAR's ethics committee may be able to help you resolve the situation.

The Light at the End of the Tunnel

Start looking for a new agent the moment you have given your first agent notice that you're leaving. Waiting until you've found a new agent to notify the first one can be embarrassing and create problems for both of them and for you. That's why agents may not talk to you until you've severed your previous connection. If your first agent gets you an offer for a book and you've just signed an agreement with a new one, you've got a problem that will anger both of them.

If your agent gives you a good reason to leave, do what will be best for you personally or professionally. Don't be too concerned about being cut adrift in the literary world. It will be easier to find your second agent than it was to find your first one.

Writers also lose agents because the agents die or go out of business. Agents expect to lose some clients because:
- they screw up
- they fail to sell a book
- a book is wildly successful
- there's no chemistry between them and a client
- the writer is getting a divorce and wants to shed an agent associated with an unhappy past
- the writer acquires a new spouse who doesn't like the agent
- the writer writes something the agent does not like or handle
- the writer stops writing

The reasons for firing agents—valid and inexcusable—are endless. One Hollywood agent believed that agents should expect to lose 10 percent of their clients a year.

Every agent who's been in business a while has been contacted by writers unhappy with their present agents. That you've had an agent gives you credibility. If you've had a book published, it will be easier still to find a new agent. And the sooner you find your next agent, the sooner you'll forget the problem that caused you to look for one.

Chapter 12
Why Hire an Agent?
Why You May Not Need an Agent and Why You May Need One More Than Ever

In an ideal world, there will be no agents because:
- writers will write their books as well as they can
- publishers will give them a fair deal without negotiating, and they'll spend whatever it takes to make their books succeed
- editors, designers, and publicists will do their best for all of their books; take all the time they need to answer all of their authors' questions; and work with them for as long as the book needs help

I hereby vow that I will give up all my royalties and sacrifice my business in a New York minute the second *this* book is no longer needed. Meanwhile, back here on earth . . .

The essence of the difference between authors and publishers is the difference between interests and agendas. Authors and publishers have the identical interest: they want their books to make money. But they have different agendas: authors are having one book published while big publishers may have a list of a few hundred books just on one of their three annual lists. And they have to resource (in publishing, it's also a verb) the books that have the greatest potential to justify their efforts. It's what any MBA worth his degree would do.

Why Magic Is a Treat, Not a Trick

One hope that sustains agents and editors is the possibility that the next manuscript they see will possess black-and-white magic. They persevere with the hope that, however quietly the book is published, it will sell like a Harry Potter book because it strikes a chord that resonates with millions of readers.

Why the World Is Wild about Harry

Harry Potter and the Sorcerer's Stone, the first book in the series, is a model for writers who want their work to appeal to a mass audience. J. K. Rowling created publishing magic by writing a magical book that:

- creates characters readers care about
- forges an unbreakable bond of friendship between the characters
- is a page-turner because it builds irresistible momentum
- is rich in character and plot
- creates a world that readers want to spend time in and return to
- is universal in its depiction of people's needs and fears
- moves readers to tears and laughter
- has an ending that is the perfect dessert after a great meal
- is so effective that it creates unstoppable magic: word of mouth and mouse

That the sixth book in the series, *Harry Potter and the Half-Blood Prince*, sold 6.9 million copies the day it went on sale is phenomenal. But even more remarkable is who bought them: a generation of kids thought to be lost in cyberspace, kids who would rather play with computer games than read. No amount of marketing can make kids get dressed in costumes in the middle of the night and go to bookstores with their parents to buy a book that runs more than 800 pages and retails for $30. Only books themselves can do that.

The franchise translates well into films that create millions of new readers. What is less well known is that J. K. Rowling spent five years writing the book, rewriting the first chapter fifteen times. Of course, you may lack her disadvantages. You probably aren't a single mom living on welfare. But if you can overcome that handicap, maybe you too can be richer than the Queen.

Writers, agents, publishers, and publicists can't make a phenomenon like Harry Potter happen. They can only do their jobs as well and creatively as they can and put their faith in readers to respond to their books the way writers want them to.

Most books fail, but the challenges and the opportunities for writers endure.

- Read what you love to read, and write what you love to read.
- Do what books you love do, only differently and better. Don't be the next anybody else, be the first and only you.

How to Make Every Book You Write a Bestseller

Although agents and publishers reject potential bestsellers, there's nothing mysterious about what makes books succeed. The elements of books that succeed and stand the test of time are in every book you love. Readers know what those elements are, so they read every book by authors whose books have them.

You know what those elements are, so do the following:

- Make a list of them.
- Put the list on your office wall next to
  - the list of your literary and financial goals described on page 247;

- the ideal review of your book;
- the ideal full-page ad for it in *USA Today*;
- the *New York Times* bestseller list with the title of your book pasted in the number one position published by the ideal publisher;
- a list of the countries you want your book to be published in;
- a list of the ideal actors you want to be in the movie based on your book.

- Make a ritual of looking at the list of elements your book must have every day before you start writing to remind yourself what you are trying to accomplish.
- Check it after you finish your proposal or manuscript to assure yourself that your work achieves your literary goals.
- Photocopy what's on your wall, and include it when you send your work to your reading network. Let your readers assure you that your book has what it takes to justify your goals.
- Don't submit it to an agent or editor until it does.
- Become a skilled promoter while you're researching and writing your book. Convince your agent and publisher that when your book is published, you will have the ability, passion, and persistence to do whatever it takes to achieve your financial goals. This will help make your publisher as committed to your success as you are.

There's nothing mysterious about agenting or publishing, only things you don't know yet. If you're a talented writer, agents and publishers need you more than you need them. You are the most important person in the publishing process because you make it happen.

Book buyers will only read your books as long as the style, content, and impact justify their time. This chapter will tell you why writers whose work isn't salable enough won't get agents, but why, when you have a salable book, you need an agent more than ever.

Nine Reasons Why an Agent Can Help You

An agent can help you far beyond the immediate goal you share of selling your books.

1. Your agent is a better judge than you are of the quality and value of your work and the best editors and publishers for it.

If your book is so brilliant that to read it is to love it, agents won't care how much money it will make. For agents and editors, love is a more compelling incentive than money. But agents can only make a living by selling books to the Six Sisters. We've sold books to more than one hundred publishers, but unless we fall in love with a book, we don't take it on because we think we can sell it for $5,000. That's no way to pay a mortgage.

The best home for a nonfiction book may be a niche, independent, or university press. Or you may want to self-publish your book to test-market it, and then sell it to a publisher. If large publishers won't be interested in your book, and they prefer to deal with agents, you may not be able to submit it to them. So finding a publisher may be easier than finding an agent. And you may be better off finding a publisher for your book then hunting for an agent, since an agent will be more likely to represent a writer whose book is already sold.

At that point, though, you may prefer to find an agent willing to take a smaller commission, or you may decide not to use an agent and just hire an agent or intellectual property attorney to review the contract at an hourly rate.

But it's my responsibility as an agent to get clients the best possible editor, publisher, and deal. So when a writer brings an offer to me before negotiating it, I will look at the proposal to see if it can be improved enough to get a better deal or a better house for the book and the author.

The idea of an agent taking an offer and then shopping the proposal to try to get more money for it angers Deb Werksman, the editor who made this edition of the book possible. By the time Deb makes an offer for a book, she has a lot of sweat equity in it. She's read the proposal, researched the market for the book, prepared a P&L, and convinced the house to buy it. So despite whatever an agent does to improve the proposal and increase its value, she won't do business with agents who waste her time by using her offer to approach other publishers.

I get letters from writers around the country telling me how they used my proposal book to sell their books. But by finding publishers who will buy their books, all writers do is prove that their work is salable. I have never met a writer whose proposal was as good as it could be or who had found the best editor and publisher for a book, let alone obtained the best deal for it.

Before accepting a deal that a writer brings in, a responsible agent will try to help make the proposal or manuscript stronger so it will be worth more and interest the best editors and publishers for it. How can you avoid or minimize the problem? Consider these suggestions:

- If you submit your book and a publisher wants to make an offer, don't discuss terms if you plan to hire an agent to negotiate the deal. You may be tying your agent's hands by responding to an offer before he or she can improve it. Say, "I'm delighted that you want to make an offer, but I'd like an agent to help me. Can you recommend one?" If you don't get an agent, an editor will take advantage of you because it's the editor's job to make as much money for the house as possible in part by minimizing what they pay authors.
- A responsible editor will suggest one to three agents for you to approach, and you can use the editor's name when you do.
- If the editor doesn't want a writer to use an agent or the house doesn't deal with agents, that's a bad sign. It usually means that the contract will unfairly favor the house. Even if you can use an agent and you still want the publisher to do your book, you can still get help with the contract and do the negotiating yourself.

- If the editor hasn't made an offer, it makes an agent's job easier. If the proposal is significantly improved, the agent may want to give the publisher an exclusive look at the revised proposal and, if the publisher makes a fair offer for the book, sell it without making the editor outbid other publishers for it.

If your agent asks you to strengthen your proposal, and the request makes sense to you, your agent can tell the editor that when the proposal is ready, your agent will resubmit it, perhaps on an exclusive basis. Should the revised proposal be worth more than the publisher can or wants to offer for it, your agent will have to try to mend fences.

- If an editor has made an offer, the agent could give the editor a topping privilege so the editor may outbid other editors by 10 percent.
- If you want a large house to publish your book, find an agent first. If you can't find an agent, it's because agents don't think they can sell the book to a big house.

Writers have come to us who regretted signing long, intimidating legal documents they didn't understand from publishers they didn't know, but they were so eager to get published that they couldn't resist. Getting a book to the right editor at the right house for the right price can make the difference between success and failure and the difference between a friendly, creative, profitable experience and pure hell.

A writer once came to us ready to quit writing. His first book had been privished (that's the opposite of published) by a small paperback house. He was never able to talk to his editor. He never saw typeset galleys of the manuscript, so he could not respond to the changes that the editor had made. He discovered that the book had been published only when he found it in a bookstore. He couldn't get his royalties. Then the publisher went bankrupt, and the author had a hard time getting the rights to his book back.

Writers are too close to their work to judge its quality or value, so they don't know if it's as salable as it can be or has to be. But you don't have to have an agent to sell your books. Writers sell thousands of books a year. Small and mid-sized publishers buy most books from writers. Even some editors at big houses accept submissions from writers.

A writer asked a critic:
"Did you read my last book?"
The critic replied:
"I certainly hope so."

2. An agent can teach you what you need to know about publishing to ensure your success.

Editors may not have time to answer all of an author's questions or to provide a lot of handholding during the publication process. Although they too are always busy, agents work for writers, so they make the time.

3. By absorbing rejections and being a focal point for your business dealings, your agent helps free you to write.

Because your agent has a fiduciary responsibility to you, you are legally entitled to see all correspondence sent or received on your behalf. However, unless a writer requests them, agents may not forward rejection slips. They don't usually provide helpful information. If they waste time reading something they don't want, why should editors (or agents) waste more time explaining why?

Some editors are more helpful than others in explaining their decisions. If they like a project enough, they'll suggest changes or another editor. In those rare instances in which editors are willing to reconsider a book if the author is willing to change it, they explain what they feel the manuscript needs. Whenever an editor writes anything that can help sell a book, we notify the writer immediately.

Elizabeth once submitted a novel to several editors. One wrote back saying that he loved the plot but hated the characters. Another rejected it saying she loved the characters but hated the plot. This convinced Elizabeth that all she needed to find was an editor who loved both. She did, so, would the writer have been better off enduring the negative reactions that the sale rendered meaningless anyway?

4. Agents are a continuing source of material for editors.

As a knowledgeable participant in the publishing process and a valuable source of manuscripts, an agent has more clout than a writer. An author represents only one book to an editor; an agent represents that book, the author's future books, and all of his or her other clients, no matter what house the editor migrates to.

5. Your agent may be the only stable element in your career.

Editors tend to work their way up the pay scale and the editorial ladder by playing musical chairs. Your agent can help start a word-of-mouth campaign going for your book in the trade. Your agent also tries to make sure that your first editor's plans for your book are carried out. This may be a challenge if the editor leaves.

Since your publisher may change hands and your editor may change jobs, your agent may be the only person throughout your career to assist you in solving the inevitable writing, selling, and publishing problems as well as personal troubles that may arise.

6. Editors at big publishers would rather receive books from agents than writers.

Agents know the publishing houses, their lists, their editors' personal tastes, and what they're looking for. Submissions from agents are better prepared and more professionally submitted than those from writers.

As I mentioned earlier, the traditional route to becoming an editor has been through the slush pile. Secretaries, now called assistants, would wade through stacks of unsolicited manuscripts, hoping to find a diamond in the rough drafts. If they found one, it might become the first book they edited.

In the early days of publishing, writers tossed their manuscripts through the transom windows above publishers' doors. Ever since, unsolicited manuscripts have been said to arrive "over the transom."

When Viking published Judith Guest's bestselling novel *Ordinary People* in the early seventies, it was the first over-the-transom book they had published in twenty-six years. Major publishers don't accept unsolicited manuscripts. Before Doubleday stopped reading unsolicited manuscripts, they received ten thousand a year, out of which three or four were published. Now they and the other major publishers rely on agents to screen manuscripts and scout for them.

Editors at large houses don't have the luxury of time to consider how a potentially salable submission might be improved. They just say yes or no as quickly as they can. Agents are filters. Editors know that if agents submit a book, the idea and the execution of it are more likely to be publishable. An agent's credibility is on the line with every submission. If agents submit lemons, editors will ignore the tree that bore them. So agents only submit a project when it's ready.

7. Agents have experience negotiating with editors.

Because they understand the give-and-take of negotiating contracts and the economics of publishing, agents can combine realism and their clients' best interests when making a deal. If they've already sold books to a publisher, they know at what points editors will have room to maneuver on a deal.

Editors know that being fair to writers helps foster lasting relationships. But editors work for publishers. As noted earlier, their job is to buy books for as low an advance as possible, keep royalties as low as possible, and keep as many subsidiary rights as possible. Fighting about a contract may hinder editors' efforts to work with writers on their books. And taking advantage of unagented writers may poison editors' relationships with them and cause writers to change publishers, depriving editors of their better and more profitable books.

As one editor-in-chief once said, "It is not the business of authors and editors to talk about money." But the only way editors can avoid taking advantage of writers is to recommend that they get an agent or an attorney to review the contract.

8. Your share of subsidiary rights will usually be greater, and you may receive it sooner if your agent, rather than your publisher, handles it.

Publishers use subsidiary-rights income to earn back advances before they start sharing them with authors. Your agent will forward it to you as it's received. Publishers may insist on waiting up to nine months until the end of the royalty period to pay your share. For rights your publisher does sell, your agent will try to have the income sent to you ASAP after your advance is earned out.

9. An agent can judge you and your work objectively.

The cliché that a lawyer who represents himself has a fool for a client also applies to writers. When you write a book, you are too close to it to judge its quality or value or speak on its behalf with objectivity; your agent can. For Bantam Executive Editor Toni Burbank, working with an agent is like having another doctor on a case who can reinforce an editor's judgment about a project or situation or offer a second opinion.

As a knowledgeable buffer between editor and writer, an agent can temper, interpret, and, if warranted, try to alter editorial and publishing decisions. When authors complain, they're nagging. When agents complain, they're just doing their job.

One Pro Deserves Another

Contrary to what you may have heard, agents are only human. They make mistakes. Like writers, editors, and publishers:
- they misjudge books, people, and situations
- they may not be available when you need them
- their email service and answering machines can screw up
- they may even add numbers wrong

Despite agents' frailties, the selling of your book deserves the same kind of knowledge, skill, professionalism, and experience that you lavish on your manuscript. An agent can't write your books as well as you can, but you can't sell them as well as an agent can.

A *New Yorker* cartoon entitled "Why the Dinosaurs Perished" shows a dinosaur holding an opened mailing bag and reading from a letter:
"Thank you for letting us consider the enclosed manuscript. Although it has obvious merit, we are sorry to say that it does not suit our present needs."

Why You Need an Agent More Than Ever

Groucho Marx once said, "We should learn from the mistakes of others. We don't have time to make them all ourselves." A competent literary agent will save you from mistakes that can cost you time and money.

Books Have More Subsidiary-Rights Potential

But those rights create responsibilities. Because there are more ways to make money from your books than ever before, you need someone to take charge of selling rights: mailing books, negotiating deals, and responding to the faxes, emails, phone calls, and paperwork from around the world that selling rights generates; and to be a knowledgeable, objective advocate on your behalf.

If you want to trade less writing time for more money and greater control over your career, you may be able to sell your books yourself. If you don't mind the trade-off, your publisher will be happy to act as your agent for subsidiary rights. But the greater a book's sub-rights potential, the more it will cost writers if their publishers rather than their agents sell them.

The Document an Editor Sees Determines What You Get

In discussing what agents do for writers, too much emphasis is given to selling the book and negotiating the deal. The fate of proposals and manuscripts is sealed along with the envelopes in which they're sent to publishers or the moment agents push the "send" button.

More than ever, it's essential for an agent to make sure that every submission is as strong as it can be before submitting it. Whatever is sent to an editor has to be right on the money or, regardless of what it's about, it will soon be history—perhaps along with an agent's credibility.

Paperwork Is Slowing Down

The bigger the organization, the more slowly paper and information make their way through it. Unless a book is a potential bestseller, the combination of overworked editors and corporate bureaucracies is slowing down the rate at which editors respond to submissions, contracts are issued, and checks are dispatched. More than ever, you need someone to follow up on payments due and the paperwork, including royalty statements, your book will generate.

Your House Is Not Your Home

Your agent may be your friend, but your publisher can't be. Major houses are parts of multinational conglomerates in which all but a few writers and editors are tiny interchangeable cogs in a huge engine of commerce.

Agents first arose because of publishers' mistreatment of authors. I believe that we are once again entering an age of imperial publishing. Bestselling authors will be able to dictate terms, but new and low-selling authors will be forced to submit to publishers trying to grab a larger slice of the larger pie created by new rights and growing markets. More than ever, writers need someone to speak on their behalf.

It's been said that left to its own devices, an industry will wind up with only three major players like Burger King, Wendy's, and McDonald's, or Ford, Daimler Chrysler, and General Motors. The fewer the major players:

- the more alike they become
- the longer it may take them to make decisions
- the more slowly paperwork moves through the maze
- the less flexible they become
- the more profit management expects books to earn
- the more likely they will succumb to doing whatever it takes to earn more profits, especially if the company exists to create ever-rising quarterly profits for stockholders

This is not an environment conducive to nurturing new writers or to treating them more fairly than they have to. The twelve largest houses publish twenty-four thousand titles a year, but independent publishers sell more books than the large houses do.

You Need Help in the Rapidly Changing World of Omnimedia

The rate at which publishing—like the rest of civilization—changes is accelerating. You want to benefit from new media and markets and the publicity and income you can earn from them. So more than ever, you need someone to keep abreast of what's going on, and the certain but unpredictable obstacles and opportunities that lie ahead.

Part 3

The Prequel: What to Know before You Go

Chapter 13
Understand How Publishers Work:
The Book Business in a Nutshell

"Communication and information are entertainment, and if you don't understand that, you're not going to communicate."

—bestselling trend mogul John Naisbitt

Who is the most important person in the publishing process?
You are because you make it go. Remember that because what you're about to read may suggest otherwise.

Taking the Helm: Controlling Your Career

It's been said that you can't control the wind, but you can control your sails. You can't control the publishing industry, but you can control your perspective on the business and what you do to ensure that your books are as good and successful as you want them to be.

You can't force people to buy your books, but you can make them want to by writing them and promoting them as well as you can. You can be committed to your future and refuse to settle for anything less than achieving your goals.

The fastest way for you to get the agent, editor, publisher, and deal you want for your book is to use the following three ways to make yourself irresistible to any agent or publisher:

1. Understand how publishers work.
2. Develop your craft.
3. Make a commitment to your career.

These are the subjects of the next seven chapters. Agents appreciate and respect writers who have an understanding of the industry and have developed their craft to a professional level. But what you know about yourself and your goals is even more important. Establishing literary and financial goals that motivate your efforts and making an unshakable commitment to reach them are as important as writing for becoming a successful author.

Publishing in an Entertainment Economy

To sound professional with agents and editors, you have to understand the economic and cultural context in which you write, agents sell, and publishers publish: the accelerating convergence of the media, computers, television, telephones, and other hand-held electronic devices.

Two kinds of companies are driving this revolution: pipes companies and content companies. Pipes companies provide the hardware, the means of transmitting information.

Content companies create the information and entertainment that whiz through the pipes: email, instant messages, text messaging, photographs, news, education, books, articles, music, radio, television shows, films, plays, sports, computer games, and online services. You are no longer a *writer*; in compuspeak, you're a *content provider*.

To this mix of content, add the endless other ways to sell ideas:

• All kinds of products that range from clothes to toys

- Commercial tie-ins with other companies
- Direct selling through catalogs, retail outlets, and online stores

Media conglomerates are transforming the United States into an entertainment economy. The goal of global media empires is the implacable logic of capitalism: vertical integration, to be both a pipes company and a content company, and to produce and profit from ideas in as many forms, media, and countries as possible.

To understand how effectively media can be integrated, consider just two engines of commerce: *Star Trek* and *Star Wars*. The books, movies, computer games, television time, and merchandising products they and their sequels have generated remain impossible to miss.

To take advantage of the opportunities that this accelerating transformation offers you, think of yourself as a multimedia, multinational conglomerate. Think about writing not one book but ten or twenty related books, each better and more profitable than the last. And don't just think books—try to generate ideas that you can sell in as many ways and places as possible.

Seduced by all of the ways that technology can inform, teach, and entertain them, consumers are spending less time reading. Only 5 percent of the population goes to bookstores—a small percentage, but still one that numbers 15 million people.

One challenge publishers face is not dividing the pie differently but enlarging the size of the pie by increasing the number of book buyers. Let's look at how this need and the context in which it grows affects you.

Caviar and Popcorn: The Clash for Cash

When RCA bought Random House (now owned by Bertelsmann), accountants were going over the house's books. At one point, one of them looked up from a ledger with a sudden sense of revelation and exclaimed, "Hey! I've got a great idea! Let's just publish the bestsellers!"

When Elizabeth and I worked in publishing, the phrase *publishing business* was an oxymoron. You could leave town June 30, return after Labor Day, and not miss a thing. Frustrated by its inefficiency, people used to complain, "Why can't they run publishing like a business?" Their wish has been granted, but it's created challenges as well as opportunities. Today, although it does slow down in the summer, publishing is a year-round business.

Like the rest of the arts, publishing must tread the tightrope between art and commerce. Publishers want to publish their books with pride and passion, but to survive, they must publish books that sell.

AAR member Ned Leavitt has observed that agents' aptitudes and inclinations range from those who are editorially oriented to those who are deal-oriented, agents more interested in words to those more interested in dollar signs.

The tension between art and commerce that agents and editors live with is captured by a cartoon in *Writer's Digest* in which an editor reassures an eager young writer across a desk from him by saying, "This is a sensitive, beautifully written story, Ms. Bentley, but don't worry, I'm sure our editors can turn it into a salable property."

Major houses have an appetite for both popcorn and caviar. They want prestigious books but must publish the commercial books that support the books that bring more satisfaction and prestige than profit. An executive vice-president of marketing at Simon & Schuster explained why: "There are three reasons to publish a book: it will make a profit, the subject is so important it has to be published, or the author shows promise. Without a profit, you can't do the other two."

The Urge to Merge:
Welcome to the Age of Omnimedia

In *Passages*, Gail Sheehy's bestselling classic about personal develop-ment, she describes passages as periods of struggle and uncertainty that we endure as we progress from one stage of life to the next.

Right now, publishing is making its way through a passage. Prodded by costs, computers, competition, and the consolidation of different media into global, omnimedia empires, the business is changing faster and more radically than at any time since it began in England more than two centuries ago.

This passage is having profound, irreversible effects on agents, authors, and publishers. The globalization of culture and commerce is shaping the future of media around the world. What happens in the areas of marketing, distribution, manufacturing, rising costs, the con-centration of publishers and booksellers, and discounting will affect your agent, your publisher, and you.

No one is in charge of this transformation, and no one knows what it will lead to. But knowing the trends and realities affecting the industry will help you clarify your goals and have a perspective that balances optimism and realism.

No Sin in Synergy

If one had to capture the essence of America in one word, it would be *freedom*. If two words were called for, the second word would be *enter-prise*. As I mentioned earlier, the multi-billion-dollar *Star Trek* empire gives added resonance to the word *enterprise*.

Pocket Books does the publishing. Paramount does the movies that are rented and sold by Blockbuster video stores and the television shows that are broadcast on United Paramount Network. That's synergy, Viacom style.

In what may be a cyclical, century-old pattern, the urge to merge caused a merger mania that is transforming American business. The rise of media conglomerates produced a competitive glamour industry with better financing and more effective marketing and management. However, by adding commas and zeroes to contracts, conglomerates have also created a bottom-line mentality that wants to minimize risks.

Media conglomerates have created Siliwood, a New York-San Francisco-Silicon Valley-Hollywood axis. These arrangements are also begetting international alliances between the worlds of film, television, publishing, and consumer electronics. Such marriages of convenience encompass books, music, journalism, television, home entertainment systems, computers, software, hardware, computer games, and cyberspace.

This is the age of the mass-market hardcover, heavily discounted million-copy-selling blockbusters by brand-name authors. Reduced overhead and economies of scale make it more profitable for publishers to print and sell one million copies of one book than ten thousand copies of one hundred books. The advances lavished on the repeaters who turn out at least one bestseller a year leave less money for new writers who need it.

Take a Bow, Ladies: The Six Sisters

In the first half of the twentieth century, hundreds of imprints were born and thrived. But agent and author Richard Curtis estimates that mergers have resulted in the loss of 90 percent of the industry's imprints. The Six Sisters publish more than 80 percent of bestsellers, and agents supply 90 percent of the books they publish. A symbolic coincidence: the zip codes of the six conglomerates start with the same number: 100.

Former Simon & Schuster President Jonathan Newcomb had a clear vision of the company's future: "There are two forces driving major change in publishing. One is technology and the other is globalization.

We want to be the major technology-driven content provider in the worldwide economy. That's how we are trying to position ourselves." How are you trying to position yourself?

Here are the Six Sisters:

- Hachette Livre USA is a part of the French publishing conglomerate Lagardere, which owns Bulfinch Press, Warner Books, and Little, Brown, and Company.

- HarperCollins, a subsidiary of News Corporation that includes Avon, Collins, HarperCollins, HarperSanFrancisco, ReganBooks, Smithsonian, and HarperMorrow. Rupert Murdoch, who controls the company as well as Twentieth Century Fox, the Fox television network, and UPN, is Australian but moved his company to the United States and became a citizen.

- Holtzbrinck Publishers, a subsidiary of a German media company, includes Farrar, Straus & Giroux; Henry Holt; St. Martin's Press; Picador; Palgrave Macmillan; and Tor Books.

- Penguin Group, which is owned by Pearson, an English media group that also owns the *Financial Times*, includes Berkley Books, Dorling Kindersley, Dutton, Gotham Books, Jeremy P. Tarcher, NAL, Penguin, Portfolio, G.P. Putnam's Sons, Riverhead Books, and Viking.

- Random House, the largest English-language publisher in the world, is a division of the German Bertelsmann Book Group, which also owns the BMG Music Group. Its major imprints are Ballantine, Bantam Dell, Clarkson Potter, Crown Publishing Group, Delacorte Press, Doubleday Broadway, Fodor's Travel Publications, Alfred Knopf, Nan A. Talese, Pantheon Books, Random House Information Group, Random House Trade Books (also called Little Random), Villard Books, and Vintage & Anchor Publishing. Random House also partners with Focus Features on books and movies.

- Simon & Schuster is owned by Viacom, which also owns Paramount Pictures, CBS, and UPN. Its imprints include Atria, Fireside Books, Free Press, Pocket Books, Scribner, and Touchstone.

Book sales are subject to the whims of luck, timing, taste, reviews, publicity, subjectivity, the economy, and natural disasters, including the weather. More than 80 percent of books fail. They sell about one thousand copies and lose money, which is not a new phenomenon. But the tremendous upsurge of self-publishing that accounts for most books shows the tremendous vitality in American writing and publishing. This is what publishing was before there was a publishing industry. Authors paid printers to print their books, and then they did what they could to sell them. The low cost of technology has made independent publishing a valid alternative to seeking a publisher.

Synergy between the disparate parts of these empires remains a work in progress. Critics say that synergy is another word for *monopoly*, but the potential for synergy and the desire to take advantage of it will help shape the future of Siliwood.

The growing consolidation of publishers raises the stakes of the publishing gamble, making it harder for new writers to break into the business with a major publisher. If you're a new writer attempting to breach the walls of fortress New York, your book must be impeccable, and you must be able to promote it. The Six Sisters publish thousands of first-time authors every year. If they can do it, you can!

The Publishing Scoreboard

The decade between 1995 and 2005 generated illuminating stats that suggest the industry's future:

- In 1995, Amazon's sales were marginal. In 2005, their sales were as much as 10 percent of total trade sales.
- In 1995, there were 46,000 publishers with at least one book out. In 2005, there were 83,000 publishers, more than 70,000 of which had ten or fewer titles.
- In 1995, 6,800 new publishers opened their doors or portals. In 2004, almost 11,500 new houses were born.

• In 1995, 114,000 books were published. In 2004, 195,000 books were published.

I saved the most sobering stat for last:
• In 1995, 2.34 billion books were sold. In 2004, 2.29 billion books were sold.

Over the last fifteen years, the amount of display space for books has quadrupled, but in 2004, the industry sold fifty million fewer books. Go figure. Despite the chain stores, the online stores, mass merchandisers like Wal-Mart and the price clubs, the number of units sold fell. Even sales of books by brand-name authors have fallen.

A Brand by Any Other Name Wouldn't Be

Big houses want brand-name authors, and they do everything they can to build writers into brand names. There's only one way to a build your brand: have enough books spend enough time on the bestseller list to grow a fan base that will buy anything with your name on it.

The pantheon of brand names includes David Bach, Dave Barry, Dan Brown, Sandra Brown, Deepak Chopra, Tom Clancy, Mary Higgins Clark, Patricia Cornwell, Catherine Coulter, Michael Crichton, Janet Evanovich, Elizabeth George, Sue Grafton, John Grisham, Carl Hiassen, John Irving, Stephen King, Dean Koontz, David McCullough, Fern Michaels, James Patterson, Ruth Rendall, Anne Rice, Nora Roberts, J. K. Rowling, Ann Rule, Danielle Steel, John Updike, and Tom Wolfe.

Books by brand-name authors are bestsellers. The only questions are how high their books will go and how long they'll stay there. Their work is distinctive enough so that whether they write fiction or nonfiction—

and several of them do both—you know what to expect from a Janet Evanovich mystery or a Tom Clancy technothriller. Sometimes titles like Harry Potter, the *Chicken Soup* books, and the Dummies series can become brands. But not all of the books in a series are bestsellers.

In *The Book Publishing Industry*, Albert Greco noted that at one point in 1993, books by only two authors took up the first six spots on *Publishers Weekly* mass-market bestseller list: John Grisham and Michael Crichton. Movies of their books helped accelerate book, audio, and wholesale price-club sales and brought new readers into bookstores and libraries.

The sustained torrent of sales catapulted Dan Brown and J. K. Rowling to brand-name status sooner than the veterans above. More than one of their books has consistently been on bestseller lists for years. When the sixth Harry Potter book was published, all six books were on bestseller lists simultaneously. The *upside* of books can be huge, and to find out the chances you have to strike it rich, keep reading.

Chapter 14
Whining and Dining on the Spaghetti Factor:
How Publishing Went from Class to Mass

"Somewhere on Earth, a woman is giving birth to a child every ten seconds. She must be found and stopped."

—humorist Sam Levenson

She may be the same person who's churning out the million manuscripts a year that make their way back and forth across the country. Nonetheless, one challenge you face is that there are far too many books being published to receive the attention they need from publishers, reviewers, booksellers, or book buyers. But this part of the book will show you how to break through the static caused by other books and media.

How Independents Test-Market Books for Chains

Out of the seventeen hundred remaining independent bookstores, four hundred fifty are the A-List stores, the *major national influential independents*. If they get behind a book with promise, especially literary fiction and nonfiction, independents can transform small books with promise into bestsellers.

Among the ways that they do this are by:
- handselling books they love to customers they know will like them
- displaying the books where they will sell best
- using the books in a window display
- using shelf-talkers—handwritten notes that hang down below the bookshelves underneath books that the staff loves
- having author events
- featuring the author in their newsletter about upcoming events
- suggesting the book to reading groups
- helping to arrange for authors to speak to reading groups
- discounting the books
- having authors sign stock and stickering the jacket
- posting author photos and reviews on walls
- taking advance orders
- using their websites to support and magnify their efforts

To get booksellers excited about books, publishers prime the pump by sending or giving booksellers advance reading copies (ARCs), the uncorrected galleys of books in trade-paperback form. They may start with a letter from someone at the house praising the book's virtues and perhaps quotes from indie booksellers.

The bitter irony for the indies is that they become victims of their own success. Once they've made a book a bestseller, the chains and big-box stores sell it at a discount and make most of the profit from it. To help their cause, the independents created Booksense to promote themselves. Booksense publishes free lists, available in stores or at www.booksense.org, of books with quotes from booksellers who nominate them for the list. At BEA, the bookseller's convention, the indies present ABBYs, the American Booksellers Book of the Year Awards.

Yes, But Can You Type? When Publishing Was a Gentleman's Business

For more than half of the last century, publishing was a *gentleman's business*. The Ivy-League-educated men who owned and ran publishing houses didn't have to worry about where their next meal would come from. They created a genteel, patrician atmosphere.

- Publishers paid small or no advances.
- There were few women in the industry who didn't make their living with a typewriter.
- Publishing was a leisurely business, especially during the summer.
- Sales reps would travel around their territory twice a year stopping in hotels, and booksellers would come to the hotel to place their orders.
- A review on the front page of the *New York Times* guaranteed best-sellerdom.
- The next best thing that could happen to a book was being made a main selection of the Book of the Month Club.

Partly sustained by their backlist, publishers were driven by the desire to provide good writing. Editors bought books they thought were worth publishing. Then the sales department figured out how to sell them.

The Spaghetti Factor was and, alas, remains the industry's guiding principle. Publishers threw six books against a wall and hoped that at least one of them would stick well enough to compensate for the others. Commerce sustained art. Successful books endowed books that deserved to be published. This is still the case, but it was easier to do then because the cost of everything was so much less.

In the sixties, the industry began to become more like a big business. Jacqueline Susann taught publishers the value of promotion by flying around the country doing publicity in a polka-dotted airplane.

The invention of the photocopy machine made multiple submissions possible. Today, they're an accepted part of how agents and writers submit their books, although editors don't want multiple submissions of a complete manuscript unless it's a potential bestseller. Computers make multiple submissions easy, and agents submit proposals as email attachments to editors.

Corporations started buying publishers with the mistaken impression that they were profitable or could be made profitable if they were properly run. This was not the case then nor is it now, which is why most of the Six Sisters are the pawns of conglomerates in search of profit and synergy.

As there was more money to be made from books and their subsidiary rights, the role of agents grew as both negotiators and editors. Because editors started working on too many books to give them the editorial attention they required, agents became more important as editors.

Why Read?

When *Publishers Weekly* polled people about why they read, they found that the most important reasons are two pleasures: first the pleasure of reading the book, then the pleasure of telling friends about it. That's why word of mouth alone can make a book successful despite the indifference with which it is published.

Simon & Schuster spent $7,500 for a book of spiritual advice by a first-time author. The first printing was five thousand copies—not an auspicious beginning for a book at a large house. But word of mouth and Scott Peck's strategy of doing three radio talk shows every day helped keep *The Road Less Traveled* on the trade paperback bestseller list for more than twelve years, a unique achievement.

A Hit-or-Miss Business

Publishing is a hit-or-miss, pre-publication-oriented business. Publishers judge a book's potential by how it picks up steam before it's even published. Without early signs for success, books either sink or swim, depending on the reception the first printing receives from:
- reviewers and book buyers
- reading groups
- word of mouth and mouse
- handselling by indies
- the author's speaking and media appearances, online or off

If a book doesn't pick up enough steam by the end of the book's one- to three-month launch window, big houses will give up on it and move on to the next book.

Uncovered at Last:
A Damsel Too Handy for Her Own Good

Publishing your book will be a personal, complex, collaborative enterprise. To have the best chance for success, your book should be well edited, copyedited, designed, produced, sold by the sales reps and the subsidiary-rights departments, distributed, promoted, reviewed, and stocked by booksellers. A multitude of things can go wrong during the publication of a book, and something inevitably will. Publishing a book perfectly is practically impossible.

During one of our spring raids on the Big Apple, during which we see an editor every thirty minutes, we were in the office of Hugh Van Dusen, well-known editor who does serious nonfiction for HarperCollins. We were surprised to see a mass-market historical romance from the company's mass-market imprint on his shelf. We asked him why it was there.

"Look at the cover," he said.

It was a typical romantic clinch showing a medieval knight kneeling with his arm around a fair damsel with long red hair and a white dress sitting on the ground in a meadow.

After inspecting the cover, we looked at him quizzically.

"Check her hands," he said.

We looked again. One hand was clasping her beloved's hand. One hand was leaning on the ground. And there, peeking out from the folds of her dress, was a third hand!

During the inevitable changes that cover art goes through, the artist had been requested to change the position of her hands. But in making the change, the artist forgot to remove the initial appendage. What's unusual isn't that the mistake happened but that the book was published and on bookstore shelves before anyone caught it.

Major publishers have spring, fall, and winter lists of books. Mass-market houses have monthly lists. After publishers inform their sales representatives about a new list, the reps fan out across the country hawking their wares. Consequently, major New York publishers want books with national interest.

One of the most fascinating and frustrating publishing truths is that regardless of how much or how little a publisher spends to buy or promote a book by an unknown writer, it is sometimes impossible to predict how the book will fare in the marketplace.

Timing Your Book

Publishers like to avoid risk. As one of our writers once said, "They'll do *anything* as long as it's been done before."

When one editor-in-chief was asked what he wanted for his house, he answered, "More of the same only different."

The comedian Fred Allen said, "Imitation is the sincerest form of television," and so it is with publishing. Publishers like to jump on bandwagons, but not too early or too late, or they land on their financial keisters. When everybody jumps, the result is bookicide: too many publishers pounce on a hot subject and suffocate it with a barrage of books. When Windows 95 arrived, so did four hundred fifty books about it!

A Returning Problem

In 1965, two years before I started working for them, Bantam Books set a world record. From accepting the proposal for *The Pope's Journey to the United States* to publishing it took them just sixty-six and a half hours.

But by the time your book is written, sold, edited, and then produced, distributed, and marketed by a large house, one and a half to two years will usually pass. Books have a shelf life of three to six months, after which booksellers return unsold books to publishers' warehouses. For mass-market books, it may only be one month.

A Burning Issue: How Random House Got 86-ed

One day eighty-six eighteen-wheel trucks pulled up to the Random House warehouse in Westminster, Maryland, with returns from just one customer: Barnes & Noble. Random House executive editor Bob Loomis went on to tell an auditorium packed with a thousand writers at the Maui Writers Conference that when Random House can't resell books, authors don't buy overstock, and the company can't even give books away, they burn them to heat the warehouse. The audience gasped when they heard this. Then a writer piped up and asked, "What's your hottest book?"

Warehouses symbolize the complexity of publishing. Every day of the week, they:

- work with thousands of books, the quantity and titles of which may change daily
- work with audio books as well as books between covers
- receive returns
- go through returns to separate books they can use
- dispatch orders of all sizes to customers of all sizes
- give priority to bestsellers to sustain their momentum and to the company's biggest customers
- receive new books from printers that they have to make room for and shelve, which changes the order in which stock pickers fill orders
- receive reprints and fill back orders for them
- receive paperback versions of hardcovers that may also still be selling
- fill orders for books that aren't earning their keep and that the house is remaindering at rock-bottom prices
- get rid of books that the publisher is declaring out of print
- establish and change the locations of books to make it as easy as possible for stock pickers to fill orders
- do the same things every day but since every order is different and the mix of books changes, do them differently
- do everything right, or suffer the consequences of shipping too few or too many books, shipping the wrong ones, or shipping to the wrong customer

Double Booking: Why Do You Think They Call It Publishing?

I once interned for the Cover to Cover bookstore in San Francisco, and one day a duplicate shipment of books arrived. When I asked the owner of the store about it, she said without hesitation: "Why do you think they call it Doubleday?"

Publishers strive to have just-in-time inventory. And they want their warehouses as empty as possible by December 31 because they pay taxes on inventory. There's an ebb and flow to publishing. For example, because of the holidays, more books are published and shipped in the fall than other seasons.

When you remember that, with the exception of Hachette USA, the Six Sisters publish and distribute more than a thousand titles a year, you begin to understand how complex just the process of warehousing books is. And warehousing is only one part of the publishing process.

To justify your book's space in a publisher's warehouse, keep reading to find out what publishers want to stock their warehouses with.

Chapter 15
The Spirit of Enterprise:
What Publishers Are Buying and Why

Investing in Authors

Po Bronson gave friends the opportunity to invest in shares of his first novel, *Bombardiers,* which is about selling bonds. The way your proposal or manuscript looks and reads must convince publishers that it's worth the investment that you want them to make in it.

Without including the variable costs of the advance and the first printing, the average investment major publishers make in a book is $50,000. Holding down advances and royalties and retaining as many subsidiary rights as possible are three ways that publishers try to protect their investment. But despite the growing value of foreign and electronic rights, publishers don't want to rely on subsidiary-rights sales to justify buying a book. They want their books to earn their keep in stores.

Two Dresses and an Escalator:
Publishers in Chains

Henny Youngman once quipped, "My wife will buy anything marked down. She just bought two dresses and an escalator."

Distribution, getting books into stores, and keeping them there is a perpetual challenge for publishers. Booksellers and the distributors who sell to them can't stock all of the books that are published. The limitations of space and budgets force booksellers to return books that don't perform well enough.

The age of the independent bookstore is over. Independent bookstores are being supplanted by superstores that mark down prices and stock up to two hundred seventy-five thousand titles. But because booksellers can return unsold books, returns are a perpetual migraine for which publishers have yet to find a cure. Alfred Knopf, who founded the company bearing his name, described this problem succinctly: "Gone today, here tomorrow." Print-on-demand will end most if not all returns.

The Spirit of Enterprise: Bottoms Up

The spirit of experimentation and independence is essential for writing to continue to flourish. But the corporate mentality and high overhead of the publishing behemoths renders them less receptive to new ideas and writers without a ready audience for their work or the proven ability to promote it. The opportunity to offer new writers and ideas is being seized by small publishers, university presses, and by authors themselves.

At the base of the publishing pyramid, computer technology, enterprising writers and publishers, and the censorship of the marketplace have created tens of thousands of independent presses and self-publishers, a booming cottage industry that will continue to grow.

The basic publishing reflex is: "I see it. I love it. I publish it." Independent publishers still follow where their passions and low overheads liberate them to go. And because they have small lists, the success of every book is important to them.

University presses started out as nonprofit enterprises publishing books by scholars for scholars. But because universities can no longer underwrite them, they are also filling the publishing vacuum for less commercial midlist books by becoming more trade oriented.

In between the large and the small publishers are the mid-sized houses that carry on without the benefit of either the resources of the large publishers or the low overhead of the small presses.

Looking Out for the Competition

"Outside of a dog, a book is a man's best friend.
Inside of a dog, it's too dark to read."

—Groucho Marx

A man's best friend is only one of the growing array of alternatives consumers have to reading your books. And when it comes to choosing which media to enjoy, consumers are surrounded by friends, so books start with significant disadvantages:

- They are black and white in the age of color.
- They have columns of type at a time in which visual appeal is an essential element in communications and marketing.
- They are motionless in the age of DSL and MTV.

Henry Youngman once admitted,

"I read about the evils of drinking so I gave up reading."

Your book will compete with all the other reasons people have to give up reading, and there are more reasons than ever, including sex, shopping, fishing, and gardening (albeit all perennial subjects for books). The competition for people's time is tougher than the competition for their money.

In one of Russell Myers's "Broom Hilda" cartoon strips, Broom Hilda is sitting at a typewriter and writes:

Dear Mr. Publisher,

Enclosed is the manuscript for my new novel. It has, I believe, everything necessary to be a bestseller. It weighs twelve pounds, eleven of which are about sex.

Fiction and nonfiction by the pound still sell, but faster reading time and lower cover prices started a trend toward shorter books. Part of the attraction of genre romance novels is that they can be read in a day while the kids are at school.

One of the reasons the *Chicken Soup* books are so successful is that the stories in them can be read anytime readers find even a few minutes to read. The chapters in *The Da Vinci Code* average three pages each. Understanding the complex, shifting cultural landscape in which you are trying to find happy homes for your books will help you take advantage of all the opportunities waiting for you to come up with the right idea.

In the age of omnimedia—all media, all the time—the form information takes is becoming irrelevant. Consumers will buy what they need depending on the information they need, the price for it, how quickly they need it, and the most effective, efficient, easy-to-use, enjoyable, and convenient way to communicate the information.

They may buy a book for a biography or a novel, an audio book if they're on the road a lot, a DVD or a downloadable version of an exercise program, and up-to-date, downloadable reference information. With the right idea, agent, and publisher, competitive media will be a source of income and publicity for you and your books. So when you're considering what to write about, try to come up with ideas that you can resell in as many media as possible.

Fiction: The Bestseller Sweepstakes

Agents and editors love gifted storytellers and are always looking for four kinds of fiction:

- Genre or category books, such as mysteries, westerns, romances, and science fiction
- Mainstream novels that have more scope and depth of characterization and broader appeal than genre fiction but are tough to sell when written by newcomers
- Literary novels that are well crafted and character-driven, and on which large hardcover houses are increasingly reluctant to lose money while waiting for new writers to build an audience
- Bestsellers, which may be genre books with enough heft, scope, and storytelling ability; mainstream or literary novels; or plot-driven commercial blockbusters

In Elmore Leonard's novel *Get Shorty*, an aspiring writer asks a Hollywood producer what kind of writing makes the most money. The producer replies, "Ransom notes."

In publishing, bestsellers make the most money. All houses want them, and in the heat of an auction, large publishers eagerly bid seven figures for them, eight on multi-book deals that will keep authors out of competitors' hands.

George Bosque robbed Brinks of $1 million, spent it in a year and a half, and then turned himself in. When he was asked how he managed to spend a million in a year and a half, he replied, "Well, I spent half of it on gambling, drink, and romance, and I guess I squandered the rest."

If publishers believe they're wagering on the next Michael Crichton or Danielle Steel, they'll let their competitive spirits seduce them into squandering a bundle in the bestseller sweepstakes.

A struggling writer calls a publisher to ask about a novel she had submitted.

"This is quite well written," admits the editor, "but we only publish work by writers with well-known names."

"Great!" shouts the writer. "My name's Smith!"

Fiction, more than nonfiction, is a brand-name business, depending on well-known names. Once authors have paid their dues to join the bestseller club by writing several novels you've never heard of, then write their breakthrough novels, they have a good shot at a lifetime membership. Seventy-five percent of the novels on the bestseller lists are by members of the bestseller club.

The *New York Times* reported that blockbusters are "all but required to keep publishers afloat." Beyond the value of the books themselves, bestsellers are important to publishers because they lead the rest of a publisher's list into the bookstore. At mass-market houses, the top books are even called "leaders."

Stat Machine

- In paperback, fiction outsells nonfiction three to one. The reverse is true in hardcover.
- Women buy 78 percent of books, including those they buy for spouses, kids, and gifts.

Nonfiction: Anything Goes

In nonfiction, publishers will take on almost anything for the general public that will sell in bookstores and that ideally has other markets, such as schools, gift stores, and libraries. Nonfiction runs the gamut.

There are frontlist books by the house's most commercial authors and those they have the highest hopes for. At the other extreme are backlist books, evergreens that sell year after year. What's the ultimate backlist book? The Bible. It's every publisher's dream. It's already sold five billion copies. It still sells millions of copies a year, and although there may be hell to pay, there are no royalties to pay on the way.

Publishers are more successful with certain subjects or kinds of books than others. So they tend to stick to the kinds of books that they sell well. This phenomenon is called *cluster publishing*.

Sandwiched in between the frontlist and backlist books are the midlist books such as new fiction by unknown writers that don't have the potential to be frontlist hits or provide sources of backlist income until an author's career takes off.

Publishers don't devote a lot of resources to midlist books, so these books usually die a quick publish-and-perish death and are forgotten unless they get unexpectedly good reviews, subsidiary-rights sales, media attention, word of mouth, or other sign that they have enough grassroots traction to justify going back to press and monitoring sales to see if they continue to grow.

The Joys of Writing Nonfiction

At the beginning of their careers, nonfiction writers are luckier than novelists because nonfiction is:

- easier to write
- easier to adapt for talks, seminars, and articles, which together with selling their books at their events can enable writers to make a living
- easier for writers to sell because it can usually be sold with a proposal instead of a whole manuscript
- easier for agents to sell because it's easier to prove the market for a book because most houses publish it, and because agents use multiple submissions
- easier to gauge the quality and value of
- easier to promote
- easier to judge how promotable authors are
- easier to know how well they'll promote the book
- easier to sell sub rights for because more media can use it
- more likely to stay on bookstore shelves longer
- easier to give a new life to with new and revised editions
- more likely to stay in print before an author is well known

Stat Machine
- About 90 percent of the books published are nonfiction.
- About 75 percent of nonfiction books are by new authors.

A Format for Every Occasion

Books are being published in more formats than ever. Competitive books will help you determine the best format for your book:

- *Hardcover.* The price and durability of hardcovers make them principally an information medium, the format for books with lasting value one wants to keep for reference. In hardcover, as mentioned earlier, nonfiction outsells fiction three to one. A year after publication, 90 percent of successful hardcover books are reprinted in paperback.

- *Mass market.* The opening salvo of America's paperback revolution was fired in 1939 when Pocket Books published ten 25-cent mass-market paperbacks. In contrast to hardcover books, mass-market books are for the most part a fiction medium. In paperback, as mentioned earlier, fiction outsells nonfiction three to one. More than half of the mass-market books sold are romances.

- *Trade paperback.* These come in any size from small gift books 3 to 11" x 14" art books or even larger. The Anchor Books imprint at Doubleday, started in 1953, is regarded as the starting point in the history of trade paperbacks, making it the newest of the three formats.

Price and the variety of formats and sizes make trade paperbacks the all-purpose medium, suitable for words and pictures, fiction and nonfiction, the serious and the frivolous, for all stores that sell books and for course adoptions, reference, and gifts.

The lower price of paperbacks means that authors receive lower royalties and publishers must sell several times as many copies for the authors to earn the equivalent of the hardcover income. But the lower the price of something, the more it is likely to sell.

A book can be published in any combination of these formats, or even, in time, all three. A publisher will do a book in whatever format works best. Since the major houses do all three, they can control the design, timing, and marketing of each edition. So, if a book becomes a blockbuster like Rick Warren's *The Purpose-Driven Life*, publishers will keep selling the hardcover until the sales indicate it's time for the paperback edition.

This flexibility came about because in the mid-sixties, mass-market publishers started publishing paperback originals to avoid the rising cost of buying paperback reprint rights. They also started or acquired hardcover imprints to produce books that could feed their paperback lines. Unable to buy a mass-market house, HarperCollins, Hyperion, Little Brown, and St. Martin's Press started lines of their own. HarperCollins later bought Avon, and Little Brown is now in the same fold as Warner Books.

The benefit to you from your house by publishing in all three formats is that when a hardcover house sells the paperback rights to a book, the income is split between the author and the publisher. If your publisher does the hardcover and paperback editions, you receive full royalties.

Rising hardcover prices have made book buyers reluctant to risk their money on new writers, especially novelists. So, unless a book has strong enough hardcover potential, it will be published in trade or mass-market paperback. It is less likely to be reviewed but more likely to sell.

Once authors have built a large enough audience or write a breakout book, the house will start publishing their work in hardcover. Genre fiction is a relatively easy way for novelists to break into the business. That's how Janet Dailey, Nora Roberts, Iris Johansen, Tami Hoag, and Sue "B-is-for-Bestseller" Grafton earned their keys to the bestseller club.

Publishing Goes Global

As if pursuing futurist John Naisbitt's dream of world peace through world trade, the globalization of publishing along with the rest of the economy is accelerating. This will continue to increase the number of readers for your books around the world. The merging of American and European media companies is one sign of this change.

Another sign was when the movie version of *Like Water for Chocolate* got the book onto the *San Francisco Chronicle* bestseller list in English and Spanish simultaneously. It symbolized the beginning of a new era of

Spanish-language publishing in *los Estados Unidos*. More publishers are doing books for America's growing Hispanic market.

The Rhythms of Publishing

Publishing has daily, weekly, monthly, seasonal, and annual rhythms.

A Daily Rhythm
- responding to mail
- responding to email from inside and outside the house
- taking calls from and making calls to authors, agents, editors, and other staff people
- attending that day's meeting(s)
- having lunch with an agent, editor, or someone else on the staff
- working with an assistant
- leaving around six or later with proposals and manuscripts to read
- going to a book signing, a party for a book or author, another publishing event, or a job-related dinner

The daily rhythm of successful authors is simple: following their daily ritual of when, where, how, and how long they write and promote their books and build and maintain their networks.

A Weekly Rhythm
The high point of an editor's weekly rhythm is the editorial board meeting at which editors make a case for buying the books they've read with the help of others who read the proposal or manuscript and agree with the editor.

Other meetings that editors might just go in and out of to discuss their books are:

- marketing meetings to decide how the house will promote forth-coming books
- cover meetings to decide how to approach the covers or jackets of their books
- reprint meetings to decide whether to reprint books and if so, how many copies

A Seasonal Rhythm

The seasonal rhythm reflects the time of year and affects the house's two or three lists. All houses have spring and fall lists. Big houses have three lists a year: January to April, May to August, and September to December.

Publishers announce each list to their reps at a sales conference, either in person or, for big houses, by teleconference. The conference for the spring list is held in December in person and, for some large houses, in a warm climate.

Preparation for the conference includes preparing a catalog for the list that sales reps can use to present the list to booksellers. Deciding what books to include in a catalog involves a balancing act between frontlist, midlist, and backlist books; between fiction and nonfiction; and between similar books.

The time between when an accepted manuscript goes into production and is sent to a copyeditor and when it's published ranges from six months to a year. But the number of books ready to be published and the best time to publish a book will also affect a pub date.

Preparing for a sales conference involves launch meetings at which editors discuss their books with the sales and marketing staff so they can decide how to present them at the conference. Among the decisions that are made are positioning the book in time and importance to the other books on the list and what the house will do to promote the book.

The house will send the reps manuscripts or galleys of the most important books on the list, so they will know about the books before the conference. The conference will focus on what the house and the reps will do to market them.

It's been said that bestsellers make their own weather. They triumph regardless of when they're published. But booksellers try to choose the best time of year to publish a book:

- January books help readers make plans for the New Year. So wedding, tax, travel, and gardening books appear early in the year as do self-help books that promise to help book buyers keep their New Year's resolutions and recover from the dissipation of the holidays. January is busy for booksellers because people are exchanging gifts and redeeming gift certificates.
- February is Black History month. Books celebrating love also appear in February.
- St. Patrick's Day and Easter books come out in March.
- In April, baseball books try to get to first base. Dads-and-grads and Mother's Day books come out in April and May.
- Beach reads, juicy novels that vacationers can indulge themselves with, appear in July and August. Old and modern classics that are on school lists that students are expected to read before school starts sell well then.
- The beginning of the school year in August and September unleashes a wave of sales of books that are required reading. But because of vacations that end after Labor Day, August is the second slowest time of the year for publishers, and the closer you get to Labor Day, the slower it gets. Most publishing people, especially those with school-age children, take their vacations during the summer. If a key person on the editorial board is away, the weekly board meeting may be postponed, so it may take longer to get decisions about buying books.
- Books by bestselling authors and books that have bestseller potential are launched in September and October with the hope that they'll keep selling through the holiday season. Halloween

books that may not stand a ghost of a chance arrive in stores in October.

- Bookstore tables are stuffed with gift books, holiday books, books by bestselling authors, and calendars in November and December, the biggest selling season of the year.
- December is the busiest month for booksellers. But between sales conferences and the holidays, it's the quietest time of the year for publishers. Big houses are even closing their doors between Christmas and New Year's.

Reps start selling the list with their master catalog that they've annotated with key selling points. Booksellers look at their copy of the catalog and make fast decisions on whether they want to buy a book and if so, how many copies to take.

An Annual Rhythm: BEA

The biggest annual publishing event is BookExpo America (BEA), held in May or June. It moves to a different city each year in the East, West, or Midwest. More than twenty thousand people come to the convention. When it's in New York, more than thirty thousand people come because publishers send their editors.

It's the only time of the year when you can see what's going on in the industry in one big room. Publishers have booths and feature their big fall books with light boxes of the covers. They also give away advance reading copies of the books they're most excited about. And one of the great perks of working in the business is being able to bring home future bestsellers. There are signings, panels, breakfasts, and lunches at which bestselling authors talk about their new books.

Going at least once is an essential experience. It will give you a humbling but inspiring perspective about the business that you're part of. The convention has a special quality to it since publishing people are there because they want to be.

There's a spirit of community, a shared sense of the value and importance of books, even with strangers. Another wonderful surprise is the people you meet accidentally, strike up friendships with, and with whom you can share your knowledge and experience. Although BEA is a trade show not open to the public, writers come and find agents and publishers.

After thirty-three publishers rejected *Chicken Soup for the Soul*, Jack Canfield and Mark Victor Hansen brought backpacks full of manuscripts to BEA, and more than one hundred more publishers rejected them before they found Health Communications. They didn't get an advance, but they were off and running, and they haven't stopped since.

With rare exceptions, publishing is not a path to wealth. People work in publishing because they like books and they like people. BEA gives them a chance to have a reunion with book people around the country that they only see once a year and to reaffirm why they're in the business.

BEA began as a trade show that was held in the Shoreham Hotel in Washington, D.C. on Memorial Day Weekend. It was always too hot and humid, and the air conditioning tended to take the weekend off. Its basic purpose was for reps to meet with bookstore owners to fix problems and take orders for fall books. Publishers would have show specials, discounts only available at the show to prod booksellers to order books.

Not much order-taking goes on now. It's more about learning about how houses are promoting books; learning how to be more profitable at breakout sessions; getting the chance to meet other booksellers; discussing problems and opportunities; and getting to hear, meet, and have books signed by bestselling authors.

Apart from the growing competition the indies face from chains, big-box stores, and online booksellers, they are facing the realities of aging readers and aging booksellers who can't find buyers for their stores. The annual meeting of the American Booksellers Association held at BEA gives them an opportunity to discuss their concerns.

Despite having fewer booksellers, BEA has grown because foreign publishers, companies that create software and other products for running bookstores, and sidelines like calendars and stationery have booths. BEA also has a foreign-rights center where agents can meet with foreign publishers and their coagents for translation rights.

BEA also attracts media like *Publishers Weekly*, which publishes a daily magazine during the conference; book-review editors; and other trade and consumer print, broadcast, and electronic media.

A Tea-rrific Event

The Northern California Book Publicity and Marketing Association (NCBPMA) puts on a "tea" at which no tea is served but local media are, which makes it a great opportunity for you to meet media people and find out what kinds of books they're interested in and how to approach them. Staff and freelance publicists attend so it also gives you a chance to meet them.

Other important annual conventions for publishers are the American Library Association (ALA) convention and the National Association of College Stores (NACS). There are also specialized conferences, on history for example, that editors who specialize in the field attend to stay abreast of what's going on in the field and to see and be seen by authors.

One way that agents and authors can prove they're serious about working in a field is by being members of professional organizations. If you're writing about food, join IACP, the International Association of Culinary Professionals.

Writer's organizations have their own rhythms of newsletters, monthly meetings, and national conferences.

Irregular Rhythms

Subjects and genre fiction have their own ebb and flow, rhythms dictated by readers' tastes. At this writing, for example, paranormal romances are hot as is romantica, a spicy blend of romance and erotica. Although popular nonfiction subjects remain stable, bestselling health and diet books have been generating millions of dollars in royalties, and the graying of America's sedentary boomers will keep lifestyle subjects popular. An event like 9/11 or a continuing source of concern like the war on terrorism can create interest in old and new books on the subject.

One challenge you face is creating daily, weekly, and seasonal rhythms that enable you to balance your desires and obligations and enable you to do justice to writing and promoting your books.

You Got Rhythm?

Create the rhythms in your life that enable you to reach your goals and look forward to getting up in the morning, knowing you're one of the luckiest people on Earth.

Chapter 16
The Editor as Hero:
An Homage to Your Other Agent

"The buying policy of this house is the sum of the idiosyncrasies of its editors."

—Hiram Hayden, former editor-in-chief of Random House

Bumpersnicker: Editors Do It Between the Lines

Your agent is a marriage broker between you and your editor. Of all the publishing realities you need to understand, none is more important to you than how editors work. Your editor will be the first, most immediate, and most vital continuing connection that you will have with your publisher, the link between you and everyone else in the house.

The endless supply of excellent editors is an endearing, enduring miracle of publishing. This fountain of youth is one of the ways in which publishing hasn't changed in decades. Although they're condemning themselves to an uncertain tenure at being overworked and underpaid, bright, likable, passionate young English majors continue to attend courses on publishing and then flock to New York in the quest for jobs.

There are three reasons why understanding how editors work will help you:

• As your in-house agent, editors will be most involved with you and your book.

- Many editors become agents, so understanding editors will help you understand agents because they have much in common.
- Knowing how editors acquire and edit books will enable you to understand how your agent works with them and how you can help your editor help you.

What roles do editors play?

Editors Are Publishers

"A competent editor is a publisher in microcosm, able to initiate and follow a project all the way through."

—Marc Jaffe, former editor-in-chief of Bantam Books

Editors know how to thrive within the rhythms of publishing. They have to be passionate, persistent, and creative in ramrodding a book through publication by:

- reading it
- doing a P&L on it
- lobbying to buy it
- rereading the manuscript, suggesting changes, and reading the rewritten manuscript
- checking the copyediting
- consulting with the art department on its design
- writing the catalog copy
- helping to generate excitement for it before, and perhaps at, the sales conference
- consulting and monitoring the planning and execution of its trade and consumer promotion
- consulting on subsidiary-rights sales
- overseeing the trade and/or mass-market paperback edition if it's a hardcover

Following through on the publication of a book may take years.

Editors Are "Intrepreneurs"

They're entrepreneurs within their houses with their own invisible imprints. Like the publishers they work for, they rise and fall on the strength of their lists.

Speaking of a novel she had rejected, editor Jane Von Mehren once said, "I liked it, but I couldn't bleed for it." Editors spend so much time shepherding a project through the publication process that they only want to work on books they love. You can't buy passion, and, especially for a small book, it's more valuable than money. But their passion also has to help keep the house afloat. If editors' books don't help fill in the black side of the ledger, they will have to find another house to set up shop in.

Editors Are Specialists

Agents know what kind of books editors like. Some editors are generalists who will consider anything their houses publish, but at big houses, most balance their passions with the house's needs.

Editors may have a passion for contemporary, historical, genre, literary, or commercial fiction. Usually one editor in a house will be responsible for acquiring books on subjects such as food, sports, health, business, child care, psychology, spirituality, gay and lesbian interests, culture issues, and fiction. Editors are hired because they've been successful with certain kinds of books.

Editors Are Book Lovers

Like agents, editors love books, and if they could write the Great American Novel, they'd be home doing it. Since they can't, the next best things are discovering and nurturing new writers. If they love a proposal or manuscript they're reading, they'll ask themselves basic questions:

- What groups of book buyers will walk into bookstores in fifty states two years from now and buy this book?
- What shelf will the book go on in the bookstore?
- What will take this book to the cash register?
- How can I convince the house to buy it?
- How much work will it need to make it as close to 100 percent as the writer can make it?

Once an editor can answer these questions, you no longer have one agent, you have two.

Editors Are In-House Agents

One of an editor's greatest gifts is the ability to be an effective in-house agent for your book. Even if an editor adores your book, that's only the first hurdle. At some houses, editors can simply take a project to their boss for a decision. But as I've mentioned, most editors must justify their enthusiasm.

First, they gather support from other editors and key people in the house they think will like it by sharing the proposal or manuscript. Then, they have to fill out a lengthy computerized P&L statement covering a book's contents, markets, the costs to buy and produce it, and its sales, subsidiary-rights, and promotion potential. There's a T-shirt that says "When all else fails, manipulate the data." If the numbers don't prove that the book will make a profit, editors massage them until they do. Finally, they (or a sponsoring editor who speaks on their behalf) discuss the book at the weekly editorial board meeting that may include other editors; members of the sales, publicity, marketing, and subsidiary-rights departments; and executives of the company, a formidable gauntlet that functions as a devil's advocate for the house.

If anyone on the editorial board can come up with a reason that seems to justify not doing a book, they'll pass on it and go on to the next book.

The more knowledgeable an agent is about a company's key players and how the acquisition process works, the better position the agent is in to influence the decision to buy a book. Since it is far simpler and easier for an editor and an editorial board to say no than yes, you and your proposal or manuscript must give the board as many reasons to say yes as possible and not one to say no.

Editors Are Visionaries

They see not just what a book is, but what it can be. One of an editor's most valuable gifts is the ability to reconcile the writer's vision with the house's and the readers' needs and desires with those of book buyers.

Editors Are Subjective Human Beings

"An editor is a person who separates the wheat from the chaff and then prints the chaff."—critic H. L. Mencken

Like the other arts, publishing is an extremely subjective business. The French author Andre Maurois once observed, "In literature, as in love, we are astonished at what is chosen by others." Art, like life, is a Rorschach. Editors see only what they're ready to see at the moment they pick up a manuscript. We've sold books to the third editor to read them at the same house to read them. Subjectivity and the group grope for the right decision are two of the reasons editors turn down books that become bestsellers.

Editors Are Overworked, Underpaid Galley Slaves

In Mark Twain's wonderful classic *Life on the Mississippi*, he describes how a riverboat captain knows every changing bend in the two thousand-mile river. He knows where he is all the time, even when he's asleep.

Editors, like agents, have to be able to stay afloat while awash in an endless deluge of meetings, phone calls, correspondence, media, junk mail, jacket proofs, galleys, submissions from agents, memos to other editors in the house to drum up support for a project, deals, and books in different stages.

It's been estimated that corporate wage slaves have only six minutes at a stretch to work before being interrupted by a colleague, a meeting, or a phone call. So, editors can't read or edit during the day; they read and edit at night, on weekends, and on vacation. The perfect title for an editor's autobiography would be *Piles to Go before I Sleep*.

An editor who won the prestigious Roger Klein Award, the Oscar for editors, guesstimated that it took him twenty minutes to edit a page. Multiply that by just two hundred and you will see how much time it takes to edit a book well. An editor may spend so much time in meetings and in acquiring books that the actual editing of a manuscript may be left to an assistant or a freelancer.

At hardcover houses, an editor may do fifteen to twenty-five books a year. The more books they do, the less time they can spend on each of them. One over-burdened editor at a mass-market house counted the number of projects he had committed to for the next three years and it was more than three hundred books. Even though many of these were reprints of hardcover books, his plate was beyond full.

Editors Are the Ultimate Middlepeople

Editors have to maintain their relationships and continually build new ones with people inside and outside of the house: authors, agents, other editors, subsidiary-rights people, sales reps and other marketing people, publicists, the advertising department, the art director, production people, and company officers on every one of their books. They are also in touch with other people in publishing, trade and consumer media, and domestic and foreign rights.

Editors Are House Hoppers

Publishers Weekly once reported that the average editor switches jobs every 2.6 years in a continuing game of musical chairs. And a book's champion leaving a house can be fatal for its future. Editors who inherit books usually don't have the passion for them that the editors who bought them do, and they may just go through the motions and let the book and the author fend for themselves.

If a manuscript hasn't been delivered, it may be possible to resell it. Your agent keeps up with what's going on with editors and publishers and will take an editor's and a house's stability into consideration when selling a book.

One editor at a major house said that editors are in a nineteenth-century job at twenty-first-century companies. They are perpetually torn between the conflicting demands of authors wanting attention, agents wanting to sell them books, and publishers wanting profits. This often leads to burnout and the need to find a new home where editors will find a happy balance between working with people they like and doing books they love.

Cyril Nelson, who edited the *Painted Ladies* books Elizabeth and I wrote for Viking Studio Books, worked in the same position for almost half a century. But Cy was an exception. Whether because of burnout; to get a raise; or to work their way up the editorial ladder from assistant through associate editor, editor, senior editor, executive editor, and editor-in-chief, editors usually have to switch houses at least a few times in their careers.

Other factors such as a house changing hands, a new editor-in-chief, editorial cutbacks or a change in direction, an editor picking more losers than winners, and personality differences may start the search for the next stop on the publishing merry-go-round.

Editors Are Insiders

Like agents, editors have their antenna open to any fact, idea, person, place, trend, or event that can wind up between covers. They know the business and the house from the inside. They understand how it works and fails and why. They live with the problems of getting a book sold, and they know what has to be done to build and maintain momentum for a book inside the house, in the publishing world, and in the marketplace.

At HarperCollins, the editorial board is called the acquisitions committee, and if you say "Acscom"—the bureaucratic shorthand for it—aloud, it has a certain Murdochian ring that doesn't sound promising. Writers may get upset or depressed when their work is rejected, but editors get shot down all the time. Peter Ginna, Trade Editorial Director at Oxford University Press, estimates that a third of the projects he proposed when he was working at one of the Six Sisters were turned down.

Every time they buy a book, editors negotiate the major points of the deal. They know where the give is in the contracts of the publishers they work for. The contracts department may finish the negotiations.

As noted earlier, editors must have a vision of not just what a proposal or manuscript is but what it can be, the ideal way to present a writer's ideas. Then they must be able to inspire, convince, cajole, criticize, praise, wait, and do whatever else it takes to help writers produce their best work and come as close to they can to achieving that ideal. Random House Executive Editor Bob Loomis says, "A good writer knows when an editor is right."

One editor rejected one of my proposals by saying, "It just didn't float my boat." Like the rest of us, editors have their own biases, intuitions, and idiosyncrasies. So, even if editors' tastes predispose them to like your manuscript, if they're feeling grumpy when they read it, they still may not be receptive to it.

A cartoon shows a wife telling her writer husband, "You got a nibble on your book . . . a paper recycling company called."

Editors Are Writers

Buying and publishing generates a heap of paperwork. Editors write emails, P&Ls, interoffice memos, copy for catalogs and jackets, letters asking for forewords and cover quotes, letters to writers asking for changes and to agents about changing contracts, and information the sales and marketing people need.

Editors Are Readers

Like agents, editors spend their lives slogging through emails and ream after ream of letters, contracts, proposals, manuscripts for which other editors are seeking support and proposals, and manuscripts from agents. They say yes or no to submissions as quickly as they can and press on to the next submission on the bottomless pile. One discouraged editor says, "I only read far enough to say no."

As I have noted, editors have editorial assistants who help them plow through the piles of manuscripts. According to Vintage Anchor Editor-in-Chief Marty Asher, "Editorial assistants determine the fate of most new writers." Editors will read their assistants' reports and either read enough of the manuscript to verify them or accept their assistants' appraisals.

One editor once told us that in the course of buying, editing, and proofing a manuscript, he read every book he bought at least seven times. One writer who sent us a manuscript admitted that he hadn't even read it once. He just typed it up and shipped it out!

Editors use computers for submissions and for communicating with colleagues, agents, writers, and the other people they know. The trade-off: when Viking Plume President Clare Ferraro returned from a week at a writer's conference, she found six hundred emails waiting for her.

Editors Are Co-Conspirators

Once a publisher acquires your book, you, your agent, and your editor are united in a conspiracy to make it as effective and successful as possible. No one else in the house will know or care as much about your book as the three of you. So despite whatever resistance and competition stand in your book's way, you must stick together when problems arise.

Editors have to be able to stand up for their books, if only because their jobs depend on their books being successful. But if they forge a solid enough track record, they may be given their own imprint, like Ann Godoff, who is president and publisher of Penguin Press.

Hail the Passionate Advocates

Agents know that a healthy working marriage between you and your editor is an essential key to your success. Indeed, your editor may be more important than everyone else in the house in determining the fate of your book. Editors also have to go with the flow, bobbing along on the swift current and dangerous eddies of uncertainty in publishing.

Editors who, despite all of their conflicting priorities, have the courage to take on the powers that be to buy a book, take the time to edit, inspire the writers they work with, and are passionate advocates for their books at every stage of publication inside and outside of the house, deserve to be regarded as the heroes of the business.

Chapter 17
Leaving Out the Parts That People Skip:
How to Make Your Craft Seaworthy

"When I want to read a good book, I'll write one."

—Benjamin Disraeli

"I try to leave out the parts that people skip."

—Elmore Leonard

As I've mentioned, one of the first questions agents and editors ask themselves about a manuscript as they read it is: how much work will it take to make this manuscript salable? The more work it will take, the less eager they will be to take it on.

So don't submit anything to an agent or editor until it's 100 percent as well-conceived and well-crafted as you can make it.

A book basically offers one of two benefits: nonfiction provides information; fiction, entertainment. Your job is to generate an idea and execute it so that your book delivers the benefit it promises as compellingly as possible. This takes craft. There are twelve steps for developing your craft:

1. Read

Ernest Gaines, author of the Oprah book club selection *A Lesson Before Dying*, created what he calls "The Six Golden Rules of Writing: read, read, read and write, write, write." He believes that you can only write as well as you read.

Writers always have reason to read: pleasure, information, inspiration, research. Ray Bradbury recommends that in addition to learning about all of the arts, writers take half an hour a night to read one poem, one essay, and one short story for pleasure, for ideas, to assimilate style, and to stoke the fires of the imagination.

An acquaintance of mine once came up to me brimming with excitement and said, "I just finished my first novel."

"That's great!" I said.

Then he asked, "What should I read next?"

If you're a novelist, you should read as many novels as you can, especially those like the one you are writing. Become an expert on the kind of book you want to write. What works for you in the books you love will work for your readers.

Keeping Up with the Tomes: Stay abreast of the endless flow of books into which yours will merge by browsing in bookstores online and off and asking booksellers about what's selling. To keep up with news about agents, writers, and publishers, read *Coda*, *Writer's Digest*, the *Writer*, *Publishers Weekly*, and the book review section of the *New York Times*. These are in libraries and at least partially online.

2. Learn to Love Words

The playwright Samuel Beckett believed that "words are all we have." Words can inform, enlighten, persuade, motivate, and inspire. They can kill and they can cure. They can make readers laugh and cry. They can transform people's lives. A book with the right words will transform your life. A book with the right words will change the world.

Your words will affect your readers in ways impossible to predict or imagine. Every word counts.

3. Understand What Makes Books Work

If you are lucky, you were born with the gift of shaping words so they sing and ignite sparks in your readers' imaginations. But even if you were born with a gift for writing, you are not born with the skill for it. But reading and writing will enable you to learn it. Analyze what makes the books you love effective, and you will be on your way to accomplishing your literary goals.

4. Get Experience Writing

"In the beginning, clips and contracts, exposure and experience are more important than money, hands down!"

—Gregg Levoy, This Business of Writing

Any kind of writing experience makes an impression on agents and editors. The longer it is, and the more relevant it is to the books you're writing, the better.

Getting experience writing will help you develop your skill, it will look good on your resume, and you may be able to use what you learn in your books. Joseph Heller wrote advertising copy for *McCall's* while he was writing *Catch-22*. Elmore Leonard recalled that before becoming solvent as a writer, "I wrote everything but cocktail napkins to make a living."

5. Come Up with Ideas

"Conception is much more fun than delivery."

—Georges Pompidou, French president

Since most books are more of the same only different, agents and editors love to find exciting new ideas. Reading books and news media is an inexhaustible source of ideas. One of my favorite *New Yorker* cartoons shows two women nursing cocktails and one is saying to the other, "I'm marrying Marvin. I think there's a book in it." There's a book in just about anything and more subjects to write about than ever.

Brainstorming with your agent and your networks about subjects you have already written about, know about, or want to know about can help you find ideas. What ideas excite you enough to make you want to research a book about them?

Someone once suggested that if you were interested in starting a magazine, you should call it *Sex and Money*, because that's what everyone wants to read about. Ask yourself: What will America be like in two years? What will its growing, multicultural population need and want to read about? Or as Bloomberg Editorial Director Jared Kieling once asked in a more practical vein, "What will people want to save money on two years from now?"

Put yourself in the position of a publisher wondering what projects to invest in, and see if your guesses lead to book ideas. Your agent will brainstorm with you, and help you mine these lists for an idea for your next book.

The High Five

The interest in fiction and perennial nonfiction subjects is timeless, but the challenge of writing a salable book grows. Why? In part because of all the competition books face from other media and pastimes, but also because every new book is in competition with every competing book that has been published or will be published.

Want your books to cut through the static of other books? Try these suggestions:

- Create a fresh idea or a fresh way to conceptualize an old idea.
- Create a platform, continuing national visibility through talks, the media, or visibility made possible by promotional partners, if talks and media exposure will be essential to promoting your book
- Create an irresistible title that compels browsers to pick up your book.
- For nonfiction, create a proposal that:
  - answers every question that agents and editors will have about the book;
  - has a promotion plan that will convince agents and editors that you will make the book as successful as you want it to be;
  - includes a sample chapter that proves why you should be the one to write your book;
  - generates as much excitement as possible in as few words as possible;
  - is an accurate blueprint of a manuscript that informs, inspires, and motivates your readers, if only to tell and email everyone they know to read your book.
- Create a niche for a series of books that you are passionate about writing and marketing.

6. Research the Subject

Ernest Hemingway believed that you should know ten times as much about a subject as you put into a book. Learning all you can about a topic enriches your writing, makes you more of an authority on the subject, and expands the opportunities to use your knowledge for articles, seminars, publicity, developing subsidiary rights, and other books. The more you learn, the more you earn.

7. Outline Your Book

Every book should have a beginning, a muddle, and an end.

—Peter De Vries

A book basically has two elements: an idea and the execution of the idea. You want your book to be the best possible embodiment of your idea. So try to make the execution of your idea as strong as the idea itself.

Elmore Leonard doesn't outline his books because, as he said, "I like to be surprised every day." Mystery writer Kinky Friedman is even more blunt: "Plots belong in cemeteries." Unless you're a novelist who has to discover what happens as you write, read AAR member Al Zuckerman's *Creating the Blockbuster Novel*. Even if you're not writing a blockbuster, it will help you create the structure for your book that best suits your plot.

Of course, you should feel free to improve the structure if a better alternative emerges.

The German poet Rilke believed that "prose should be built like a cathedral." So when you set out to construct an enduring edifice of prose word by word, brick by brick, give yourself a solid foundation on which to build.

8. Establish a Work Style

*"All my major works have been written in prison . . .
I would recommend prison not only to aspiring
writers, but aspiring politicians, too."*

—Indian statesman Jawaharlal Nehru

A popular and sought-after playwright, Edmond Rostand was forced to write *Cyrano de Bergerac* in his bathtub, because it was the only place where his endless callers would leave him in peace.

What do you need in order to write?

Do you write better early in the morning?

During the day?

At night?

Do you have an office where you can write undisturbed?

Mystery writer James Frey protects his privacy with this sign on his door: "Disturb this writer and die."

Do you use a tape recorder?

A typewriter?

A computer?

A pencil?

Like John Steinbeck, Ernest Hemingway, Norman Mailer, Joseph Heller, and Alice Walker, Barnaby Conrad, the author of more than thirty books and founder of the Santa Barbara Writers Conference, writes with a pen because he feels that a machine gets in the way of his thoughts and feelings.

If you want to be a successful author, you have to pay your dues to the muse by making writing a daily ritual. Push yourself with an attainable goal for the number of pages you crank out a day and a deadline for finishing your projects. Even a page a day is a book a year.

The only right way for you to write is in whatever way enables you to produce your best work. So, find the time, place, and writing tools that spur your best efforts. Sticking to the work style that works for you will boost your effectiveness, morale, and professionalism.

9. Write

In reporting on his progress, a writer once told me with an air of confidence, "I've got all the pages numbered. Now all I have to do is fill in the rest." That's where craft comes in. The prose of pros is an inseparable, indistinguishable blend of art and craft, poetry and carpentry, vision and revision.

Craft leaps off the page instantly. Agents and editors are suckers for good writing. They will be delighted if, after reading your first paragraph, they can exclaim to themselves, "At last! This one can really write!"

One weary editor noted that "you don't have to eat all of an egg to know it's rotten." Agents and editors only read far enough to make a decision. So starting with your query letter, every line you write must motivate them to read the next line. The essential virtue of salable prose is that it keeps readers turning the pages. If you can keep your readers turning the pages, it doesn't matter what you write about.

The first and last pages of a novel can be vital to its success. Mickey Spillane once said, "The first page sells the book. The last page sells the next book."

When movie producer Samuel Goldwyn was asked what he wanted in a script, he replied that he wanted "a story that starts with an earthquake and works its way up to a climax."

Writing at its best also has passion, vision, and vigor. Bantam Executive Editor Toni Burbank once remarked about a manuscript:

"There was nothing wrong with it, but there was nothing right with it either." Or as author Cyra McFadden once lamented about another failed effort, "The prose just lay there, dead on the page."

Make your writing live for agents and editors, and if you have a salable idea, your manuscript will sell. Write as if your future depends on it—it does.

Charles Dickens wrote his early novels in monthly installments. Nobody thought he was writing *literature*, just damn good stories that made his fans eager to read the next chapter. He proves that the pulp fiction of one generation may become the literature of the next.

You Yin, Me Yang

Balance is an essential virtue for successful authors. They have to balance the time they allot to writing and promoting their books with their personal and professional lives and goals. Jack Canfield talks about balance as the yin and yang of writing. The yin or feminine aspect of the craft is when you're at home in your cave, invoking your muse and giving birth to your manuscript, in total control of your book. Everything that happens after that is yang, your continuing encounter with the world outside your cave:

- Building your networks
- Creating a website that will be your primary medium of service to the world and communication about you and your books
- Finding an agent and publisher
- Helping your publisher to midwife your book
- Promoting your book

Successful authors achieve the balance between yin and yang they need for bringing up baby.

10. Revise

"The writer's best friend is a wastebasket."

—Isaac Bashevis Singer

"I write the first draft to get the meaning, the second draft to put in everything I left out, the third draft to take out what doesn't belong, and the fourth draft to make it sound like I just thought of it."

—mystery writer Margery Allingham

Ray Bradbury summed up writing in two verbs: "throw up" and "clean up." Think of writing has having two stages. The first challenge isn't getting a book right; it's getting it written. First, you have to get something, anything, down on paper, and then massage it until it's one hundred percent.

11. Share Your Work

"You cannot correct your work well until you've forgotten it."

—Voltaire

New writers are often too eager to get published to take Voltaire's advice, or the most modest proposal of Vintage & Anchor Editor-in-Chief Marty Asher: "Put your novel under your bed for thirty days."

So here's a suggestion from the great Russian ballet star Nijinsky, who explained his ability to remain aloft by saying, "I merely leap and pause." After your creative leap, it's time for you to pause. Give yourself a break and share your manuscript with six kinds of readers who can advise you on how to improve it.

1. Friends and family, who will tell you they like it, because they like you. After all, what are friends and family for? But you need unconditional praise, so revel in it.

2. Potential readers: they may not know good writing, but they know what they like. Would they buy your book if they found it in a bookstore?

3. Literate, objective readers who may not know about the kind of book you're writing, but who know about writing, and can advise you about what's wrong with your manuscript as well as what's right with it.

4. Experts who are knowledgeable about the subject of your book or the kind of novel you are writing. Ask for feedback from authors in your networks who have had similar books published. If you are developing a controversial thesis, find a member of the opposition to go over it for you and try to poke holes in it. You may not gain a convert, but you might avoid embarrassing yourself later.

5. The most valuable person of all: a devil's advocate, a mentor who can and will combine truth and charity, and spot every word, idea, character, punctuation mark, sentence or incident that can be improved or removed. Devil's advocates are worth their weight in royalties.

6. If you're writing fiction, or nonfiction that you want to read like it, join or start a critique group, a table full of writers that get together every week online or off and discuss each other's work.

Spare the Reader, Not the Writer

Write the injunction above in large letters on every copy of the proposal or manuscript that you share and include as fancy a red pen as your budget allows.

If you can't find anyone else, use your networks or *Literary Market Place* to locate an experienced, reputable, affordable freelance editor to help you polish your manuscript.

12. Do a Final Revision

Since reactions, especially to fiction, are subjective, receiving more than one will prepare you for the varying responses your book will arouse. Follow only the advice that makes sense to you. As in all things, you must trust your instincts and your common sense.

Once you've sorted out the opinions of others and feel ready to return to your manuscript with a fresh eye, do a final revision. Then it's time to see if the world agrees with you. Only your devotion to your career should be as great as your devotion to your craft.

Chapter 18
The Difference between a Pig and a Chicken:
Why Your Goals Will Determine Your Future

In the making of ham and eggs, do you know the
difference between the pig and the chicken?
The chicken is involved, but the pig is committed.

"The world always steps aside for people who know where
they're going."

—Miriam Viola Larsen

Understanding how publishers work and developing your craft are essential to your success. But you are the most important factor in your success. So, the third way to make yourself irresistible to any agent or publisher is to make a commitment to your career. The next three chapters will show you how.

Know Yourself and Your Goals

"You can't have everything. Where would you put it?"

—Ann Landers

"Vision is the art of seeing things invisible."

—Jonathan Swift

Life, like art, should be the celebration of a vision. Sue Grafton believes that "writing isn't something you do; it's something you are." To be a successful writer, you must know who you are and what you want. Tom Clancy once said, "Nothing is so real as a dream." So, create a waking dream, a vision of yourself and your goals as a person and a writer.

Mozart said, "When I am . . . completely myself, my ideas flow best and most abundantly." Well, on the literary chorus line of life, who are you, anyway? When a friend of Dorothy Parker had a baby, Parker sent her this telegram: "Dear Mary: Good work. We all knew you had it in you."

What have you got in you? What are the strengths you need to be a writer? A knowledge of books, writing, and what you're writing about? A desire to teach? Make lists of your personal and professional strengths and frailties.

Also, make lists of the joys and hazards of being a writer. They must convince you that you have what it takes to make the grade. They must also justify your efforts. Keep these lists handy and revise them as needed.

Bestselling novelist Susan Isaacs once remarked that "hot fudge fills many needs." What needs does writing fill for you? Keeping in mind the need to harmonize the short view and the long view, make lists of your immediate and long-term personal goals. Does writing fit into them well?

The German poet Goethe believed that "life is the infancy of our immortality." Love, money, the need to communicate, and the hope of immortality inspire writers to ply their craft.

When asked why he wrote the bestseller *The Name of the Rose*, Umberto Eco replied, "I felt like poisoning a monk." Stephen King once admitted, "People ask me why I do this, why I write such gross stuff. I like to tell them that I have the heart of a small boy, and I keep it in a drawer in my desk."

Goals to Go: The Most Valuable Information in This Book

The answers to the following eleven questions will be the most valuable information you will take away from this book. I mentioned that as a writer, you are the most important person in the publishing process because you make it go. So what you know about yourself is far more important than what you know about writing, agents, and publishers. Your answers will paint a portrait of who you are and what you want to accomplish as an author.

Your agent may ask you these questions, and you will come across as a professional if you have ready answers. The answers will also clarify what you want your agent to accomplish for you.

In a William Hamilton cartoon, a young writer is musing wistfully to a companion: "Fame is such a hollow goal. Cult figure may be enough."

Every writer marches to the beat of a slightly different drummer. What's the beat of your drummer? What are your literary and financial goals? You can sum up your literary and financial goals and how you will achieve them with the answers to these eleven questions. Start each answer with the word *I* and be specific.

1. Why do you want to write?

After you list the joys of writing that I suggested earlier in the chapter, ask yourself: What makes you write? What drives you to be a writer?

Your reasons for writing may be any combination of those below, or you may have other reasons. But whatever your reasons for writing, put your list on the wall where you write. If you ever question what you're doing, look at the list. Change it whenever you wish. The only criterion for why a reason should be on the list is that it motivates you to keep going.

Do any of these reasons to write strike a chord with you?

- You were born to write.
- You love doing it.
- You can't help it.
- You love to read, and the books you love inspire you to write.
- You are committed to writing out of the best that's in you to reach and inspire the best of what's in your readers.
- You're not writing for agents, editors, publishers, critics, or money, only for your readers.
- You're committed to writing books that have lasting value.
- You want to harness the power of your words to change minds, hearts, and lives.
- Your readers will enjoy and benefit from reading your books.
- You're so excited about the value of your ideas that you're eager to write and promote your books.
- You're fulfilling your obligation to take a stand about what you believe in.
- You have an idea for a series of books that will enable you to reach your literary and financial goals.

If you have other reasons for writing, I hope you'll share them with me.

2. What literary forms—poetry, novels, nonfiction, plays, screenplays—do you want to write in?

The easiest question.

3. Whom are you writing for?

An editor once told writer Arky Gonzales, "The subtle difference between a writer and an amateur is that amateurs feel and write for themselves; professional writers write for somebody else. This difference comes across in the very first or second line of an outline or manuscript."

Are you writing to write or to be read? Are you writing for yourself or your readers? The right answer to both questions is *both*. What you write will be an expression of who you are, of your knowledge, your experience, your imagination, your gift for writing, and your desire to reach readers who will enjoy your work.

The Unsigned Contract between You and Your Readers

Jonathan Franzen, author of the bestseller *The Corrections*, believes that there are two models for novelists: the status model and the contract model.

The status model is that of artists who write what they must, regardless of who enjoys it or even understands it. If Umberto Eco wants to start a novel with six lines of Hebrew and you don't know Hebrew, tough darts. His job is to write the best book he can; what readers get out of it is their business.

The other model is the contract model: when readers sign the credit card slip, an author has made a contract to entertain them enough to justify their expenditure of time and money. And every contract writers make with readers is a one-book contract. The first book by an author readers don't like is the last book by that author they read.

You are free to write whatever you wish. But to be a successful author, you have to write what people want to read. Deciding whom you want to write for will determine what you write and how. That's why the simplest way to figure out what to write is to read what you love to read and write what you love to read. What is written with passion as well as craft will find an audience.

4. What do you want your writing to communicate?

What do you want to share with your readers?
• Your knowledge?
• How readers can make their lives or communities better?
• Your philosophy?
• Your perspective on the human condition?
• A story that conveys the inexhaustible variety and richness in people and life?

5. What do you want your writing to achieve?

How do you want your books to benefit your readers?
• Provide pleasure?
• Bring about social change?
• Enable them to enjoy better lives?

6. Where do want you and your books to be in the literary landscape?

Pick the books and the author that embody your goals. The books don't have to be by the author you choose. You may want to write books like those of Tom Wolfe but have Tom Clancy's position in the industry or write like Molly Ivins and be Suze Orman. Feel free to pick a combination of a man and a woman or a kind of novel with a nonfiction writer's place in the literary pantheon.

The only criteria for the books and author you choose is that they motivate you to get to your computer every day and do whatever it takes to write the kind of books and rise to the preeminence that you aspire to.

52 Words to Upwardly Mobile Authors

Einstein said that "everything should be as simple as possible but no simpler." Following bestseller lists, which haven't changed significantly in a century, will convince you that the more readers you want for your nonfiction books, the simpler your ideas and your writing must be.

7. What advances would you like for your books?

"I don't have to sell my work. I've got dental benefits."

—poet, novelist, and professor Mary Mackey

Establish financial as well as literary goals for your career. If each of your books sells better than the previous one, your advances will reflect your success. But you will reach a plateau at which bigger advances won't be justified by sales or inspire greater commitment from your publisher. And as mentioned earlier, you may also need to defer income for tax purposes. (I know that's a problem you'd love to have!)

But once you decide on what you want your annual income to be and the amount of the other sources for it, you will arrive at the advances you want for your book. Even big houses don't spend big bucks on most books. But don't think about what you can get, only about what you want. I'm talking desire here, not realism, so choose a sum with as few or as many zeroes as you wish.

8. How much money do you want to earn a year from your writing?

Decide how much you want to earn from each book you write, and what you want your annual income to be. There are no wrong answers, but all answers have consequences. Whether you'd be happy earning no money, just writing for the pleasure of it, or you want to earn $15 million a year, again pick a round number with as few or as many zeroes as you wish.

All answers are equally valid. If you don't care how much money you earn a year from your writing, you have total freedom. You can write anything you want, because there are no economic consequences. But if you want to earn a million dollars a year and you want to write poetry, you've got a problem.

Mark Twain once confessed, "I'm opposed to millionaires, but it would be dangerous to offer me the position." If you want the position, there's only one kind of book you can write: bestsellers. So pick any number you want and write to that number. But make sure that it strikes a realistic balance between writing for yourself and writing for readers.

Advances, royalties, subsidiary rights, giving talks, and selling books and audiobooks are five ways your books can help you generate income. Track competing authors and use your networks to help you come up with realistic but motivating goals for how soon you can expect these five revenue streams to flow, how soon, and how fast.

Doubling Your Income Instantly: Give Yourself a Raise

After you pick a number for your annual income, double it. Even if you only earn half that much, you'll still reach your original goal. And who knows? You may surprise yourself. The clearer and larger your vision, the more your life and what comes into it will align itself with your goals. (I get to write things like that because I live in California.)

*Chicken Soup*ermen Jack Canfield and Mark Victor Hansen urge writers to have giant goals. They want to sell a billion books by 2020. Since they've sold one hundred million in ten years, I wouldn't bet against them.

9. How involved do you want to get with the writing process?

There's a *New Yorker* cartoon showing a patient sitting in his doctor's examination room after being examined, and the doctor says to him, "I'm afraid that novel in you will have to come out."

There are more ways to get that nonfiction book out of you than ever. You can:

- write it yourself
- use a freelance editor or book doctor to help you
- collaborate with a writer
- hire a ghostwriter

Got a "master piece" in you? The word *masterpiece* originated with the medieval guilds. Boys would apprentice themselves to craftsmen for no pay to learn the craft. They proved they were ready to join the guild when they produced a master piece.

If you're a doctor or executive who has only one book's worth of information in you, you may not want to go through the apprenticeship of learning the craft of writing. Your assets are the information you have to share, your credibility, and your ability to promote your book. How you write your book is your business.

An editor once approached a movie star about writing a book, and the star said, "Write a few chapters, and I'll see if I like it." No one expects Hollywood biographies to be written by movie stars. Agents, editors, and readers just want the book to deliver.

10. Do you want to self-publish, pay to be published, or be paid to be published?

As I mentioned in Chapter 1, you have more options than ever for getting your book published online and off: self-publishing, subsidy, and vanity publishing; a small house, a large one; a regional publisher, a national one; a scholarly or university press, a publisher who does professional books, a niche publisher; an audio publisher, a POD publisher, or an e-book publisher.

You have to decide how involved you want to get with the publishing process.

11. How will you support your writing until it can support you?

Writer's Digest once ran a cartoon in which a wide-eyed lady is sitting next to a man at a party and says, "I'm so thrilled to meet an author. What do you do for a living?"

Most writers don't earn enough income to liberate themselves to write. This helps explain why a freelancer has been called a writer with a working spouse. After deciding what they want to write, the next question most writers have to ask themselves is: "How am I going to support the habit?"

To help you weather the rough spots, take Sue Grafton's advice: create a five-year plan for your career. Decide where you would like to be five years from today, and then plan what you have to do *now* to reach that goal. Heed the wisdom in this Chinese proverb: "The two best times to plant a tree are twenty years ago and tomorrow."

The answers to these questions should produce a coherent picture of your literary and financial goals. They should strike a realistic balance between writing for yourself and writing for the marketplace. They will make you sound more professional when agents and editors ask about your future.

Put this list on the wall where you write. Make it your personal set of affirmations, your literary mantra (more California talk). Whenever you begin to wonder who you are or why you're writing, read the answers aloud to yourself. If the answers stop inspiring your best work, find new answers or another line of work.

You need to forge an identity that is durable, marketable, flexible, enduring, and, ideally, original. When Carthaginian general Hannibal decided to cross the Alps with his elephants, he said, "We will either find a path or we will make one." Writers have to do both. Emulate successful books and authors until you know it's time to stop being the next somebody else and start being the first you.

Chapter 19
English Lit—How about You?
Reinventing Yourself as an Authorpreneur

Reinvent Yourself as an Authorpreneur

A *New Yorker* cartoon shows two scarecrows standing in a cornfield, and one is saying to the other, "English Lit. How about you?"

After knowing yourself and your goals, the next way to make a commitment to your career is to rethink yourself. It's been said that if writers were good business people, they'd have too much sense to be writers. It's important for you to think about business as well as writing. You are part of an entrepreneurial explosion that is one of the most hopeful signs for America's future.

Despite the jokes about the hazards of being a literary entrepreneur that are scattered throughout this chapter, start thinking of yourself as an entrepreneur: a self-employed professional running a small business. Balance your desire to write something and the satisfaction of doing it well and seeing it published against your potential compensation and how the project will help develop your craft and your career. Your agent and editor will respect your professionalism.

Do you have business cards saying you're a writer? Vistaprint.com will give you the first two hundred fifty free. If you write every day, you're a writer. Convincing others will help you convince yourself.

Beyond thinking of yourself as an entrepreneur, think of yourself as an *authorpreneur*, a word coined by author and speaker Sam Horn. Authorpreneurs devote their careers to making and taking:

• Making a living by coming up with ideas and communicating them in as many forms, media, and places as possible

• Taking responsibility for making sure their books sell

From Pitchecraft to Nichecraft: The Quest for Seamless Synergy

There are contradictory approaches to developing your career, both of which have merit:

• Don't get fixed on one subject, or one kind of fiction, or even one kind of writing. There are many subjects and kinds of writing that can be developed to make a living. If editors are willing to pay you to learn about a subject that interests you, why not? Novelist Fenton Johnson recommends that writers diversify by writing fiction and nonfiction.

• The second approach is a faster, more effective way to ensure your success, which is why it's used by publishers, booksellers, writers, and even some agents: practice nichecraft. Develop a specialty. Once you've done one book on a subject, you're an authority and can present yourself as an expert when you try to sell your next book on the subject.

Jay Conrad Levinson's *Guerrilla Marketing* series creates synergy by helping to sell each other, the sub-rights income they generate, and the talks by Jay and his coauthors.

As an author, your capital is your:

• time

• ideas

- knowledge
- creativity
- ability to turn your ideas into books
- zeal for promoting your books

As I suggested earlier, examine your ideas with an eye to recycling them in as many media as possible:

- Articles in trade and consumer print and broadcast and electronic media that you can rewrite and resell
- Excerpts and serializations of your books
- Columns, blogs, and newsletters
- E-zines
- Software
- Movies
- DVDs
- Podcasts
- Radio and television shows

As the audience for your work grows, the income from your books will also grow, as will the ways in which you will make money from them.

Pick the right subject or kind of novel, and you will create a seamless synergy in which everything you do sells everything else you do. You will build your own brand and carve a career out of it. Doing a series accelerates this process because once you hook readers with one book, they'll want to read the other books in the series, which is why as backlist books, novels are more profitable than nonfiction. It also explains why at airports, the mass-market racks have more books by fewer authors—the brand-name authors.

After you've written one book, you can go from book to book and advance to advance. If you, your agent, or your editor has ideas, and you write proposals about them, you can jump from one project into the next. But you have to keep generating ideas and proposals for nonfiction or whatever your editor needs to see for novels. And you can't assume all of them will sell. Danielle Steel once recalled that after her first novel was published, she wrote five more that have never been published.

A possible trade-off to practicing nichecraft, especially with fiction, is that once you become established as an author of a certain kind of book, you risk becoming typecast (pardon the pun), making it harder to switch subjects or the kind of fiction you are writing.

One way to get around this is to use a pseudonym. When Anne Rice wants a break from writing about vampires, she uses two others names for her erotica. It's not a secret, but the pseudonyms still help separate her two literary lives.

To be a successful author, you have to combine yin and yang, art and commerce, writing and selling. To do that, you have to be an authorpreneur.

Chapter 20
You Deserve All the Help You Need:
Mobilizing Your Networks

Mobilize Your Networks

There's a cartoon showing two Native Americans looking at a mountain in the distance from which puffs of smoke are rising. One of them is saying, "Makes you wonder how we ever lived without it."

Bestselling business author Harvey Mackay asks his audiences, "What's the most important word in the English language?" His answer: "Rolodex." Harvey's has more than twelve thousand names in it.

Lily Tomlin advises us to "remember, we're all in this alone." Unless you collaborate, she's right about writing: it's a solitary endeavor. But that's the only part of being a writer that you have to do alone. Your networks will help you with every other aspect of writing, publishing, and promoting your books.

A cartoon in the *New Yorker* showed two disreputable-looking guys in a bar. One of them says to the other, "I tried victimless crime, but I'm a people person."

If you want to be a successful author, you have to be a people person. Bestselling novelist Jacqueline Susann had a Christmas mailing list with nine thousand names on it. She took great pains to cultivate everyone in the business who could help her and they did. This is one reason why *The Valley of the Dolls* has sold more than twenty million copies.

Why Network + Net Speed = Net Profits

You need sixteen overlapping, international networks online and off that will be as essential to your career as writing and promoting your books, because neither will be effective without them:

1. Your personal network: your family and their friends, your relatives, your neighbors, your friends, schoolmates, and the people you work with.

2. Your writing network: professionals with whom you can talk shop.

3. Your reading network: a variety of readers from whom you can get feedback on your work, an idea I discussed in Chapter 19.

4. Your field network: every key person in the field you are writing about in the media, academia, and government, as well as professionals working in the field. Every field has its own events, media, merchants, organizations, promotional partners, authors, and opinion-makers. Whether you're writing mysteries or histories, get to know as many colleagues as you can who can help you.

5. Your publishing network: writers, editors, sales reps, members of writer's organizations, writing teachers, librarians, reviewers, sales reps, and publicists. Go to literary events. Scour the Web for kindred spirits. Collect business cards.

6. Your promotion network: everyone who can help you promote your book—authors, publicists, reviewers, talk-show hosts and producers, trade and consumer writers in your field, other media people, and tour escorts who take visiting authors around major markets.

7. Your speaking network: speakers, audiences, speakers' bureaus, meeting planners who can book you, businesses and nonprofits that do book you, and members of Toastmasters and the National Speaker's Association.

8. Your network of fans who read your books, attend your events, and buy your products and services.

9. Your reading-club network: groups of readers who read and discuss your books; when possible, join the conversation by phone, computer, or in person. Your website can provide a reading group guide and be a clearinghouse for people who want to join or start a group. This idea isn't suitable for all books, but if it's possible, it has the potential to generate significant sales.

10. Your network of booksellers: your own chain of bookstores—booksellers who will welcome you back every time you have a new book because they like your work and because you put cheeks in seats. Try working in a bookstore or being an unpaid intern. Get to know booksellers and make allies of them. They may share your love of books and can be valuable sources of information and encouragement. They may be able to help you find an agent. And one day, you will be asking them for a book signing!

11. Your network of champions: a relatively small group of people who adore you and your work and promote you, your books, and your services online and off, wherever they are, whenever they can. They are the knights of your round table. They can't be bought, but you can do everything possible to justify their ardor and reward their efforts.

12. Your mastermind network: a group of five to nine people in publishing or other fields who meet by phone or in person every other week, serve as a board of directors for each other, and hold each other accountable for their commitment to use the advice they receive.

13. Your Net network: an ever-growing email list of people around the world from your networks who you serve with an e-zine, answers to their questions, and an irresistible website that provides a forum for discussion. The two most important things they can do for you are buy your books when and where you ask them to and be your viral marketing department by forwarding what you email them to their email lists. It's faster and easier than coining money and has the same effect.

Gaming the System: E-Blasting Your Way to the Bestseller List

Two reasons to build your networks are that if they're big enough you can use them to make your book a bestseller on pub date. You want to make your own email list as long as you can, and you also want to be able to ask your networks to email their email lists about your book.

You also want to be able to ask your networks to email you hot articles and information that you can value collectively at a four-figure sum. You can create a file of this information and use it to entice people to buy your book when you ask them to. You can use that information, your list, and their lists to make your book an online bestseller on pub date. Write to your list and offer $X,000 worth of information if they buy your book on pub date from an online bookseller. When you receive the email confirmation of an order, you email the person the link to the information. Because Barnes & Noble's online store is smaller than Amazon, it takes fewer sales for your book to be a bestseller.

When Jill Lublin and Rick Frishman, my coauthor on *Guerrilla Marketing for Writers*, were promoting *Networking Magic*, their networks sent an email about the book to their lists. They reached two million people and made their book a #1 bestseller at Barnes & Noble's online store, a fact they use every time they can, including on the cover of the book.

14. Your major-market network: people around the country who help you with info on local media, authors, booksellers, speaking venues, and sources of information as well as potential members for your other networks. They can also give you a place to lay your head when you are researching and promoting your books.

15. Your network of suppliers: purveyors of the products and services you use should be champions for each other.

16. Your tech network: you may not even want to use technology, but if you want to be a successful author, you can't compete or even cope with the demands of being a writer without it. Competing authors are using it, and their success reflects how well they use it. If, like me, you're not a techie, assemble a network of wizards who love technology, keep up with the latest and greatest products and services, and can:

   - create, host, and update your website
   - set up a blog for you
   - research other authors' sites so they can continue to make yours more effective
   - establish reciprocal links with as many sites as possible for as many products, services, and kinds of information you offer as possible, adding new links ASAP
   - set up a podcasting system so you can use your computer like a radio station
   - show you how to promote your books, your blog, your podcasts, your teleseminars, and whatever else you sell (or do it for you)
   - answer any question at any hour of the day
   - fix problems by phone or in person
   - set up and maintain a shopping cart

- integrate your phone, camera, music equipment, computer, website, and hand-held electronic devices so they're as easy to use as possible in your office and when you travel
- advise you on the hardware and software you need to maintain secure, state-of-the-art technology
- tell you the best way to buy them or handle the transaction for you
- install what you buy
- barter their services for yours if necessary
- do whatever else you need that I couldn't think of

The Big Payoff

There are more ways for your networks to help you than we can list, but these are also worth mentioning:

- Buying whatever you have to sell and asking everyone they know to buy it
- Selling what you create at their presentations
- Giving you leads and recommend you for speaking engagements
- Doing seminars with you
- Connecting you to potential members of your networks
- Exchanging (e)mailing lists with you
- Giving you ideas and sending you information that you can use for talks, books, and articles

You have direct and indirect networks. Your direct networks are everyone *you* know; your indirect networks are everyone *they* know. Editor and author Richard F. X. O'Connor wrote that we all know two hundred fifty people. This means that you are two emails away from millions of people: yours to two hundred fifty people and theirs to two hundred fifty people.

To build your networks, join local and national writers' organizations and a critique group online or off. Writers' organizations are listed in

Literary Market Place. You can also attend classes, seminars, conferences, and publishing institutes.

Organizations and events that will help you build your networks are listed in *Literary Market Place.* You can also attend classes, seminars, and conferences.

Don't ask anything of the people in your networks that you wouldn't do for them. Stay in touch with them with an e-zine. Pass on good news that confirms their judgment to help you. As long as it isn't in a story involving a felony, people love to see their names in print. So thank people in your books in a way that's commensurate with their help and be creative in how you reward their efforts.

Word of mouth is the best promotion, and thanks to technology, word of mouse can let the world know about our books instantly. Your networks will be a powerful force in helping your books generate "The Big Mo," momentum. They are an essential element in your quest for success, and technology makes it easier than ever to build and maintain them. Think of it as your *Net*work.

Continue to build your networks throughout your career, and be grateful that technology makes building and maintaining them easier than ever. Your networks will repay the time you spend on them many times over. Relationships are media. The more people you know, the farther you'll go. And thanks to word of mouse, the faster you'll get there.

The next challenge you face is to focus all of your brains, creativity, passion, persistence, and networks on doing everything you can for your books. No one will do more than you will. Read on to find out how to help your manuscripts as they make their way from a pile of pages into a book.

Chapter 21
From Slo-Mo to Promo:
Kicking Your Book's Promotion Campaign
into High Gear

Pure Yang

Once your manuscript is accepted, it usually takes nine months for it to reach bookstore shelves. The process is so long that it seems your book is being published in slow motion. But your book is passing through the hands of more than a hundred people at a big house and outside its walls before it leaves your publisher's warehouse.

Writing and selling your first book elevates you to a higher level of achievement, from being an aspiring writer of articles or short stories to being a published author. But your new status confers on you another set of challenges to meet. And to meet them, you have to devote some, if not all, of the time and energy you devoted to writing your book to promoting it. So, the next two chapters are about bringing your baby into the world with as much passion, persistence, and creativity as you can call on.

Make it your mission to do everything you can for your books. Like your agent, you have to be the advocate for your book. You can do a dozen things to help make the birth of your baby a celebration:

- If editors are interested in acquiring your book, visit them if you can. Editors will have varying degrees of passion for a book and houses will have different levels of commitment to it, depending on their response to your book and their success with similar books. Meeting editors and their colleagues will give you a good idea of how happy your working marriage will be. The more impressed they are with you and your future, the better the offer they'll make. And the relationship you establish with the editor and other people in the house may be more important to you than what the house can offer for your book.

- Make sure the nonfiction manuscript you write fulfills and, if possible, exceeds the promise of your proposal or that you use your editor's advice to make your book better than either of you thought it could be. Make your manuscript impeccable in form and content. The harder editors have to work on a manuscript, the more discouraged they may become about the book.

- Ask for a timeline on the publication of your book and monitor its progress as it makes its way through the process.

- If you have an idea for a jacket or cover, send the editor a note about it, do a rough sketch, or if you have access to an artist, have a design done. It probably won't be used, but it will at least give the cover designer something to go on and may inspire a better idea.

Make the design the size you envision the book being. The standard size for a hardcover or trade paperback is 6" x 9". Before you spend money on the cover, try the design out on authors, booksellers, and graphic artists. People spend their lives doing cover designs, and they still don't get it right every time. Most books don't have the best possible cover or titles, just the best that the publisher could come up with in the time allotted for it. Worst off are authors whose publishers can't think of an image for the cover, so they wind up with a tombstone cover that, like a tombstone, is all type—not a propitious symbol of what lies ahead.

The simplest description of screenwriting is producer Robert Greenbaum's take on it: substituting images for words. That's what cover art should do: use an image to capture the essence of your books in a positive way that helps the title to sell your books.

- Write the jacket or cover copy for your book. It may not be used, but it will give your publisher something to improve on.
- Ask for samples of your publisher's publicity materials and create a press kit including a news release, list of questions and answers, and your bio. There's more about press kits later in this chapter.
- Visit your publisher after your book has been accepted but before the marketing plans are set. Ask to meet all of the staff members involved with the editing, production, and marketing of your book. Discuss the marketing plan for your book. Ask them how you can help make your book sell. Express your gratitude for their efforts on your behalf.
- Take your local sales rep to lunch and absorb all you can about the business and how you can help. Publishers don't usually like authors talking to reps and may not even want you to know who your rep is. Local booksellers and your regional booksellers' association, which is listed in LMP, will know who they are. Sales reps are the publishers' grunts, the men and women on the front lines who know what gets books into and out of stores. And like agents and editors, sales reps' credibility rides on every book they sell. They gain leverage by being right, and will be ignored if they're not.
- Visit independent booksellers and get them excited enough about your book so that their staffs will "handsell" it.
- Ask your editor to help you monitor sales.
- Buy a lifetime supply of your books. If your publisher sells out and decides not to go back to press, you will not have the chance to buy a stash of them for future use. However, if you can resell the book, or if it becomes a print-on-demand title, its future is assured.

Part of the challenge is being an advocate for your book without becoming obnoxious. Don't badger anyone with phone calls. Use email and create a paper trail with faxes that keeps everyone in the house up to date. In the course of following these suggestions, you will discover other opportunities.

After writing your book as well as you can, promoting it is the most important way that you can help your book succeed. So, the next way to make a commitment to your career is to promote your books.

Two cannibals are having dinner and one says to the other, "You know, I don't like your publisher."

"Okay," the other cannibal replies, "then just eat the noodles."

"Marketing has long been the industry's weakest link."

—John Dessauer, *Book Publishing: The Basic Introduction*

The most common reason authors become disenchanted with their publishers is lack of promotion. Unless a book is one of the few big titles on a list or the publisher has high hopes for it, authors are usually dissatisfied with what their publishers do to promote their books.

The Literary Life and Other Curiosities includes this anecdote: "In promoting Simon & Schuster's children's book *Doctor Dan, the Bandage Man*, publisher Richard Leo Simon decided to give away six Band-Aids with each copy. 'Please ship half a million Band-Aids immediately,' he wired a friend at Johnson & Johnson. He soon received the reply: *Band-Aids on the way. What the hell happened to you?*"

Three months after your book is published, you may feel like you need some emotional Band-Aids. The silence that greets most books can be deafening and disheartening. After *Chicken Soup for the Soul* was published, Jack Canfield found that being published felt just like not being published. The goal of this chapter is to help you to launch your book in a way that does justice to its quality and its commercial potential.

How Promotable Are You and Your Book?

Promotion is essential for all books, but not all books and authors are equally promotable. Based on tracking similar books and how their authors promoted them, you have to make a realistic assessment of you and your book's promotional potential.

Publishers do some trade and consumer promotion for their books:
- They put them in their catalogs and on their websites.
- They list hardcovers and trade paperbacks in house ads in *Publishers Weekly* to announce each season's list.
- If a book and author have the potential for national TV shows, a publicist will send a book to the shows.
- They send books to reviewers.

If you're writing one of the more than fifteen hundred cookbooks that are published a year, you want news about your book to be on the Food Network, in food and women's magazines, and in the Wednesday food section in newspapers, not in the book review section.
- They may contact media in the author's hometown.
- If authors give themselves a national tour, their publishers may piggyback on their travels for a certain amount of time in a certain number of major markets.
- If a book has enough radio talk-show potential, publicists may contact at least some of the country's more than nine hundred phoners, talk shows you can do in your PJs.

Gift and Humor Books

Authors don't go on tours for short gift and humor books. The low cover prices won't justify the cost of a national tour. Nor do they usually lend themselves to talks at which authors can sell them. Gift books are impulse items. The key to their success is placement. The closer to the cash register they are, the better they sell.

Publishers may do trade promotion that can include more space in the publisher's catalog and an extra discount.

If books are part of a series, publishers will devote more resources to establishing the series. So if books are part of a series, they will benefit from the success of previous books.

Reference Books

Reference books usually don't lend themselves to consumer promotion. Publishers buy them because they have the potential to backlist. Publishers count on libraries as a continuing source of sales for reference books.

Some consumer reference books, like a guide to buying cars, have talk-show potential, so the publicist will send books to reviewers and perhaps publicity media that cover cars.

Serious and Literary Books

Publishers don't expect authors of literary biographies or books about popular science to have national platforms. They should belong to organizations in their field, speak at conferences for professionals in the field, and have a field network of key people.

Novels and Narrative Nonfiction

The key to the success of novels and narrative nonfiction that read like novels is the writing. Does it keep readers turning the pages, and does it have enough impact that readers tell everyone they know that they have to read it? If the answers to all these questions is an enthusiastic yes, publishers will do at least some promotion.

The promotion possibilities for these books include:
- a website, which is essential for these kinds of books because there are fewer ways to promote them
- doing a reading-group guide and contacting groups about choosing the book
- readings in bookstores
- talks at writer's conferences

How-To and Self-Help Books

If you want to write how-to and self-help books with a large potential readership, your promotion plan has to be as long and strong as you can make it.

Bookstore shelves are always full, so you have to convince agents and editors that your book and your efforts to promote it will guarantee space for it on bookstore shelves despite the past, present, and future books that will compete for space with it. If your book is published in hardcover, what your publisher will do for the paperback edition depends on the sales for the hardcover edition.

Selling More Books to Fewer People

The smaller the number of potential readers, the fewer books you can expect to sell. The logic of this is irrefutable, but sales will also depend on your ability to reach potential buyers. As I mentioned, every field has its own set of:
- events
- media
- organizations
- merchants
- promotional partners
- authors and other opinion-makers

And the smaller the field, the easier it is to reach the people in it. So, it may be possible to sell more books to a smaller group of potential buyers than a larger group of people that is harder to reach. For example, if you were writing a book for military wives, it would be relatively easy to reach them through:

- the stores they shop in
- the media that reaches them
- the organizations they belong to
- the businesses and nonprofits that might help you promote your books
- the events they attend

Top-Down and Bottom-Up Books

Bill Petrocelli, co-owner of Book Passage, a bookstore in Corte Madera, California, says there are two kinds of books: top-down and bottom-up. Less than one percent of books that are published are top-down books by brand-name authors who benefit from six-figure promotion campaigns. Their books have lay-down dates. The boxes they arrive in have a date on them, before which booksellers are not allowed to sell them.

On pub date, booksellers pile 'em high and watch 'em fly. This creates such an explosion of sales that the books not only get on bestseller lists but may land as close to the top of the list as they are likely to get. Top-down books may work their way down the bestseller's list.

The other 99 percent of books published are bottom-up books, "make" books that have to buck the odds and take their best shot at making potential buyers hit the stores or at least punch the right keys. The tiny percentage of bottom-up books that become bestsellers work their way up the list.

Tweeners: Books with a Shot at the List

Sandwiched between the small number of top-down books by best-selling authors and all of the bottom-up books are a small group of "tweeners." Tweeners are books that have breakout potential.

Bestsellers like *Emotional Intelligence, Snow Falling on Cedars, Cold Mountain*, and *The Lovely Bones* started out with twenty-five thousand-to thirty-five thousand-copy first printings but were published in a way that attests to their publisher's belief that they can become bestsellers. *French Women Don't Get Fat* started out with a fifty thousand-copy printing, an optimistic but not top-down printing.

Publishers send the manuscripts of tweeners to their reps to read before sales conferences, telling them that the books have breakout potential. At sales conferences, executives make the case for the book and gauge the reactions of the sales force. The reps choose one book on each list as a "rep pick." And each rep can pick a book as their own pick. Both of these designations are meaningful to booksellers because the reps are staking their credibility on steering their customers right.

Publishers hope that reviews and word of mouth and mouse will build a critical mass of passionate readers that will catapult the book onto the bestseller list.

Publishers may also:
- send authors on a pre-publication tour to meet booksellers
- do advanced reading copies (ARCs) and send them to:
    - booksellers to help get them excited about the book
    - review media to help ensure a review
    - publicity media
    - subsidiary-rights buyers such as movie people and foreign publishers or to the coagents who sell these rights
- give away galleys at BEA if it's a fall book
- display the cover art for the book in a light box at BEA
- send the author on a tour

When an Author Grabs the Brass Ring

When books take off, publishers:
- advertise them in newspapers to help sustain their momentum

- keep sales reps in the loop about sales and publicity
- send authors to more cities
- watch sales closely so they can reprint in time to ensure that book-sellers will continue to be able to buy books as they need them

In *The Writer's Quotation Book: A Literary Companion*, editor Jim Charlton quotes humorist Robert Benchley: "It took me fifteen years to discover I had no talent for writing, but I couldn't give it up because by that time, I was too famous."

If fame is your goal, and you don't want to wait fifteen years for it, give yourself a promotion. Sandra Dijkstra thinks that making a book successful requires overcoming indifference in agents, publishers, and book buyers.

A recreational pilot once observed that "in flying an airplane, the hardest thing you have to deal with is the ground." The hardest thing in writing is getting a book off it. Writing a book, getting an agent, and selling a book are easy compared to making the book succeed. It's been said that building momentum for a book is like getting a 747 off the ground. It takes a heap of energy, but once aloft, the sky's the limit.

You can take one of two opposite views about promotion. One is that of marketing pro Carl Lennertz, who says, "I truly believe that a wonderful book will succeed with no marketing whatsoever." You can do nothing and hope that lightning strikes. And there are bestselling authors who are so well established that they don't have to promote their books, which become bestsellers anyway.

You can also adopt the opposite view. Accept that every book is a stepping-stone to the next one. Assume that if you don't promote your book, it won't get done, and your book will fail, making your next book harder—if not impossible—to sell.

No amount of promotion will make a bad book sell. Publishers spend millions of dollars a year trying in vain to disprove this, but they can't. So the most common reason good books fail is lack of promotion.

Fortunately, there are more ways for you to promote your books than ever, and a promotable author is the (pun intended) best selling tool a publisher has. As Vintage & Anchor Books Editor-in-Chief Marty Asher says, "The best promotion department for your book is you." But many authors can't promote their books; others won't—and without a news angle or a famous or promotable personality behind them, novels are tougher to publicize than nonfiction.

Want to know how to make a small fortune? Start with a large fortune and write full-time. James Patterson started writing bestsellers armed with the money he had made in advertising. He spends a million dollars advertising every book, but his efforts only increase his fortune.

It's been said that 80 percent of a major publisher's annual promotion budget goes to 20 percent of its books. That leaves 20 percent of the budget for the other 80 percent of the list. Assume that no one in the house knows or cares as much about your book as you do and that only your editor has read it.

Assume that communications between the advertising, editorial, publicity, and sales department, although improved by email, are not perfect, if only because everyone is involved simultaneously with many past, present, and future books. This means that if you want the public to find out about your book, you either have to let fate take its course or work as hard as you can to promote it.

Publishers have both a short-term and long-term perspective on promotion. They're eager to find writers whose livelihoods depend on their going around the country giving seminars and selling books at them. That's a lifetime promotion plan for every book they write.

Most books have a one- to three-month launch window, a fleeting opportunity for them to sink or swim in the continuing deluge of books, remaining afloat through reviews, word of mouth and mouse, and promotions that generate sales. That window opens on pub date when books are in stores and reviews start to appear. One sure way to impress an agent is with your plans for promoting your book.

Labors of Love

Jack Canfield and Mark Victor Hansen spent fourteen months promoting *Chicken Soup for the Soul* before it hit the bestseller list. They advise writers to spend 90 percent of their time promoting their books.

Romance author Debbie Macomber was a housewife with a rented typewriter who spent five years writing four novels that didn't sell. But she persevered and created every writer's dream. Her books have sold more than sixty-five million copies. At first she spent 10 percent of her income on promotion. Now she spends 25 percent. She has online and four-color printed newsletters. When she signs books, she gives away pens, bookmarks, and bags with tea, coffee, or hot chocolate.

One of her continuing characters has a yarn store, and her novels include knitting patterns that fans knit and bring to her appearances. Debbie also gives free knitting lessons to people who help her knit afghans for a charity called Warm Up America! For more information, visit www.debbiemacomber.com.

She calls writer's conferences "dreamer's conferences," because new writers have the same dream. Debbie has a gift for connecting with writers because she started out just like them. And she makes writers believe if she can do it, they can. She doesn't have "fans," she has "friends," and she reads every letter and email they send her. Does life get better than being able to do well and do good? Like Jack and Mark, Debbie is an author you can emulate with pride.

Making Your Free Talks Pay

Someday you may be in the rare, enviable position of being able to set up paid talks when and where you want them and get the organizations you speak for to pay for first-class airfares and hotels.

Until then, you're among the vast majority of authors who can't afford the cost of a national tour. Tours are expensive and authors won't get enough publicity, and the publicity they do get won't sell enough books to justify the expense. But authors have to take the long view as well as the short view about the value of a tour.

If you can get yourself around the country, you can use your tour for more reasons than just publicity, the most important being as a reason to invite everyone in a city you want to know about you and what you have to offer to hear you speak. You will be laying down track and making contacts that you can use for the rest of your career as an author and, perhaps, speaker. This is worth all of the time and money authors are willing to invest.

The publication of a book is the best opportunity most people have to make everyone in the country and abroad aware of them and their services. The best time to promote a book is when it's new: it's news to the media, and it will probably have maximum exposure on bookstore shelves.

So, authors have to make maximum use of their book's once-in-a-lifetime launch window to generate publicity for their book and themselves in as many cities as possible.

Like writers, speakers learn their craft by doing it for free. But here are ways to make free talks pay for themselves:

- Invite the media and potential speaking clients.
- See if someone can feed you and put you up, perhaps even for more than one night if you want to stay in the area.
- If not, ask your contact if anyone in the organization has a connection with a hotel or B&B that will give you a room or a special rate. Offer to thank and praise the place in the talk, and give the person who gives you a room a signed copy of your book.

- Get a testimonial letter from the organizations you speak to.
- Ask the audience if they know of other organizations who might be interested in hearing your talk.
- Write the intro your host will use so that it includes your products and services. Also, give your host an "outro" designed to get your eager listeners to buy your book after you speak.
- Sell products and services.
- Get your host to let your listeners know in advance that you are available to do one-on-one coaching or consultations before or after you speak.
- Ask the organization to buy a specific number of copies of the book to justify your expenses.
- Ask the person who books you to let those who can't make your talk know that if they buy the book in advance, you will personalize and autograph it.
- Ask listeners to sign a pad or give you their business cards if they want free info or to subscribe to your e-zine.
- Give audiences your business card so they can visit your site and call you after your talk with questions.
- Make appointments with anyone in the area who can help you or who you want to meet for personal or professional reasons.
- Contact authors in your field in cities you'll be visiting.
- Use the national roster of writer's organizations to find people around the country to help you.
- If you do the free talk, ask if there's another talk you can get paid to give, or with your host's help, set up another talk that attendees will have to pay for.
- Try out new material.
- Invite speakers to give you feedback on your talk.
- Visit bookstores with your book, meet the book buyers, sign books, and ask if they will put "Autographed Copy" stickers on them and give them more and better display space.

• Ask if organizations will print handouts. If they will, ask how many pages they can do, and make sure your product, services, and contact info is unobtrusive but on every one.

This is a starter set of ideas. You're only limited by your imagination.

A *Writer's Digest* cartoon shows a guy sitting at a bar, lamenting to a fellow tippler, "Since I started freelancing full-time, I've made quite a few sales . . . my house, my car, my furniture."

The Big Picture

Take the long view about promotion. Look at it as a lifelong challenge at which you will become more effective with each book. When reporters and talk-show hosts invite you back and your promotional efforts boost the sales of your book, you will find the process exciting.

Trying to convince book buyers across the country to buy your book will probably be the hardest thing you have ever done. So, set realistic goals for what to expect of your book and yourself. But also take Israeli President David Ben-Gurion's advice: "To be a realist, you have to believe in miracles."

Authors who succeed often have a lucky break to thank for their success. Cherie Carter-Scott and Broadway Books did a great job with her book *If Life is a Game, These are the Rules.* But the reason it became a number one *New York Times* bestseller is that Oprah was starting a series of change-your-life shows the month the book was published. Having the right book at the right time got Cherie on the show. The great job she did on the show along with Oprah's praise for the book did the rest. They story of Cherie's big break is in *Guerrilla Marketing for Writers.*

Don't get involved with promotion halfheartedly. You've got to convince yourself and your publisher that you harbor a consuming drive to succeed, and that you will do whatever it takes to make your books sell. Unless you surrender to the process and jump into promotion body and soul, you may be better off working on your next book.

Let your agent help you be realistic about balancing your efforts against the sales they may generate, how you feel about doing it, and the need to use your time as productively as possible.

Depending upon your goals, your personality, the kind of books you write, and your need to earn a living, you might be right to decide that you, your publisher, and your readers will be better served if you keep your cheeks glued to a chair and your hands chained to a keyboard.

When you submit your proposal or manuscript, describe your speaking, media, and promotional experience. Present a plan listing what you will do to promote your book. Your eagerness and ability to promote your work will be a major factor in determining the editor, publisher, and deal you get for your book.

As its title suggests, the most comprehensive guide to ways to promote your books is John Kremer's *1001 Ways to Market Your Books*.

A poet laments to a friend, "Burglars broke into my house last night."

Friend: "Yes? What happened?"

Poet: "They searched through every room, then left a five-dollar bill on my dresser."

—*10,000 Jokes, Toasts, and Stories*

Keep Growing

Don't let your desire to be a writer turn you into a one-sided personality. Strive to develop all your potentials as a human being. Your writing will mirror your personal growth.

In his excellent book, *This Business of Writing*, Gregg Levoy writes, "The depth of your writing is a function of how absorbent you are. Writers must first inhale the world, and then exhale it in writing. Art, it has been said, is the discharge of experience, and the more deeply informed you are by your receptivity, by your life's experiences, the richer your writing.

"Imagine your body as a prism that the light of experience flows through and emerges as art. The more of the world you 'inspire' (literally 'breathe in'), the more you are capable of inspiring the world."

Let Nothing Stop You

"The surest way to kill an artist is to give him everything he wants."

—Henry Miller

"To make your dreams come true, you have to wake up."

—Paul Valery

It's been estimated that less than 1 percent of the practitioners of the arts make a living at it. But *Writer's Digest* estimated that 6 percent of writers are successful. And writing is the easiest of the arts to enter. You just sit down and start writing. It's easier to succeed as an author than as an artist, actor, dancer, musician, or composer. But like the other arts, writing requires an apprenticeship and a huge effort to go from being unknown to being well-known. If you get discouraged about the demands of the writing life, consider becoming a dancer.

Two of the reasons why now is the best time ever to be a writer is that there are more subjects to write about than ever and more ways to approach them. There are more forms of fiction to write in and more ways to approach nonfiction subjects. So all writers have to do is to figure out what kind of writing excites them the most, and reading will answer that question.

Chapter 22
Building Your Platform and Converting It into Your Promotion Plan

If books like yours depend on author promotion to succeed and you want to sell your book to a New York house, you will need a national platform or profile before you sell it. Your platform will affect the agent, editor, publisher, and deal you get for your book. Borrowed from the world of speaking, platform is the magic word for opening publishers' doors for how-to and self-help books, the largest categories of books that require authors to be the center of attention.

What's a platform? It's continuing visibility. Different books need different platforms. A platform can be:

- local, regional, national, or international
- in an author's field
- in cyberspace
- the number of people an author speaks to a year
- how many people read an author's blog, column, or newsletter
- how many people listen to an author's podcast or broadcast radio show
- how many viewers watch an author's television show
- how much time and space an author or a book can command in the media

One Talk at a Time:
How to Build Your Platform

How do you build a platform? Start small: write for and do appearances in small media. Start speaking in small venues. When you're ready, you'll find opportunities to move up to the next level, and they'll find you. You're an amateur speaker until someone offers you money. When you and your message are potent enough, they will.

If, for example, you're writing a guidebook about your city, your platform could be your visibility through:

- talks for the trade and the public in your city
- trade and consumer travel media in a column or radio or TV show that you appear on regularly or host
- media contacts who have agreed to do a review, an excerpt, or an article about you or the book
- a promotional partnership with a travel-related business such as a tour company or a nonprofit such as a visitor-and-convention bureau

The platform you need depends on the kind of book you're writing and your literary and financial goals. If your goal is to be a successful author and be on the A-list in your field, you must seize every opportunity to become and remain as visible as you need to be to achieve your goals. You can:

- study your way to your platform and make yourself an authority figure in your field by doing research and getting a PhD on the subject, and by reading articles in trade and consumer on- and off-line magazines, newsletters, and blogs to stay on top of developments in your field
- write your way to your platform with academic and professional books on your subject, reviews of books in your field, articles, short stories, op-ed pieces, letters to the editor, postings to sites in your

field, a (self-)syndicated column, and contributions about your subject to Wikipedia

- talk your way to your platform with a radio or television show, or with talks, classes, workshops, seminars, webinars, teleseminars, and by coaching, consulting, and training for businesses, nonprofits, conferences, and conventions. You can send a speaker's kit to speaker's bureaus, meeting planners, CEOs, and other people who can hire you to speak when you can command four-figure sums
- publicize your way to a platform by periodically emailing or snail-mailing a news release to media
- network your way to your platform by befriending and earning the respect of opinion-makers in your field so you're regarded as an equal and can obtain cover quotes from them
- host your way to a platform by having a website so helpful and enjoyable to visit, it's always one of the top-rated links to your subject on Google
- winning your way to your platform with contests, prizes, and awards
- partner your way to a platform with a business or nonprofit whose support gives you national visibility
- serve your way to your platform by participating, as an officer if possible, in organizations in your field and community groups

All of these opportunities will make you and your book more visible, and they'll also create synergy with your books and what you do to promote them. So make it a goal to take advantage of as many of these opportunities as you can. Concentrate on those that offer the best opportunities for maximizing your visibility and that of your books.

Building your platform will:
- help you test-market your book, your talks, and your press kit
- lead to invitations to give more talks

- add to your stature in your field
- generate media interviews, requests for articles, and sales of your books, products, and services
- help you build your networks
- help you add links to your site

Your efforts and their affects will continue to grow in their power and value the more things you do and the longer you do them. Never stop building or maintaining your platform or fine-tuning how you do it, but only do things in which you have a genuine interest that justify your personal or professional time.

In a nonfiction proposal, your platform comes just before your promotion plan because your plan has to be a logical, believable extension of what you're already doing. You can't say you'll do fifty talks a year when you've only done five. Publishers won't accept that math. If you're already giving talks, your publisher will believe that increasing your fees and selling books will give you the incentive to keep doing them.

Just before your promotion, describe your platform by listing what you have done and are doing to promote your work and yourself.

Two Ways to Write Your Promotion Plan

There are two ways to write your promotion plan:

The Simple Way

If you're writing a book for which author promotion isn't a major concern or you don't have promotion or speaking experience, and you will be approaching small, mid-sized, or university presses about your book, just list in descending order of impressiveness what you will do to promote your book and mention your eagerness to do what your publisher asks of you. If you can afford a budget, cost out the best way to use it and say that you will pay for what's in your plan.

The Serious Way

If you're writing a book aimed at a wide national audience that you want to be published by a big house, you will need a promotion plan that is as long and strong as you can make it. To create one, list in descending order of importance what you will do to promote your book during its one- to three-month launch window and after.

The four most important commitments in your plan will be the number of:

- your matching promotion budget, which is optional because few writers can afford one
- major markets you will go to on publication
- talks you'll give a year
- books you will sell a year, assuming that one out of four listeners at your talks buys a book

An agent or editor can tell just from these numbers whether a big house is likely to buy a book. Again, these numbers apply to promotion-driven books. They aren't expected for literary books, serious books, gift books, and most reference books. And it's not just a question of whether a publisher buys your book but how they buy it. Unless the house falls in love with a book, they won't get behind a book unless they spend enough money to force them to try to earn it back. And if Lady Luck doesn't bless a small book on a big list, it will get lost in the shuffle.

"The author will match the publisher's, out-of-pocket, consumer promotion budget up to $XX,XXX on signing." Using your advance for promotion is a good idea, but don't mention it because nobody knows what it will be, and you have to cost out your promotion plan. As important as having a budget is proving that you're a guerrilla marketer who knows how to get the biggest bang from the littlest buck.

If it's $15,000 or less, don't mention the amount, just list what you will do, and that you'll pay for it. Making a financial commitment is the best way to justify one from your publisher, but even large publishers may not match your budget.

If you find a publisher who will, ask them for the plan they will carry out with their budget. Don't mention a budget to a mid-sized or small house; they won't expect it or match it.

Hiring a publicist to generate publicity is usually the biggest chunk out of a budget. If you can do it, mention who it is and how he or she will help you. If your budget allows, aim for a firm like Planned Television Arts that is well known to New York editors.

PTA offers writers a menu of services, and based on the nature of their book and the size of their budget, clients choose the most effective ways to use it. Other publicists charge a monthly retainer for their services. Google, *Literary Market Place*, and your networks will lead you to the publicist you need.

Publishers know that most writers can't afford a budget, and that's okay. Publishers won't buy your book because you have a budget or reject it because you don't. It's the following commitments that are crucial:

- "On publication, the author will give talks and do publicity in the following XX major markets . . ."

Follow this with a list of the cities that you will get yourself to. If you can't hire a publicist but you can give yourself a national tour, a staff publicist may piggyback on your travels at least shortly after publication. This assumes that you can get paid enough to justify giving talks around the country.

- "The author will continue to give XX talks a year."

You will find out how many talks you want to give a year by giving them and asking yourself:

"How much money do I want to earn a year from speaking and selling books?"

"How many planes do I want to get on a year?"

"How often do I want to leave my family?"

If you don't have a video of you speaking on your website, have a talk on a DVD ready to mail to editors, and assume that they will want to meet you if you can visit them on your dime.

- "The author will sell X,XXX books a year."

Business authors sell books to about 25 percent of their audiences. You're probably not writing a business book, but it's not an unreasonable expectation for most books. Large houses will have four-figure expectations.

- A wild card: if you can, establish a partnership with a business or nonprofit organization that will commit to:
  - buying a large quantity of books to sell or give away
  - sending you around the country as a spokesperson
  - featuring you or your book in its advertising and on its website
  - lending its name to the book
  - sponsoring an (annual) event connected to the book and making you a part of the event or mentioning you and the book in its publicity and advertising

List what your partner will do, and end the list by writing, "The last page of the proposal is a letter from [your partner] about their commitments to the book."

This is not easy to do, and it's more likely to happen for experienced professionals who have nurtured business relationships than for someone closer to the beginning of a career than the end of it. But businesses and nonprofits are always open to win/win ideas. A partner who can give you a powerful national platform will guarantee that your book will sell to a publisher and the public. And you can enlist as many noncompetitive partners as you can.

- List the ways that you will promote your book online and how you will use your website for promotion.

- If you have a large emailing list that you will sell books to, mention the size of the list.
- List your contacts at impressive media outlets who have told you they will do a review, an article, or an interview on publication.
- List what your media/speaker's kit will contain.
- Give round numbers for the lists of media people to whom you will send the media kit. Indicate which of these people will receive a promotional copy of the book. Your publisher will supply a certain number of free promotional copies, a number negotiated on signing. If possible, say that you will provide those that they can't.
- List trade and consumer conferences and conventions at which you know that you will be able to speak during the first year after publication and, if impressive, the number of people who will attend them.
- List opinion-makers whose names will give your book credibility and salability in fifty states two years from now who, based on reading your proposal, will give you quotes for your book after they read your manuscript.
- Mention special-interest magazines that will trade ads for stories you write.
- Mention magazines that will do per-order ads for which the magazine supplies the space, your publisher the books, and they share the profits.
- Mention a commitment to run a column you will write that will give your book as much exposure as possible, online or off, for cash or in exchange for a bio you will write to promote your book and yourself.
- Continue the list with anything else that will impress editors or agents. This means that people you'll contact about an idea come last.
- Consider doing two promotion plans: one for after your book is published, and a lifetime plan.

- End your promotion plan like this: "The author will coordinate [his/her] plans with the publisher's."

Publishers only respond well to the word *will* and numbers. They want to know things will happen and how many of them they'll be. Assume that your publisher will include a promotion budget and the number of books you will sell a year in their contract. So exaggerate nothing. But don't be discouraged if you don't have numbers that will excite publishers. You will in time if that's your goal.

From Vertical to Horizontal: Transforming Your Plan from Theory into Action

When you're submitting your work to publishers, your plan is a selling tool so it's a vertical list in descending order of importance that agents and editors will only read enough to know you're for real.

Once your editor accepts your manuscript, and it goes into production, you will have at least nine months to ramp up your promotion campaign. To do that, you have to make your vertical plan horizontal by transforming it into a timeline that shows you what to do when. Your publicist and your networks will help you do this. For example, you or your publicist may have to contact long-lead magazines as much as nine months ahead of publication.

There are more ways to promote books than ever before. You are only limited by your time, energy, knowledge, and imagination. Keep in mind that you will carry out your plan eighteen months to two years from now when your book is published.

If you don't need an advance to write your book and you don't have to be concerned about competitive books, consider patience: build your platform, finish your book, and test-market it, if only by selling your manuscript in a loose-leaf binder at your talks. Then you will be well positioned to sell your book in the most advantageous way.

The bottom line: the greater the continuing national impact you can give your book, the better agent, editor, publisher, and deal you will get for it, and the greater its chances for success.

Chapter 23
Writing High:
The End of the Beginning

"The greatest opportunity in business today is having a clean sheet of paper."

—Michael Treachy, coauthor of *The Discipline of Market Leaders*

"A good book is the purest essence of the human soul."

—Thomas Carlyle

Why Now Is the Best Time Ever to Be a Writer

If you are writing to meet the needs of the marketplace, and you have the ability to promote your work, now is the best time ever to be a writer. More than ever there are:

- subjects for you to write about
- books and authors to serve as models
- formats for your book to be published in
- media for communicating your ideas
- countries for your books to be published in
- agents
- publishers
- writers' groups, classes, conferences, organizations, publishing institutes, magazines, and newsletters

- ways to get your books written
- options for getting your books published
- bright, dedicated editors
- good books being published
- ways to test-market your books
- ways to promote and profit from your books
- ways to use technology to write, research, promote, and profit from your ideas; earn a living; and build and maintain your networks

What publishers call *the upside* is greater than ever. Thomas McCormick, the former President of St. Martin's Press, made the company consistently profitable with this philosophy: "Take care of the downside, and the upside will take care of itself."

Why Now Is the Most Exciting Time to Be Alive

"We are as gods and might as well get good at it."

—Stewart Brand, *The Whole Earth Catalog,* 1968

"Information is coin of the realm in cyberspace."

—Charles Rubin, coauthor of *Guerrilla Marketing Online: The Entrepreneur's Guide to Earning Profits on the Internet*

Thomas Jefferson thought that a revolution every so often can be a good thing. But a revolution won is a revolution lost. Enjoying the fruits of what the revolution was fought for saps the commitment to its spirit. It can dissipate the commitment to do anything but enjoy life. What we need is revolutionary fervor without revolutionary excess. And books are a way to build and sustain that fervor.

Technophiles believe that the three great events in human history are the invention of writing, machinery, and the computer. For them, computer technology has sparked the greatest revolution in communication since Gutenberg's printing press five hundred years ago. But history is only a warm-up act for a future. The only thing that we can confidently predict about the future is that we can't predict the future.

Lines of Sight

Beware of straight-line thinking. At the end of the nineteenth century, shortly before the building of the first subway, New Yorkers believed that the city could never grow to a million people, because there wouldn't be enough room to stall the horses. The future will not be just the extension of present conditions, and writers and other artists have to tell us what it will be because they are the visionaries who can see it.

Seeing the Future with Crystal Clarity

"Civilization is limited only by its imagination."

—Napoleon

Now is the most exciting time ever to be alive. Civilization is either at the beginning of the end or the end of the beginning. It's reinventing itself before our eyes. Life itself is miraculous. But we are living in the age of miracles. The continual breakthroughs in technology and biotechnology are astonishing.

Microcomputer efficiency is doubling every eighteen months. This enables computers to transform the way books are written, edited, designed, manufactured, sold, promoted, and used. They are also enlarging the markets both for books about the new technology and for electronic media such as software, databases, CDs, DVDs, computer games, and online services such as eBay, Google, and America Online. Computers have also all but eliminated the drudgery of writing.

Technology can also lead publishers into blind alleys. When they discovered CD-ROMs, it was love at first byte. With the zeal of kids in a candy store, they sunk millions into "new media" departments until they realized they can't create or sell CD-ROMs effectively. Millions of dollars later, they quietly closed up shop and got back to the business of publishing.

The Tao of Technology

Technology takes a path from the mind of its creators into the future:

- Two passionate guys in a garage create something new that they think people will buy. Think Apple.
- They create a business model: they figure out a way to *monetize* their invention and build a company to make it happen.
- The promise of the new technology entices many players to join the game.
- If a company grows big enough, it recruits corporate managers who know how to run a business.
- Companies either grow big enough to survive as independent enterprises, or they are bought by larger companies as investments or by companies that need the technology.
- Over time, the field is reduced to a few major players who must innovate continuously and successfully to keep their jobs and keep their companies going.

Technology continues to evolve at an accelerating rate, making it impossible to understand its social and spiritual consequences. The telephone is more than a century old, but we still don't fully understand its implications. Micro-loans to Indian villages to buy cell phones enables them to start a business selling phone calls. But phones have been banished from men's locker rooms because they can take pictures. Predicting how creativity and advances in technology will add to the ways people can use phones is impossible, let alone what those changes will mean to us as individuals or citizens.

The Yankee great Yogi Berra once said, "Predictions are hard, especially about the future." Technology is heartless and mindless. It can only do what we enable it to do. There are people who spend their days in Silicon Valley working with technology who, to get away from it, don't use electricity in their homes. Imagine your life without electricity.

One lesson writers can learn from this is that a fad, trend, or successful idea begets its antithesis as surely as Queen Anne Victorians begat the Bauhaus. When everyone is looking one way, look the other way. One way to find clues about where the culture is heading is to read between the lines of people's lives. How they work, play, and domesticate themselves will give you insights into the future.

There's a *New Yorker* cartoon showing two dogs sitting in front of a computer and one is saying to the other: "On the Internet, nobody knows I'm a dog."

Why Content Is King

"It is only with the heart that one can see rightly;
what is essential is invisible to the eye."

—*The Little Prince*, Antoine Saint-Exupery

"Inner space is the real frontier."

—Gloria Steinem

Despite the miracles that are transforming our lives, people continue to need:
- physical and financial security
- spiritual, physical, and mental health
- a network of friends, family, and colleagues
- meaningful work
- sexual satisfaction
- the opportunity to develop all of one's potential
- an environment conducive to fulfilling one's needs
- hope for the future

After basic needs are met, the most important things in life are abstractions: love, faith, virtue, beauty, creativity, friendship, peace of mind, a sense of achievement, and a spirit of community.

What does all this mean to you as a writer? It's been said that luck is ability meeting opportunity. If this is true, then you are part of the luckiest generation of writers that ever lived.

Information is doubling every eighteen months. You absorb more information in a month than people in the 1800s received in their whole lives. The Age of Information, which is just beginning, has to be the age of the writer.

In one of Bruce Springsteen's songs, he complains about fifty-seven channels with nothing on. Before long, you may have a thousand channels to choose from. Author Steven Levy predicts that as television and computers merge, the World Wide Web will unleash five hundred thousand channels. That's why content is king. Somebody has to fill the pipes.

Bookstores already have books on all of the needs mentioned above. They encompass endless possibilities for fiction and nonfiction. And books about them will continue to be published because what you need and care about are the same things that everyone else in the human family needs and cares about.

This includes the inevitable problems that technology creates. You can tell that the Internet is starting to come of age when there is a twelve-step program for overcoming addiction to it!

Change is the sacrifice required for progress. So as a Texas adman put it, "You have to learn to kiss change on the lips." But whether you're writing fiction or nonfiction, you can help us understand what to do, how to do it, and what it means.

Books and the Other Four B's

In the 1890s, people thought that books were in jeopardy because bicycles were so popular. In 1900, an article in a St. Louis newspaper expressed concern for the future of books because people were spending so much time riding the new streetcars.

Around this time, Congress considered a bill abolishing the patent office because some members felt that nothing more could be invented. The bill failed but the inventions that followed continued to alarm book lovers.

According to the doomsday prophets, the radio, movies, television, and the computer were all supposed to sound the death knell for books. Books survived, and are reused more than any of the other media. Can you imagine an officer of the court holding out a CD of the Bible so witnesses can take an oath on it?

For a medium of communication to become integrated into our lives, it has to be usable in the four B's: bed, bath, beach, and bus. You can order books online and download them in seconds. But I can't imagine the day when readers would rather curl up with a flat screen of any size to read *War and Peace*.

Rather than being a threat to books, technology will liberate the medium to do what it does best. Nothing else offers the tactile feeling and experience of reading a book. As an affordable, efficient, portable, durable, sometimes beautiful, sometimes sacred means of communication, books will remain part of our lives.

Despite the growing interest in electronic media, former Simon & Schuster President Jon Newcomb spoke for all publishers when he vowed that at S&S, "Books will always be our cornerstone."

Graduation Day

Bob Hope once gave a talk at a college graduation, and he was asked to give the graduates some advice about going out into the real world. His advice was "Don't go."

But if you are going out into the real world of publishing, and you want to be a successful author, there are six challenges for you to meet. You have to:
1. write every day
2. take the long view as well as the short view in developing your books, your craft, and your career
3. set literary and financial goals for yourself that inspire you to produce your best work
4. keep writing books that you are proud of and that you can promote and sell in as many media and countries as possible
5. never submit anything until it's 100 percent—as well conceived and crafted as you can make it
6. always be committed to achieving your goals

You know more and care more about your books and your career than anyone else, so you must be committed to your success.

The strongest hope your books will have of reaching their literary and commercial potential is for you to stretch your abilities to their limits. Conceive and craft your books as well as only you can. Submitting only your best work will bring out the best in every agent and editor who reads it.

Writing as if Books Mattered

"Artists are the antennae of the race."

—poet Ezra Pound

For the first time, technology, the media, universal concerns, and the globalization of culture and commerce are uniting the human family. As the planet hurtles through time and space on this voyage of transformation into an unknowable future, Spaceship Earth has no more valuable passengers than its artists and writers who should be its copilots.

The ancient Greek philosopher Heraclitus believed that "Only change endures." Because the world is changing faster than ever, readers of all ages around the world need reporters and storytellers to explain what's going on and how to live long and prosper as the Age of Information transforms our lives. Ideas travel and transform readers just as they are transformed by the media that communicate them.

Rarely has there been greater need for calming, reassuring, inspiring words that help us understand ourselves and the world around us. We need your voice, your vision, your passion, and your humor as much now as they were ever needed. Former New York mayor and bestselling author Ed Koch once said: "Books are not the foundation of civilization, they *are* civilization."

Max Perkins was a legendary editor who worked for Scribner's. In a career that spanned three decades, he edited the work of Ernest Hemingway, F. Scott Fitzgerald, and Thomas Wolfe. In *Max Perkins: Editor of Genius*, Scott Berg's inspiring biography, Perkins says, "There is nothing so important as the book can be."

The right book will change the world. Norman Mailer believes that "only great fiction can save the world . . . for fiction still believes that one mind can see it whole."

Even if you are not fated to write books that improve the human condition, writing any book well is an achievement you can be proud of. Writing is a courageous calling, and if you can add to the world's store of pleasure and information, of beauty and truth, your future is assured.

If your books are touched with magic because of their ideas or their style; if you capture people, places and situations in a compelling, timeless, universal way, your books will find their audience no matter how they are published, and they will endure. What greater challenge could you ask for? What greater achievement could you hope for?

Author Barry Lopez wrote, "Sometimes a person needs a story more than food to stay alive." People everywhere are hungry for information and understanding, and the more they know, the more they want to know.

A Fork in the Road

Writers ask agents, "What do editors really want?" What editors really want is writers like:

- Humorist James Thurber, who said, "If I couldn't write, I couldn't live."
- Isaac Bashevis Singer. When the Nobel-Prize-winning author was born, the midwife brought him to his mother, and she asked, "Is it a boy or a girl?"

"Neither one," replied the midwife. "It's a writer."

- The woman at a writer's conference who admitted, "My husband just ran off with the baby-sitter, and I'm trying to figure how to use it in my novel."
- Isaac Asimov, who wrote and edited four hundred seventy books and anthologies without an agent and once said, "If the doctor told me I only had six minutes to live, I'd type a little faster."

Editors and agents are looking for writers who love to write, who *live* to write. As San Francisco Bay Area agent Felicia Eth said, they're looking for "writers who make them forget that they're in the business and make them remember *why* they're in the business."

As a writer, you are the most important person in the publishing process because you make it go. The more competitive the book business gets, the more agents' and editors' jobs hinge on their ferreting out good books and new writers.

Promising new writers are the lifeblood of the publishing business, and discovering them is the best part of the job. Agents and editors are as delighted to find promising new writers as new writers are to be published. Selling a well-conceived, well-written book that satisfies the growing, insatiable need for understanding and entertainment of readers around the world is easier than ever.

Baseball great Yogi Berra once said, "When you come to a fork in the road, take it." I hope that this book will be a fork in the road for you. Whether it inspires you to hit the keys or take up plumbing, it will have served you well.

The Chinese sage Lao-Tse taught that "he who obtains has little. He who scatters has much." The simplest recipe for happiness that I know of is to find your unique gift, the song that only you can sing, and give it to the world.

If you are lucky enough to be able to write, you have been endowed with a wonderful gift. You owe it to yourself and posterity to develop your gift to its fullest, to place your life in the service of your gift, your ideas, your books, and your readers. You have the opportunity to use your gift not just to make a living but to make a difference.

The right combination of talent, luck, and perseverance will lead to success. The only absolute about writing, agenting, and publishing is to trust your instincts and common sense and do whatever works. The best piece of advice we've ever heard about becoming a writer came from an editor who said, "If anything can stop you from becoming a writer, let it. If nothing can stop you, do it and you'll make it."

Good luck!

Appendix 1:
The AAR Checklist of Questions for Authors
(and a Few More to Fill in the Blanks)

The AAR offers this helpful guide on what to ask an agent who wants to represent you. I have added a few more questions you may want to ask.

The following is a suggested list of topics for authors to discuss with literary agents with whom they are entering into a professional relationship.

1. Is your agency a sole proprietorship? A partnership? A corporation?
2. Are you a member of the Association of Authors' Representatives?
3. How long have you been in business as an agent?
4. How many people does your agency employ?
5. Of the total number of employees, how many are agents, as opposed to clerical workers?
6. Do you have specialists at your agency who handle movie and television rights? Foreign rights? Do you have sub-agents or corresponding agents overseas and in Hollywood?
7. Do you represent other authors in my area of interest?
8. Who in your agency will actually be handling my work? Will other staff members be familiar with my work and the status of my business at your agency? Will you oversee or at least keep me apprised of the work that your agency is doing on my behalf?
9. Do you issue an agent-author contract? May I review a specimen copy? And may I review the language of the agency clause that appears in contracts you negotiate for your clients?
10. What is your approach to providing editorial input and career guidance for your clients or for me specifically?
11. How do you keep your clients informed of the activities on their behalf? Do you regularly send them copies of publishers' rejection letters? Do you provide them with submission lists and rejection letters on request? Do you regularly, or upon request, send out updated activity reports?
12. Do you consult with your clients on any and all offers?
13. Some agencies sign subsidiary contracts on behalf of their clients to expedite processing. Do you?
14. What are your commissions for: 1) basic sales to U.S. publishers, 2) sales of movie and television rights, 3) audio and multimedia rights, 4) British and foreign translation rights?
15. What are your procedures and timeframes for processing and disbursing client funds? Do you keep different bank accounts separating author funds from agency revenue?
16. What are your policies about charging clients for expenses incurred by your agency? Will you list such expenses for me? Do you advance money for such expenses?
17. How do you handle legal, accounting, public relations, or similar services that fall outside the normal range of a literary agent's functions?

18. Do you issue 1099 tax forms at the end of each year? Do you also furnish clients upon request with a detailed account of their financial activity, such as gross income, commissions and other deductions, and net income, for the past year?

19. In the event of your death or disability, or the death or disability of the principal person running the agency, what provisions exist for continuing operation of my account, for the processing of money due to me, and for the handling of my book and editorial needs?

20. If we should part company, what is your policy about handling any unsold subsidiary rights to my work that were reserved to me under the original publishing contracts?

21. What are your expectations of me as a client?

22. Do you have a list of Dos and Don'ts for your clients that will enable me to help you do your job better?

The following questions will also help you find out about the agent's personality and credentials:

- How did you become an agent?
- What kinds of books do you handle?
- Who are some of the publishers you have sold to?
- About how many books are you working on now?
- Are you a member of [organizations in your field]?

The following questions will help define your working relationship:

- Do you receive a commission on short pieces I sell?
- What are the chances of you selling my book?
- How long do you think it will take to sell?
- How much of an advance should I expect for it?
- How will you go about placing it?

Since personal relationships with editors are essential, if the agent is outside of New York, ask, "How often do you go to New York?"

Before you approach the agent, your research in directories and on the Web will answer some of these questions. For best results, be discreet about asking them questions. Don't give agents the impression that you're grilling them or reading off a list of questions. Assume that even if they're not AAR members, they're aware of the questions.

The more established and successful agents are, the less willing they may be to be questioned. But you're hiring someone to work for you, so you are entitled to know what you feel you have to so you won't be surprised later about how, for example, your agent works or when you can expect to hear from her or him.

Appendix 2:
Two Agents' Clauses

The following two agency clauses, the second one ours, are used in publishers' contracts. Agents who don't have written agreements with their clients may, as in the first example, spell out their compensation in the agent's clause of the publisher's contract more completely than would otherwise be necessary.

First Agency Clause
The Author hereby irrevocably appoints _____ as his sole and exclusive agent with respect to the said Work and authorizes and directs the Publisher to make all payments due or to become due to the Author hereunder to and in the name of the said agent, and to accept the receipt of the said agent as full evidence and satisfaction of such payments. As sole and exclusive agent, the said agent is authorized to negotiate for the Author throughout the World as to the disposal of all other rights in and to the said Work. The said agent is further empowered to engage sub-agents for the sale of British Commonwealth and/or translation rights in and to the said Work and to pay such sub-agents a commission of up to ten percent (10%) of the monies collected from the disposition of any such British Commonwealth and/or translation rights through such sub-agents. In consideration for services rendered, the said agent is entitled to receive or retain as its commission fifteen percent (15%) of gross monies paid to the Author hereunder and from all other rights in and to the said Work (including the said optioned works), except that such commission shall be reduced to ten percent (10%) as to those monies out of which a sub-agent's commission of five percent (5%) or more is also paid, the said ten percent (10%) to be computed after deduction of the sub-agent's commissions. The provisions of this clause shall survive the expiration of this Agreement.

Second Agency Clause
The Author irrevocably assigns to Michael Larsen/Elizabeth Pomada Literary Agents, 1029 Jones Street, San Francisco, California 94109 ("the Agent"), 15% of all monies due to the author under this Agreement. The Author authorizes the Agent to receive all monies payable to the Author through this Agreement. The Agent is authorized to act on the Author's behalf in all matters arising out of this Agreement. This clause will survive the termination of this Agreement.

The following is the code of ethics that all AAR members must agree, in writing, to uphold.

ASSOCIATION OF AUTHORS'S REPRESENTATIVES, INC.
Canon of Ethics

1. The members of the Association of Authors' Representatives, Inc. are committed to the highest standard of conduct in the performance of their professional activities. While affirming the necessity and desirability of maintaining their full individuality and freedom of action, the members pledge themselves to loyal service to their clients' business and artistic needs, and will allow no conflicts of interest that would interfere with such service. They pledge their support to the Association itself and to the principles of honorable coexistence, directness, and honesty in their relationships with their co-members. They undertake never to mislead, deceive, dupe, defraud, or victimize their clients, other members of the Association, the general public, or any other person with whom they do business as a member of the association.

2. Members shall take responsible measures to protect the security and integrity of clients' funds. Members must maintain separate bank accounts for money due their clients so that there is no commingling of client's and members' funds. Members shall deposit funds received on behalf of clients promptly upon receipt, and shall make payments of domestic earnings due clients promptly, but in no event later than ten business days after clearance. Revenues from foreign rights over $50 shall be paid to clients within ten business days after clearance. Sums under $50 shall be paid within a reasonable time of clearance. However, on stock and similar rights, statements of royalties and payments shall be made not later than the month following the member's receipt, each statement and payment to cover all royalties received to the 25th day of the previous calendar month. Payments for amateur rights shall be made not less frequently than every six months. A member's books of account must be open to the client at all times with respect to transactions concerning the client.

3. In addition to the compensation for agency services that is agreed upon between a member and a client, a member may, subject to the approval of the client, pass along charges incurred by the member on the client's behalf, such as copyright fees, manuscript retyping, photocopies, copies of books for use in the sale of other rights, long distance calls, special messenger fees, etc. Such charges shall only be made if the client has agreed to reimburse such expenses.

4. A member shall keep each client apprised of matters entrusted to the member and shall promptly furnish such information as the client may reasonably request.

5. Members shall not represent both buyer and seller in the same transaction. Except as provided in the next sentence, a member who represents a client in the grant of rights in any property owned or controlled by the client may not accept any compensation or other payment from the acquirer of such rights, including but not limited to so-called "packaging fees," it being understood that the member's compensation, if any, shall be derived solely from the client. Notwithstanding the foregoing, a member may accept (or participate in) a so-called "packaging fee" paid by an acquirer of television rights to a property owned or controlled by a client if the member: a) fully discloses to the client at the earliest practical time the possibility that the member may be offered such a "packaging fee" which the member may choose to accept; b) delivers to the clients at such time a copy of the Association's statement regarding packaging and packaging fees; and c) offers the client at such time the opportunity to arrange for other representation in the transaction. In no event shall the member accept (or participate in) both a packaging fee and compensation from the client with respect to the transaction. For transactions subject to Writers Guild of America (WGA) jurisdiction, the regulations of the WGA shall take precedence over the requirements of this paragraph.

6. Members may not receive a secret profit in connection with any transaction involving a client. If such a profit is received, the member must promptly pay over the entire amount to the client.

7. Members shall treat their clients' financial affairs as private and confidential, except for information customarily disclosed to interested parties as part of the process of placing rights as required by law, or, if agreed with the client, for other purposes.

8. The AAR believes that the practice of literary agents charging clients or potential clients fees for reading and evaluating literary works (including outlines, proposals, and partial or complete manuscripts) is subject to serious abuse that reflects adversely on our profession.

For this reason the AAR discourages that practice. New members and members who had not, before October 30, 1991, registered their intent to continue to charge reading fees shall not charge such fees. Effective January 1, 1996, all AAR members shall be prohibited from directly or indirectly charging such fees or receiving any financial benefit from the charging of such fees by any other party.

Until January 1, 1996, AAR members who, in accordance with the registration provisions of the previous paragraph, do charge such fees are required to comply with the following:

A. Before entering into any agreement whereby a fee is to be charged for reading and evaluating any work, the member must provide to the author a written statement that clearly sets forth: (i) the nature and extent of that report; (ii) whether the services are to be rendered by the member personally, and if not, a description of the professional background of the person who will render the services; (iii) the period of time within which the services will be rendered; (iv) under what circumstances, if any, the fee charged will be refunded to the author; (v) the amount of the fee, including any initial payment as well as any other payments that may be requested by the member of additional services, and how that fee was determined (e.g., hourly rate, length of work reviewed, length of report, or other measure; and (vi) that the rendering of such services shall not guarantee that the member will agree to represent the author or will render the work more saleable to publishers.

B. Any member who charges fees for such services and who seeks or facilitates the member's inclusion in any published listing of literary agents, shall, if the listing permits, indicate in that listing that the member charges such fees. Apart from such listings, members shall not solicit reading fee submissions.

C. The rendering of such services for a fee shall not constitute more than an incidental part of the member's professional activity.

Appendix 4:
A Bill of Rights for Writers and
a Bill of Rights for Agents

Whomever you choose to represent you, however the agent operates, and whether your contract with your agent is written or oral, both of you have certain "inalienable rights."

Ken Norwick, the legal counsel for the Association of Authors' Representatives and coauthor of *The Rights of Authors, Artists, and Other Creative People: The Basic ACLU Guide to Author and Artist Rights*, was kind enough to review this book. He noted that these aren't all legal rights. But they are what you and your agent have a reasonable right to expect from each other. With rights come responsibilities. As you maintain and improve your relationship with your agent, you create obligations that you have to fulfill.

A Writer's Bill of Rights
1. As long as your expectations are realistic, you have a right to be satisfied with what happens with your work.
2. You have the right to approve of how your agent is handling your work.
3. You have the right to expect honesty and professionalism in your agent's relationships with publishers and with you.
4. You have the right to see all correspondence about your work.
5. If your agent declines to handle a project, you have the right to sell it yourself or hire another agent.
6. If your agent exhausts all the possibilities for your work and can do no more to sell it, you have the right to take the project back and try to sell it yourself or through another agent, whether or not you continue to work with your first agent.
7. You have the right to be informed promptly about all offers for and helpful responses to your work.
8. You have the right to receive prompt replies to your letters and phone calls.
9. You have the right to understand and approve agreements negotiated on your behalf.
10. You have the right to receive money due you promptly.
11. You have the right to have your business affairs kept confidential.
12. You have the right to ask your agent for news and encouragement.
13. You have the right to have reasonable changes made in your agency agreement at any time.
14. You have the right to stop working with an agent who is not representing you to your satisfaction.

15. If you end your relationship with your agent, you have the right to receive your work back, with rejection letters.

An Agent's Bill of Rights

1. Your agent has the right to work however he or she wishes.
2. Your agent has the right to expect the same degree of professionalism from you that you expect from your agent.
3. Your agent has the right to represent a book that competes with yours, provided that handling the competing book doesn't lessen your agent's ability to represent your book.
4. If a buyer approaches you about your work or writing services, only your agent has the right to negotiate on your behalf.
5. Except for work you agree to exclude, your agent has the right to be the only person to represent all of your work for every commercial use.
6. Your agent has the right to continue trying to place a project as long as the agent is competently and conscientiously trying to do so.
7. Your agent has the right to be spared excessive letters, phone calls, and visits.
8. Your agent has the right to be spared requests that are not part of an agent's job.
9. In contracts negotiated for you, your agent has the right to include an agent's clause specifying the commission, the agent's right to receive income and mail for you, and the right to act as agent on your behalf.
10. Your agent has the right to keep earned commissions if you return your advance.
11. If a problem develops between you and your agent, your agent has the right to discuss it with you and to try to help solve it to your mutual satisfaction.
12. Your agent has the right to stop representing you at any time.
13. If your agent does a good job for you, the agent earns the right to keep you as a client.
14. Your agent has the right to keep his or her home address and phone number private.

Appendix 5:

Three Author-Agent Contracts

The following three sample author-agent contracts will give you a sense of the range that these agreements can take.

First Sample Agreement

It is agreed that _____ (hereinafter referred to as the Client) does grant _____ (hereinafter referred to as the Agent) the exclusive right to represent the Client in any and all negotiations for the sale of _____ (hereinafter referred to as the Work) to a publisher and, thereafter, for the sale of any and all rights related to the Work as well as all other books and/or projects as shall be mutually agreed upon.

The Client does hereby warrant that He/She is the author and sole owner of the Work; that it is original and that it contains no matter unlawful in the content nor does it violate the rights of any third party; that the rights granted hereunder are free and clear; and that the Client has full power to grant such representation to the Agent.

The Client agrees that the Agent shall receive 15% (fifteen percent) of the gross of all monies earned from the sale of the Work. It is also agreed that the Agent will receive from the sale, licensing option, or other disposition of any foreign language rights (including British rights) when negotiated without an overseas subagent a commission of 15% (fifteen percent) of the gross; when foreign language volume rights (including British rights) are negotiated with an overseas subagent the total commission will be 20% (twenty percent) of the gross: 10% (ten percent) for the Agent and 10% (ten percent) for the sub-agent. Further, if the Agent should use the services of a sub-agent for the sale of movie and/or television rights the total commission shall be 20% (twenty percent): 10% (ten percent) for the agent and 10% (ten percent) for the sub-agent . . . all from the gross.

The Client does hereby empower the Agent to receive all monies due to him under any contractual arrangements related to the Work and the Agent warrants that her receipt shall be a good and valid discharge. The Client further empowers the Agent to deal with all parties on his behalf in all matters arising from the Work. The Client agrees that this agreement shall be binding on his/her estate.

The Agent agrees to remit all monies due to the Client, less the Agent's stipulated commission, within thirty (30) days of the receipt of any monies earned from the sale of any rights related to the Work if said monies are paid in U.S. currency. Otherwise, the Agent will remit all monies due to the Client, less the Agent's stipulated commission, within thirty (30) days of the conversion of said monies to U.S currency.

If either Client or Agent should desire to terminate this agreement, either party must inform the other, by certified mail, of such intent, and the agreement shall be considered terminated sixty (60) days after receipt of such letter. It is, however, understood that any monies due after termination whether derived from contractual agreements already negotiated or under negotiation by the Agent when the agreement is terminated shall be paid to the Agent who will then deduct her commission and remit to the Client as outlined above.

If the foregoing correctly sets forth your understanding, please sign both copies of this letter where indicated, retaining one copy for your files and returning the other copy to me for mine.

Second Sample Agreement

Another agent drew up the following agreement with the help of a literary lawyer. This agent uses an American foreign rights representative who charges 20% to help sell foreign rights, so the commission rises to 30%.

Dear writer:

On the following terms, I hereby propose to act as your agent to seek publication of your book and works derived from it, tentatively titled _____ and referred to below as the "Property."

1. EXCLUSIVE AGENT I will be your exclusive agent for the Property and any sequels to it (works on the same subject as the Property, making use of the same themes, and written for the same market) for an indefinite period beginning today, _____ (date). However, I will be entitled to commissions beyond termination according to paragraph 5 below.

2. TERMINATION This agreement can and will be terminated by either party upon mailing a written 90-day notice to terminate to the other party. However, I will be entitled to commissions beyond termination according to paragraph 5 below.

3. REASONABLE EFFORTS I will make every reasonable effort to obtain the best possible offer for the Property. I will report to you immediately any offer that I obtain, and will generally keep you informed of my activities under this contract.

4. AUTHORITY Any offer that I may succeed in obtaining will be subject to your written acceptance, and will have no binding effect on you otherwise. You will be free to accept or reject any offer. My authority will be limited to obtaining offers. I will have no power or authority to close any sale or to make any binding commitment of any kind on your behalf.

5. COMMISSIONS If during the period of this agreement I bring you an offer that you accept in writing, and you and the publisher execute the publishing agreement, you will pay me a commission equal to fifteen percent of all proceeds received from the publisher. In addition, you will pay me a commission equal to thirty percent from sales throughout the rest of the world and from the sale of any serial, merchandising, or dramatic (motion picture, television, radio) rights when a sub-agent is required to negotiate the deal. In addition, I will receive the same percentages (15%

when a subagent is not used and 30% when a sub-agent is used) of all proceeds obtained from any subsequent sale of rights that derives from the initial sale of the Property, including, but not limited to the following: condensation, translation, anthology, periodicals, electronic formats and reproductions, television, audio and video recordings, paperback, and commercial.

If you sell or transfer publishing rights in the Property to a person or company to which I submitted a proposal for the sale of those rights during the term of this agreement, I will be entitled to my full commission even though the sale or transfer of rights takes place after the agreement terminates. My right to compensation for a sale or disposition of rights under this agreement, once earned, will continue even after the agreement terminates, and in case of my death or disability, my successor in interest will have that right and will administer the receipt and disbursement of funds under this agreement.

6. PROCEEDS I will be entitled to collect on your behalf all proceeds derived from the sale of the Property. I will deduct my commissions and forward all sums due to you along with any statements from the publisher or licensee within three weeks of my receipt of proceeds or statements from the publisher or licensee.

7. COSTS You will repay me for all postage, copying, telephone, travel, and other costs specifically related to the sale of the Property. These costs will not exceed $300 without your consent. I will be entitled to deduct these costs, as well as my commission, from the proceeds derived from the sale of the property if you have not reimbursed me already.

8. COMPETING WORKS As a literary agent, I may represent clients whose work competes with yours. You agree that I may do so.

9. ARBITRATION We will arbitrate any dispute arising under this agreement before an arbitrator in San Francisco, California, under the rules for commercial disputes of the American Arbitration Association then in effect. If we cannot agree on the arbitrator, each of us will appoint one representative, and the representatives will choose the arbitrator. The arbitration award will be enforceable in any court with jurisdiction.

10. ATTORNEY'S FEES If any dispute is referred to arbitration or results in litigation, the party who wins shall be entitled to reasonable attorney's fees from the other party.

11. ASSIGNMENT Neither party will assign or pledge his or her rights under this agreement without written consent of the other party.

12. INDEMNIFICATION You represent and warrant to me that you have the right to make this agreement without impairing anyone else's rights, and you agree not to make any commitment about the Property or works derived from it that conflicts with this agreement. You will indemnify me and hold me harmless against any claim based on your breach of the provisions of this paragraph.

13. ENTIRE AGREEMENT This agreement supersedes any and all other agreements between us with respect to the Property and is the only agreement between us on its subject. It may be amended only in writing signed by both of us.

If the above terms are acceptable to you, please indicate by signing below and returning this agreement to me. It will then constitute a binding agreement between us.

Third Sample Agreement
Michael Larsen/Elizabeth Pomada Literary Agents

Dear Michael and Elizabeth:

While trust, friendliness, and confidence are the basis for our relationship, I have read your website, and I am ready to put our commitments to each other in writing:

I appoint you my sole agent to advise me and negotiate sales of all kinds for all of my literary material and its subsidiary rights in all forms and media and for all future uses throughout the world. You may appoint co-agents to help you. If you say that you can't handle a property, I shall be free to do as I please with it without obligation to you.

If a potential buyer for my literary work or writing services approaches me, I will refer the buyer to you.

If an idea is mine and we do not develop it together, only I have the rights to the idea or any basic variation on it. However, if another writer approaches you with the same idea or a similar idea, you are free to represent the project.

If the idea for a project is yours, only you have the rights to the idea or any basic variation on it. You may represent a project competitive to mine, provided that we agree that it doesn't lessen your ability to represent my work.

You will pay for all expenses that arise in selling my work except photocopying my work; mailing it abroad or on multiple submissions; buying galleys and books; and legal assistance. I must approve all expenses of more than $50 for which I will be responsible.

You may receive on my behalf all money due me from agreements signed through your efforts. This includes all sales for which negotiations begin during the term of this agreement, and all changes and extensions in those agreements, regardless of when they are made or by whom.

You are irrevocably entitled to deduct 15% commission on all gross income earned through your agency for my writing services. For foreign rights, you may deduct 20%, 30% in Asia, which includes 10% for your co-agents. All commissions you receive will not be returnable for any reason.

I must approve all offers and sign all agreements negotiated on my behalf. Michael Larsen/Elizabeth Pomada Literary Agents will be named as my agency in all agreements I sign on all projects that you represent.

You will remit all money and statements due me within 10 working days of receiving them.

You may respond to mail received on my behalf unless it is personal, in which case you will forward it to me promptly. I will notify you promptly if I change my phone number or address.

I realize that it may take years to sell a book, and you agree to try as long as you believe it is possible. You will notify me promptly when you can no longer help on a book. Then I may do as I wish with it without obligation to you.

If a problem arises about your efforts or our relationship, I will contact you, and we will conscientiously try to solve the problem with fairness to both of us. A problem we can't solve will be resolved with a mediator or arbitrator we choose.

You or I may end this agreement with 60 days' notice by registered mail. However, you will be entitled to receive statements and commissions on all rights on properties on which you make the initial sale, whether or not the agency represents me on the sales of these rights.

This agreement is binding on our respective personal and business heirs and assigns, and will be interpreted according to California law.

I am free to sign this agreement and will not agree to a conflicting obligation. I will sign two copies, and each of us will have one. Both of our signatures are needed to change this agreement.

We sign this agreement with the hope that it will symbolize our mutual long-term commitment to the development of my career and to sharing the rewards of this growth.

Acknowledgments

Huge thanks to my editor, Deb Werksman, whose faith in the book made this edition possible and whose forbearance enabled her to cope with my changes. You as well as I have reason to be grateful to Deb because her discerning suggestions made the book more helpful and more enjoyable to read.

My gratitude goes to Tara VanTimmeren for the arduous task of copyediting the book and then gracefully enduring another round of changes, and to Dawn Pope for designing the cover.

My great gratitude goes to the agents and editors kind enough to give quotes for the book.

Many thanks to my faithful readers: our agency reader and friend Adele Horwitz, our associate agent and techie from heaven Laurie McLean, and our interns Claire Cavanaugh, Emily Thompson, and Candace Finn, who graduated to William Morris. Very special thanks to Antonia Anderson, our faithful, perennial reader, friend, and assistant, who helps make our life possible because she's always there when we're not.

We are blessed with more ways to learn about writing, agenting, and publishing than it's possible to make use of. Any mistakes in the book are mine, but what you find helpful will be in part the knowledge and wisdom of all the people we've had the pleasure of knowing and learning from.

Thanks to agents Andree Abecassis, Carole Bidnick, Andrea Brown, Kimberley Cameron, Nancy Ellis, Cathy Fowler, Candace Fuhrman, Donna Levin, Jillian Manus, Kendra Marcus, Linda Mead, Karen Nazor, Robert Shepard, Bob Stricker, and Ted Weinstein, and to other members of the Bay Area, Southern California, and New York agenting communities for their continuing help and support. Thanks also to Oregonian agent Natasha Kern.

Our warm appreciation also goes to the following New York and Los Angeles agents: Marcia Amsterdam, Barbara Braun, Sheree Bykofsky, Richard Curtis, Sandy Dijkstra, Jane Dystel, Arnold and Elise Goodman, Joel Gotler, Ashley Grayson, Jeff Herman, Fred Hill, Julie Hill, Wendy Keller, Milly Marmur, Lori Perkins, Susan Ann Protter, BJ Robbins, Rita Rosenkranz, Katharine Sands, Ken

Sherman, Bobbe Siegel, and the Other Agents Group. My thanks also to AAR for being a source of state-of-the-art information about publishing and agenting.

I'm indebted to the following editors for their insights over the years: Marty Asher at Vintage Anchor, Tracy Bernstein at New American Library, Hillel Black at Sourcebooks, PJ Dempsey, Eamon Dolan at Houghton Mifflin, Jennifer Enderlin at St. Martin's Press, George Gibson at Walker, Michaela Hamilton at Kensington, Mike Hamilton at John Wiley, Bob Loomis at Random House, Alan Rinzler at Jossey-Bass, Jon Segal at Knopf, Geoff Shandler at Little Brown, Matthew Shear at St. Martin's Press, Trish Todd at Fireside, Charlie Winton at Avalon, and George Witte at St. Martin's Press. Apologies to those whose names I've overlooked.

For their knowledge of the business, my gratitude goes to John Baker, Michael Cader, Jack Canfield, and Dan Poynter.

My appreciation also goes to the AAR Counsel Ken Norwick for his input.

To the clients who had faith in us and whose questions as well as those of other writers helped me write the book by finding answers for them, I am very grateful.

Large thanks also to Barnaby and Mary Conrad of the Santa Barbara Writers Conference, Bill and Elaine Petrocelli at the Book Passage bookstore, Jan and Terry Nathan of Publishers Marketing Association, John and Shannon Tullius of the Maui Writers Conference, and the other writers' conferences that helped us to keep learning by teaching.

Starting our own conference also helped us zero in on what new writers need to know and how best to provide it. We are greatly indebted to cofounder Wendy Nelder, Barbara and Richard Santos, agents John and Francesca Vrattos, Ray and Gwen Cipolla, children's book whiz Andrea Brown and her husband David Spiselman, and our passionate intern Robin Carpenter and house techie Laurie McLean for their tremendous help as well as that of our board of directors, our speakers, and our volunteers in making the conference as good as it is.

We owe a great deal to our friends and families for their love and support, foremost among them my brother Ray and his wonderful wife Maryann. Ray helped me understand the parallel challenges in the toy and publishing industries. He also helped keep a roof over the agency's head, for which our gratitude is greater than my words can tell.

Many thanks also to Carol and Don Kosterka, and to Rita Pomada, the matriarch of the family, for always asking, "When's it going to be finished?"

And last but most, to my Queen Elizabeth, who makes all things possible and knows when to pull the plug!

Index

About the Author

After working for six New York publishers, Michael Larsen and partner Elizabeth Pomada started their San Francisco literary agency in 1972, and it has sold books to more than one hundred publishers. Mike is a member of the Association of Authors' Representatives, and he handles general nonfiction that will interest New York publishers or that he can't resist.

Michael is the author of the third edition of *How to Write a Book Proposal*, which has sold more than one hundred thousand copies. With Jay Levinson, author of *Guerrilla Marketing*, and Rick Frishman, president of Planned Television Arts, Mike coauthored *Guerrilla Marketing for Writers: 100 Weapons for Selling Your Work*. With Hal Zina Bennett, he coauthored *How to Write with a Collaborator*.

His agency must find new writers to stay in business, so Michael welcomes the chance to give you feedback on your ideas and your writing. He also welcomes the chance to mentor you by answering your questions. For more information, visit www.larsen-pomada.com.

Michael and Elizabeth are cofounders of the San Francisco Writers Conference, which takes place on President's Day Weekend in February. For more information, visit www.sfwriters.org.

All Mike needs to write is an irresistible idea; a computer; Bach, Mozart, and jazz to provide the soundtrack; and enough time—which, for him, is an oxymoron.